Grade 3

First Stop
on Reading Street

D1404921

Glenview, Illinois • Boston, Massachusetts • Chandler, Arizona
Shoreview, Minnesota • Upper Saddle River, New Jersey

ISBN-13: 978-0-328-50447-3
ISBN-10:   0-328-50447-5

3 4 5 6 7 8 9 10 V064 14 13 12 11 10
CC1

Any Path, Any Pace

PEARSON

Find Your Place on Reading Street!

Who leads the way on

YOU ARE HERE!

SCOTT FORESMAN
READING STREET

FIRST**STOP**

GRADE
5

My Teaching Library
PEARSON

Any Path, Any Pace

My Teaching Library
The ultimate find-your-place case! It stores all your Teacher's Editions in one space.

First Stop on Reading Street
It's your how-to guide, coach, and roadmap.
Find your place on *Reading Street*.

- Research into Practice
- Teacher Resources
- Professional Development
- Pacing Charts
- Reteach Lessons (and more!)

"Start here, go there, you see a chicken anywhere?"

Print • Online • CD/DVD • School to Home • English/Spanish

Reading Street?
Teachers Do.

How can something be slim and chunky?

The Teacher's Edition is slim, so it won't weigh you down. It's chunky, because it "chunks" the curriculum in manageable, three-week increments.

It's a Snap!
Snap-in tab to bookmark DIFFERENTIATING INSTRUCTION

Differentiating Instruction

UNIT 1
VOLUME 1

SCOTT FORESMAN
READING STREET
GRADE 5

Where are all my teaching resources?
On disk or online— all the time!

Three Weekly Lessons
Considerate design that's manageable and doable

Customize Literacy
Mini skill lessons to use with a variety of text sets

Customize Writing
21st Century Writing Projects and Writing Process lessons

Any Path, Any Pace

Who thrives on

All Children.

Every Child.

Every Single One.

"Hey, what about chickens? You didn't mention chickens!"

PEARSON

SCOTT FORESMAN

Print • Online • CD/DVD • School to Home • English/Spanish

Reading Street?

Let's read it and write it and think it and do it!

Let's
Go Digital
See It! Hear It! Do It!

Let's
Write
Weekly Writing

Let's
Learn
Application and Transfer

Let's
Listen
Phonemic Awareness

Let's
Talk
Oral Vocabulary/ Amazing Words

Let's
Envision
Visual Skills and Strategies

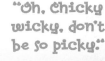
Let's
Think
Personalized Reading Coach

"Oh, Chicky wicky, don't be so picky."

Any Path, Any Pace

What makes Reading Street

"A sweet, humble cow. Now that's a WOW! So long, Chicky."

PEARSON Rules!

A day, a week, a unit, and a year!
Connect and scaffold learning

On *Reading Street* everything is neat. The unit concepts connect the curriculum from start to finish, scaffolding children's prior knowledge. Sustained concept and language development accelerates children's ability to comprehend, discuss, and write about what they're reading. Neat? *Sweeeeet.*

"Build your unit around one idea with power, an idea that helps learners make sense of otherwise isolated content."

Grant Wiggins
Coauthor with Jay McTighe of
Understanding by Design
Exclusive Pearson Consulting Author

strong?

Sustained Concept and Language Development.

Big Ideas
Consider big questions

Language
Hear and use sophisticated language

Envision It
Envision new ways of thinking

Team Talk
Share information every day

Unit Concept

Writing
Write to share what you know

Text Sets
Read related text sets

Science and Social Studies
Transfer concepts and language to content areas

Print • Online • CD/DVD • School to Home • English/Spanish   Any Path, Any Pace

What makes Reading Street

PRIORITY SKILL	SUCCESS PREDICTOR
PHONEMIC AWARENESS	Blending and Segmenting
PHONICS	Word Reading
FLUENCY	Words Correct per Minute
VOCABULARY	Word Knowledge
COMPREHENSION	Retelling

1 **Monitor Progress with Success Predictors**
Check students' progress of each priority skill with
research-based predictors of reading success.

2 **Don't Wait Until Friday!**
Prevent misunderstandings
right away with on-the-spot
reteaching and prescriptions.

Print • Online • CD/DVD • School to Home • English/Spanish

work?

The Right Skills at the Right Time.

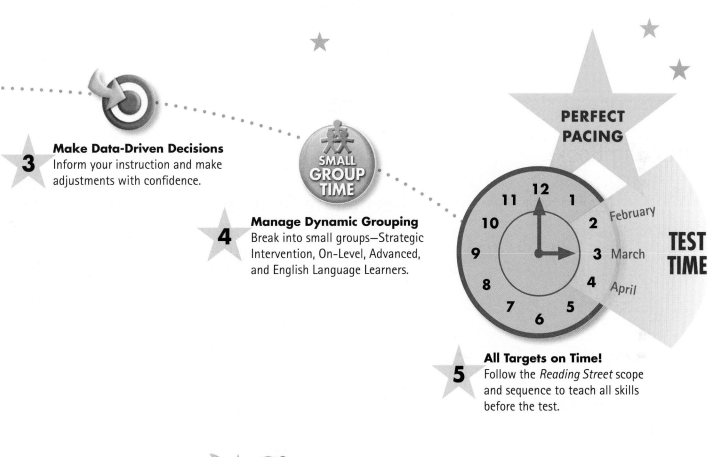

3 **Make Data-Driven Decisions**
Inform your instruction and make adjustments with confidence.

SMALL GROUP TIME

4 **Manage Dynamic Grouping**
Break into small groups—Strategic Intervention, On-Level, Advanced, and English Language Learners.

PERFECT PACING

TEST TIME

February
March
April

5 **All Targets on Time!**
Follow the *Reading Street* scope and sequence to teach all skills before the test.

"Sure a cow can talk the talk, but can a cow ride a bike?"

PEARSON
SCOTT FORESMAN

Any Path, Any Pace

What do readers read

Funny Stories   Myths   Caldecott Winners   Classic Literature

Multicultural Literature   E-mails   Big Books

Online Directories   Trucktown Readers   Adventure Stories

Nonfiction   Online Sources   Informational Text

Little Big Books   Concept Literacy Readers   Biographies

Narrative Fiction   Decodable Readers   Newbery Winners

Poetry   Trade Books   Mysteries   Realistic Fiction

English Language Development Readers   Historical Fiction   Blogs

Legends   Recipes   Search Engines   News Stories

Pourquoi Tales   Fables   Tall Tales   Fantasy Stories

Nursery Rhymes   Web Sites   Drama   Trickster Tales

"I prefer doggy stories over chicky stories."

Print • Online • CD/DVD • School to Home • English/Spanish

on Reading Street?

Grade 3 Literature Selections

"I like horse stories. Say, Chicky, do you have any spare hay?"

Any Path, Any Pace

What do writers write

Narrative Poems   Invitations   Research Papers

Blogs   Classroom Newsletters   Realistic Stories

Adventure Stories   Compare and Contrast Essays   Lists

Friendly Letters   Online Journals   Online Forums

Persuasive Essays   Formal Letters   Steps in a Process

Expository Compositions   Podcasts   Captions

Personal Narratives   Multi-paragraph Essays

Drama Scenes   E-mail Pen Pals

Fiction   Peer Revisions   Responses to Prompts

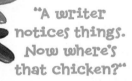

"A writer notices things. Now where's that chicken?"

Print • Online • CD/DVD • School to Home • English/Spanish

on Reading Street?

Customize Your Writing

21st Century Writing Projects
The writing section in your Teacher's Edition also provides collaborative writing projects that use the Internet to develop new literacies. Go digital! You choose.

Writing Process
Turn to the writing tab in your Teacher's Edition. A writing process lesson helps children learn the process of writing. Use as a Writing Workshop or customize to your needs.

The Internet Guy
Donald Leu, Ph.D.

The Write Guy
Jeff Anderson, M.Ed.

"Chicken stories are for the birds. I'll write about acorns."

Any Path, Any Pace

Who said so?

The Leading Researchers,

Program Authors

Peter Afflerbach, Ph.D.
Professor
Department of Curriculum
and Instruction
University of Maryland
at College Park

Camille L. Z. Blachowicz, Ph.D.
Professor of Education
National-Louis University

Candy Dawson Boyd, Ph.D.
Professor
School of Education
Saint Mary's College of California

Elena Izquierdo, Ph.D.
Associate Professor
University of Texas at El Paso

Connie Juel, Ph.D.
Professor of Education
School of Education
Stanford University

Edward J. Kame'enui, Ph.D.
*Dean-Knight Professor of
Education and Director*
Institute for the Development of
Educational Achievement and
the Center on Teaching and Learning
College of Education
University of Oregon

Donald J. Leu, Ph.D.
*John and Maria Neag Endowed
Chair in Literacy and Technology
Director, The New Literacies
Research Lab*
University of Connecticut

Jeanne R. Paratore, Ed.D.
Associate Professor of Education
Department of Literacy and
Language Development
Boston University

P. David Pearson, Ph.D.
Professor and Dean
Graduate School of Education
University of California, Berkeley

Sam L. Sebesta, Ed.D.
Professor Emeritus
College of Education
University of Washington, Seattle

Deborah Simmons, Ph.D.
Professor
College of Education and
Human Development
Texas A&M University

Alfred W. Tatum, Ph.D.
*Associate Professor and Director
of the UIC Reading Clinic*
University of Illinois at Chicago

Sharon Vaughn, Ph.D.
*H. E. Hartfelder/Southland
Corporation Regents Professor
Director, Meadows Center for
Preventing Educational Risk*
University of Texas

Susan Watts Taffe, Ph.D.
Associate Professor in Literacy
Division of Teacher Education
University of Cincinnati

Karen Kring Wixson, Ph.D.
Professor of Education
University of Michigan

Consulting Authors

Jeff Anderson, M.Ed.
Author and Consultant
San Antonio, Texas

Jim Cummins, Ph.D.
Professor
Department of Curriculum,
Teaching and Learning
University of Toronto

Lily Wong Fillmore, Ph.D.
Professor Emerita
Graduate School of Education
University of California, Berkeley

Georgia Earnest García, Ph.D.
Professor
Language and Literacy Division
Department of Curriculum
and Instruction
University of Illinois at
Urbana-Champaign

George A. González, Ph.D.
Professor (Retired)
School of Education
University of Texas-Pan American,
Edinburg

Valerie Ooka Pang, Ph.D.
Professor
School of Teacher Education
San Diego State University

Sally M. Reis, Ph.D.
*Board of Trustees Distinguished
Professor*
Department of Educational
Psychology
University of Connecticut

Jon Scieszka, M.F.A.
*Children's Book Author
Founder of GUYS READ
Named First National Ambassador
for Young People's Literature 2008*

Grant Wiggins, Ed.D.
Educational Consultant
Authentic Education
Concept Development

Lee Wright, M.Ed.
Pearland, Texas

xvi

Practitioners, and Authors.

Consultant

Sharroky Hollie, Ph.D.
Assistant Professor
California State University
Dominguez Hills, CA

Teacher Reviewers

Dr. Bettyann Brugger
Educational Support Coordinator—
Reading Office
Milwaukee Public Schools
Milwaukee, WI

Kathleen Burke
K–12 Reading Coordinator
Peoria Public Schools, Peoria, IL

Darci Burns, M.S.Ed.
University of Oregon

Bridget Cantrell
District Intervention Specialist
Blackburn Elementary School
Independence, MO

Tahira DuPree Chase,
M.A., M.S.Ed.
Administrator of Elementary
English Language Arts
Mount Vernon City School District
Mount Vernon, NY

Michele Conner
Director, Elementary Education
Aiken County School District
Aiken, SC

Georgia Coulombe
K–6 Regional Trainer/
Literacy Specialist
Regional Center for Training and
Learning (RCTL), Reno, NV

Kelly Dalmas
Third Grade Teacher
Avery's Creek Elementary, Arden, NC

Seely Dillard
First Grade Teacher
Laurel Hill Primary School
Mt. Pleasant, SC

Jodi Dodds-Kinner
Director of Elementary Reading
Chicago Public Schools, Chicago, IL

Dr. Ann Wild Evenson
District Instructional Coach
Osseo Area Schools, Maple Grove, MN

Stephanie Fascitelli
Principal
Apache Elementary, Albuquerque
Public Schools, Albuquerque, NM

Alice Franklin
Elementary Coordinator, Language
Arts & Reading
Spokane Public Schools, Spokane, WA

Laureen Fromberg
Assistant Principal
PS 100, Queens, NY

Kimberly Gibson
First Grade Teacher
Edgar B. Davis Community School
Brockton, MA

Kristen Gray
Lead Teacher
A.T. Allen Elementary School
Concord, NC

Mary Ellen Hazen
State Pre-K Teacher
Rockford Public Schools #205
Rockford, IL

Patrick M. Johnson
Elementary Instructional Director
Seattle Public Schools, Seattle, WA

Theresa Jaramillo Jones
Principal
Highland Elementary School
Las Cruces, NM

Sophie Kowzun
Program Supervisor, Reading/
Language Arts, PreK-5
Montgomery County Public Schools
Rockville, MD

David W. Matthews
Sixth Grade Teacher
Easton Area Middle School
Easton, PA

Ana Nuncio
Editor and Independent Publisher
Salem, MA

Joseph Peila
Principal
Chappell Elementary School
Chicago, IL

Ivana Reimer
Literacy Coordinator
PS 100, Queens, NY

Sally Riley
Curriculum Coordinator
Rochester Public Schools
Rochester, NH

Dyan M. Smiley
English Language Arts Program
Director, Grades K-5
Boston Public Schools, Literacy
Department, Boston, MA

Michael J. Swiatowiec
Lead Literacy Teacher
Graham Elementary School
Chicago, IL

Dr. Helen Taylor
Director of Reading/English Education
Portsmouth City Public Schools
Portsmouth, VA

Carol Thompson
Teaching and Learning Coach
Independence School District
Independence, MO

Erinn Zeitlin
Kindergarten Teacher
Carderock Springs Elementary School
Bethesda, MD

Any Path, Any Pace

Any Path, Any Pace

Find Your Place on Reading Street!

"On Reading Street, you can do anything and go anywhere."

"Tell me and I forget. Teach me and I remember. Involve me and I learn."

—Benjamin Franklin

Welcome! You've arrived on Reading Street

You're about to take your class on a rich instructional journey. As students explore the world that reading opens to them, they will look to you for guidance and support. You, as their teacher, can make the difference in their literacy experience. To help you, *Scott Foresman Reading Street* has paved the way with solid, research-based instruction. This support will be your clear path to success.

Now it's time to discover what you can expect in the materials and professional support that *Reading Street* offers. It's time to make your *First Stop on Reading Street!*

First Stop on
Reading Street: Grade 3

From Our Authors...

Dear Third-Grade Teacher,

"Welcome to third grade!" These four simple words contain a lifetime of possibilities. New potentials are in the air as students first walk into your room, seeing new friends, a new teacher, and a new classroom. A special magic surrounds the beginning of the school year!

Your Students

Who are these students? The answer is wonderfully different for every teacher. Thank goodness, too, since the diversity that defines us also enriches us. Still, there are common elements that generally describe students at this developmental level.

Your students are doers! Third graders are a most active bunch. They learn by doing and by communicating what they have learned. One way to understand them is to realize that they are young scientists, interacting with the world around them, testing out hypotheses and drawing conclusions:

> "Let me push that. What happens?"
> "Voy a probar esto. ¿Qué es esto?"
> "Let me do that. How does it work?"

Observe your students carefully. They will teach you important lessons about what they know and how they learn.

Your students are thinkers! Third graders are incredibly curious. They think about everything—sometimes all at once. They also begin to think in more abstract ways, a developmental milestone that will lead to important new understandings.

Your students are talkers! Yes, I know, I know. "If they would only talk a little less and listen a little more." Be thankful that your students talk so much. It is how they learn. Use this to discover important insights about them. Later, they do not always tell us.

Your students are readers! Oh, the places your students will go in reading this year! They can travel to the moon, dive deep under the sea, and climb the highest mountains simply by reading a good book. Your students love to read, even those who are reluctant readers. All students can be motivated by your approach to reading. Your enthusiasm is contagious. Ensure that reading forms the heart and soul of your third-grade curriculum. It will make an important difference in students' lives.

Donald J. Leu, Ph.D.

Your Curriculum

What is the reading curriculum in third grade? Perhaps most important to consider is that your curriculum may contain the broadest set of skills of any grade level. You may have a few students still acquiring elements of phonemic awareness, and you will certainly have students developing phonics skills. Most students, though, will require focused instruction in three areas: fluency, vocabulary, and comprehension.

Fluency. We want students to automatically recognize the words they encounter so that they can spend more time thinking about what the words mean. We teach fluency to support better comprehension; we do not teach fluency for fluency's sake alone. Fluency does not ensure good comprehension; it simply makes it more likely.

Vocabulary. The more words students understand, the better they will be at comprehension. Word meanings count. Students will learn many new words and meanings through their reading adventures; they will learn others from your lessons.

......the diversity that defines us also enriches us.

Comprehension. This year, your students will begin the transition from learning to read to reading to learn. Comprehension is at the heart of this transition. You will help students to comprehend an increasingly wide variety of genres, especially informational text. Making inferences, drawing conclusions, predicting outcomes, evaluating information, and summarizing will be the cornerstones of success. Comprehension will also take on new dimensions as your students learn how to read and comprehend information online. These new literacies will be critical to their future.

Welcome to Third Grade!

This may be the most important year in the lives of your students. It is one of transition to greater independence in reading and in daily life. You have an opportunity that few others ever realize—you can change the world by teaching each one of your students to become a better reader. Best wishes on this important journey. I salute you!

Cordially,

Donald J. Leu

Donald J. Leu
John and Maria Neag Endowed Chair in Literacy and Technology
Professor of Education, University of Connecticut

Research into Practice
on Reading Street

Section 1 is your tour of the daily lessons on *Scott Foresman Reading Street.* When you make each of these stops, your third grade instruction is successful.

- Get Ready to Read

- Read and Comprehend

- Language Arts

- Wrap Up Your Day

Along the way, you'll learn more about Oral Language, Text Comprehension, and other research building blocks of literacy. You'll discover that every activity and routine in the daily lesson is there because research has shown that it's important for your teaching practice.

This Research into Practice section presents a representative sample of lesson pages for one week of instruction. Where pages from the Teacher's Edition are not shown for a given week, those pages are listed with references to research supporting the instruction.

The Building Blocks of Research in Literacy

Oral Language

Phonemic Awareness

Phonics

Decodable Text

Fluency

Oral Vocabulary

Language Arts

Reading Vocabulary

Comprehension

Academic Vocabulary

Informational Text

21st Century Skills

Writing

Differentiated Instruction

English Language Learners

Success Predictors

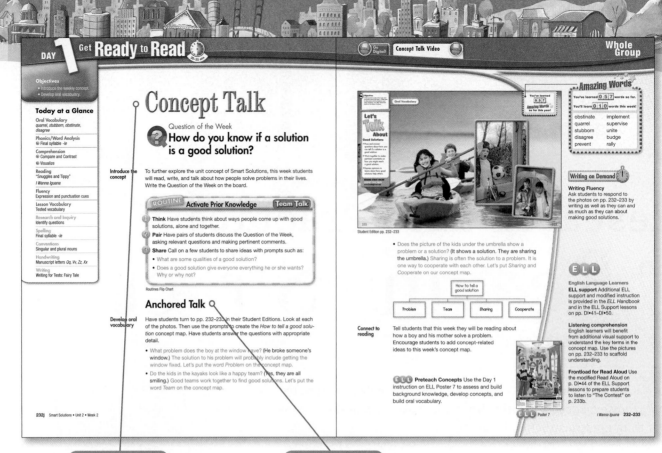

ORAL LANGUAGE

In Reading Street

Concept Talk To begin each day, students come together for a brief, whole-class, rich, oral language experience. Discussion of the Question of the Week guides students to activate prior knowledge and develop new knowledge and understanding of the unit concept. Each Concept Talk throughout the week includes opportunities for reviewing skills.

Because Research Says

Reading instruction builds especially on oral language. If this foundation is weak, progress in reading will be slow and uncertain. Students must have at least a basic vocabulary, a reasonable range of knowledge of the world around them, and the ability to talk about their knowledge. These abilities form the basis for comprehending text. —(Anderson, Hiebert, Scott, and Wilkinson, 1985)

ORAL LANGUAGE

In Reading Street

Anchored Talk During the week, the class creates a concept map to build comprehension of the week's concept. The map first takes shape as students explore their prior knowledge and discuss visual cues. Throughout the week, students add related concepts based on their reading and their life experiences.

Because Research Says

Semantic maps address the relationships between words and concepts. Relational charts allow students to generate new information based on their reading and learning. —(Blachowicz and Fisher, 2002)

Text discussions should go beyond answering comprehension questions. Discussing text with students requires that teachers understand that meaning is not in text per se, but is to be found in the text and the experiences the reader brings to it. —(Tatum, 2005)

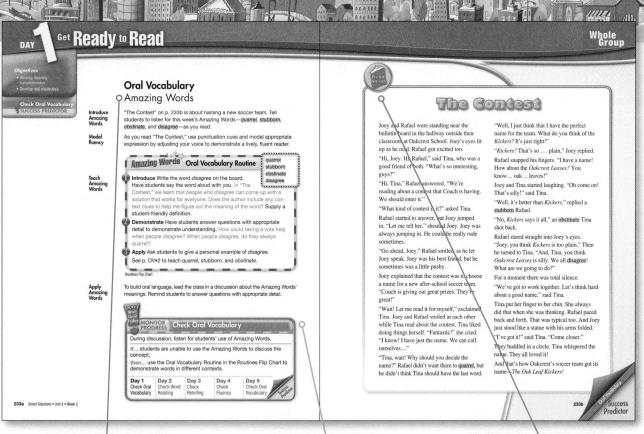

ORAL VOCABULARY

In Reading Street

Amazing Words Each week students learn a set of conceptually related Amazing Words, generally beyond their reading ability, selected from shared literature. Throughout the week students use the words in multiple contexts: in conversations about text, in retelling a story or summarizing a text, in their daily writing, and in the end-of-day discussions.

Because Research Says

▸ A robust approach to vocabulary involves directly explaining the meanings of words along with thought-provoking, playful, and interactive follow-up. —(Beck, McKeown, and Kucan, 2002)

SUCCESS PREDICTORS

In Reading Street

Monitor Progress Throughout the week, teachers do quick checks in the context of classroom instruction to monitor students' progress in core areas of reading instruction such as oral vocabulary, fluency, and retelling/summarizing. Don't Wait Until Friday/Monitor Progress features provide *if . . ., then . . .* statements to help teachers evaluate the skills and respond to students' difficulties on the spot.

Because Research Says

▸ Comprehension instruction should be accompanied by ongoing assessment. Teachers should monitor students' use of comprehension strategies and their success at understanding what they read. Results of this monitoring should, in turn, inform the teacher's instruction. —(Duke and Pearson, 2002)

COMPREHENSION

In Reading Street

Read Aloud Each week of instruction begins with a read-aloud that supports the concept of the week, addresses the Question of the Week, and includes Amazing Words that build background for the lesson's reading selections.

Because Research Says

▸ Teacher read-alouds can be a good starting point for introducing critical strategies for comprehension. That is, just by listening first, students can focus on the strategy being introduced without actually having to read. —(Ivey, 2002)

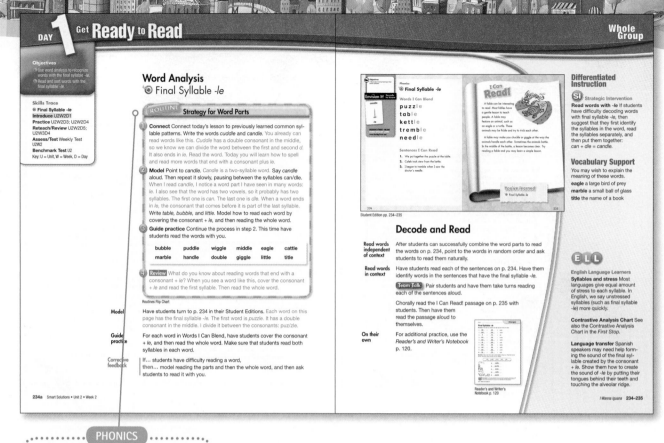

In Reading Street

Blending Strategy This routine provides explicit instruction for sound-spellings and word parts. Students develop an understanding of the alphabetic principle as they are led to use and point to letters as words are written, and then to blend, or decode, words.

Because Research Says

Segmenting words into phonemes and blending phonemes into words contributes more to learning to read than any other phonological awareness skills. —(Vaughn and Linan-Thompson, 2004)

Objectives
• Apply knowledge of sound-spellings to decode unknown multisyllabic words when reading.
• Decode and read words in context and independent of context.
• Decode and read words with the final syllable -le.
• Practice fluency with oral rereading.

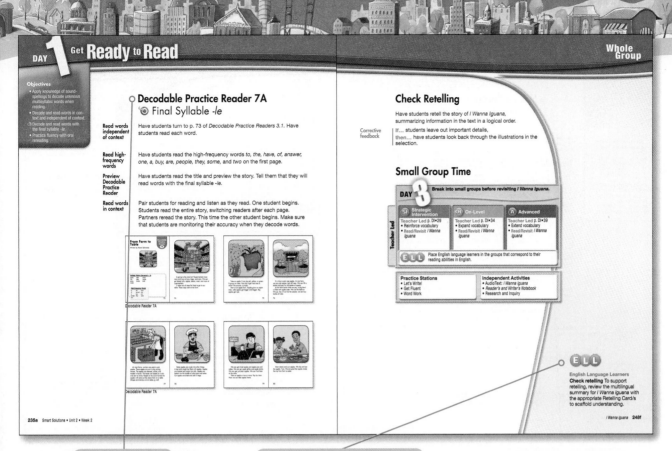

Decodable Practice Reader 7A
Final Syllable -le

Read words independent of context
Have students turn to p. 73 of *Decodable Practice Readers 3.1.* Have students read each word.

Read high-frequency words
Have students read the high-frequency words *to, the, have, of, answer, one, a, buy, are, people, they, some,* and *two* on the first page.

Preview Decodable Practice Reader
Have students read the title and preview the story. Tell them that they will read words with the final syllable -le.

Read words in context
Pair students for reading and listen as they read. One student begins. Students read the entire story, switching readers after each page. Partners reread the story. This time the other student begins. Make sure that students are monitoring their accuracy when they decode words.

Decodable Reader 7A

Decodable Reader 7A

235a Smart Solutions • Unit 2 • Week 2

Check Retelling

Have students retell the story of *I Wanna Iguana,* summarizing information in the text in a logical order.

Corrective feedback
If... students leave out important details,
then... have students look back through the illustrations in the selection.

Small Group Time

DAY 3 Break into small groups before revisiting *I Wanna Iguana.*

Teacher Led

SI Strategic Intervention	OL On-Level	A Advanced
Teacher Led p. DI•29	Teacher Led p. DI•34	Teacher Led p. DI•39
• Reinforce vocabulary	• Expand vocabulary	• Extend vocabulary
• Read/Revisit *I Wanna Iguana*	• Read/Revisit *I Wanna Iguana*	• Read/Revisit *I Wanna Iguana*

ELL Place English language learners in the groups that correspond to their reading abilities in English.

Practice Stations	Independent Activities
• Let's Write!	• AudioText: *I Wanna Iguana*
• Get Fluent	• Reader's and Writer's Notebook
• Word Work	• Research and Inquiry

ELL
English Language Learners
Check retelling To support retelling, review the multilingual summary for *I Wanna Iguana* with the appropriate Retelling Card/s to scaffold understanding.

I Wanna Iguana 248f

DECODABLE TEXT

In Reading Street

Decodable Practice Readers
Students use readers to practice the weekly target phonics skills. Students can read these texts with a high potential for accuracy because they are at least 80 percent decodable—that is, at least 80 percent of all words are based on previously taught phonics elements. The remaining words in the readers are previously taught sight words.

Because Research Says

Learning letter-sound relationships in isolation is necessary, but not enough. Students must know how to apply their knowledge to reading text. They should begin by reading decodable text comprised largely of words containing previously taught letter-sound relationships and gradually move to less controlled text as their ability and confidence grow. —(Vaughn and Linan-Thompson, 2004)

ENGLISH LANGUAGE LEARNERS

In Reading Street

Support for English Language Learners Throughout the lesson, teachers are offered strategies and activities that help scaffold and support English learners in reading, writing, listening, and speaking at all levels of English proficiency.

Because Research Says

All the preliteracy skills, such as the development of concepts about print, alphabet knowledge, phonemic awareness, writing, and environmental print, are important for ELL students to be exposed to and to learn. —(Tabors, 1997)

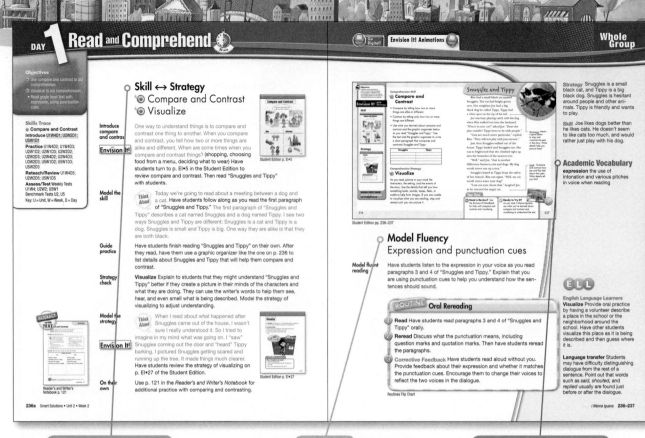

In Reading Street

Comprehension Skills and Strategies Using the Student Edition lesson, the teacher explicitly instructs students in key comprehension skills and strategies using a think-aloud. Students apply the skill first through a guided practice, and then independently.

Because Research Says

Think-alouds have been shown to improve students' comprehension both when students themselves engage in the practice during reading and also when teachers routinely think aloud while reading to students. —(Duke and Pearson, 2002)

In Reading Street

Model Fluency As the teacher reads, he or she models one aspect of fluent reading (e.g., accuracy, appropriate rate, attending to punctuation, expression, expressing characterization). The teacher also models prosodic features such as tone of voice, use of pauses, volume, phrasing, emotion, and dialogue. After listening to the teacher model the skill, students engage in guided oral reading practice with feedback.

Because Research Says

Repeated reading practice produces significant improvement in reading speed, word recognition, and oral reading expression. Repeated reading and assisted readings may enable students to read more difficult material than they might otherwise be able to read. —(Samuels, 2002; Kuhn and Stahl, 2003; National Reading Panel, 1999)

In Reading Street

Academic Vocabulary During the week, the teacher directly teaches a limited number of academic vocabulary words related to reading and language arts concepts. Lessons also offer multiple strategies for developing an understanding of this academic vocabulary.

Because Research Says

When choosing words for direct instruction, include those that lead to conceptual understanding. Students need to understand these words beyond the sense of the general concept and be able to provide precision and specificity in describing the concept. The most productive direct vocabulary instruction aims at words that are of high frequency for mature language users and are found across a variety of domains. —(Beck, McKeown, and Kucan, 2002)

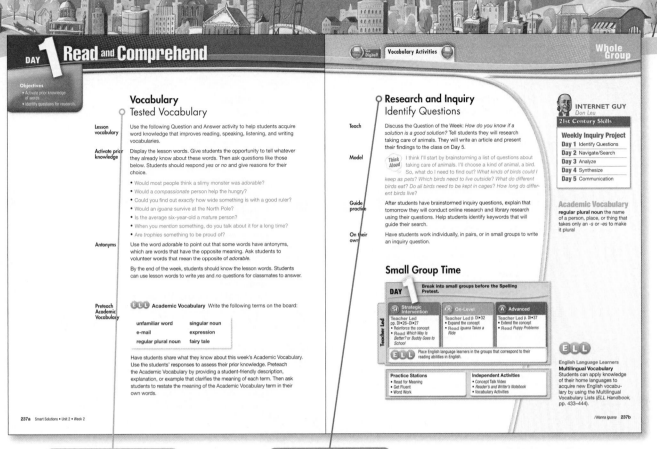

In Reading Street

Tested Vocabulary The teacher introduces the lesson vocabulary words and engages students in an activity to develop word meaning.

Because Research Says

The effective vocabulary teacher presents new vocabulary in ways that model good learning. This type of instruction involves developing learners who are active, who personalize their learning, who look for multiple sources of information to build meaning, and who are playful with words. Good learners are active. As in all learning situations, having the learners actively attempting to construct their own meanings is a hallmark of good instruction.
—(Blachowicz and Fisher, 2002)

In Reading Street

Research and Inquiry Students conduct a 5-day inquiry project connected to the weekly lesson concept. Each day, activities provide step-by-step instructions for formulating inquiry questions, navigating a student-friendly search engine, analyzing acquired information, synthesizing research, and communicating findings.

Because Research Says

The new literacies of the Internet include the skills necessary to successfully use and adapt to rapidly changing information and communication technologies and contexts. These skills allow us to use technology to identify important questions, locate information, critically evaluate the usefulness of that information, synthesize information to answer those questions, and then communicate the answers to others.
—(Leu, Kinzer, Coiro, and Cammack, 2004)

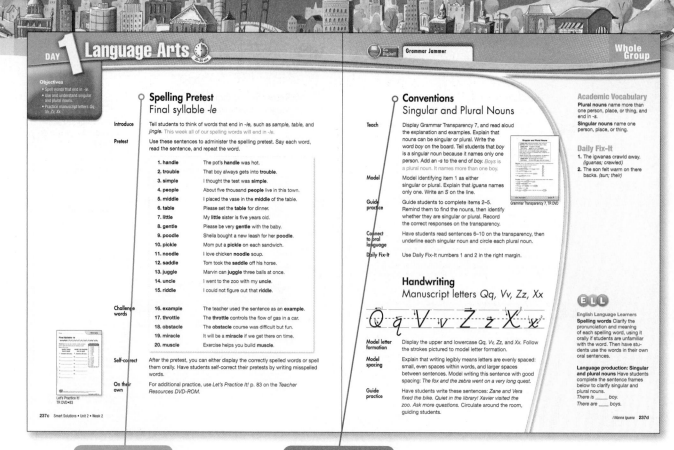

Objectives
- Spell words that end in -le.
- Use and understand singular and plural nouns.
- Practice manuscript letters Qq, Vv, Zz, Xx.

Spelling Pretest
Final syllable -le

Introduce Tell students to think of words that end in -le, such as *sample*, *table*, and *jingle*. This week all of our spelling words will end in -le.

Pretest Use these sentences to administer the spelling pretest. Say each word, read the sentence, and repeat the word.

1. handle	The pot's **handle** was hot.
2. trouble	That boy always gets into **trouble**.
3. simple	I thought the test was **simple**.
4. people	About five thousand **people** live in this town.
5. middle	I placed the vase in the **middle** of the table.
6. table	Please set the **table** for dinner.
7. little	My **little** sister is five years old.
8. gentle	Please be very **gentle** with the baby.
9. poodle	Sheila bought a new leash for her **poodle**.
10. pickle	Mom put a **pickle** on each sandwich.
11. noodle	I love chicken **noodle** soup.
12. saddle	Tom took the **saddle** off his horse.
13. juggle	Marvin can **juggle** three balls at once.
14. uncle	I went to the zoo with my **uncle**.
15. riddle	I could not figure out that **riddle**.

Challenge words

16. example	The teacher used the sentence as an **example**.
17. throttle	The **throttle** controls the flow of gas in a car.
18. obstacle	The **obstacle** course was difficult but fun.
19. miracle	It will be a **miracle** if we get there on time.
20. muscle	Exercise helps you build **muscle**.

Self-correct After the pretest, you can either display the correctly spelled words or spell them orally. Have students self-correct their pretests by writing misspelled words.

On their own For additional practice, use *Let's Practice It!* p. 83 on the *Teacher Resources DVD-ROM*.

Let's Practice It!
TR DVD•83

237c Smart Solutions • Unit 2 • Week 2

Conventions
Singular and Plural Nouns

Teach Display Grammar Transparency 7, and read aloud the explanation and examples. Explain that nouns can be singular or plural. Write the word *boy* on the board. Tell students that *boy* is a singular noun because it names only one person. Add an -s to the end of *boy*. *Boys* is a plural noun. It names more than one boy.

Model Model identifying item 1 as either singular or plural. Explain that *iguana* names only one. Write an *S* on the line.

Guide practice Guide students to complete items 2–5. Remind them to find the nouns, then identify whether they are singular or plural. Record the correct responses on the transparency.

Grammar Transparency 7, TR DVD

Connect to oral language Have students read sentences 6–10 on the transparency, then underline each singular noun and circle each plural noun.

Daily Fix-It Use Daily Fix-It numbers 1 and 2 in the right margin.

Handwriting
Manuscript letters Qq, Vv, Zz, Xx

Qq Vv Zz Xx

Model letter formation Display the upper and lowercase Qq, Vv, Zz, and Xx. Follow the strokes pictured to model letter formation.

Model spacing Explain that writing legibly means letters are evenly spaced: small, even spaces within words, and larger spaces between sentences. Model writing this sentence with good spacing: *The fox and the zebra went on a very long quest.*

Guide practice Have students write these sentences: *Zane and Vera fixed the bike. Quiet in the library! Xavier visited the zoo.* Ask more questions. Circulate around the room, guiding students.

I Wanna Iguana 237d

Academic Vocabulary
Plural nouns name more than one person, place, or thing, and end in -s.
Singular nouns name one person, place, or thing.

Daily Fix-It
1. The igwanas crawld away. *(iguanas; crawled)*
2. The son felt warm on there backs. *(sun; their)*

ELL

English Language Learners
Spelling words Clarify the pronunciation and meaning of each spelling word, using it orally if students are unfamiliar with the word. Then have students use the words in their own oral sentences.

Language production: Singular and plural nouns Have students complete the sentence frames below to clarify singular and plural nouns.
There is _____ boy.
There are _____ boys.

PHONICS

In Reading Street

Spelling Instruction in spelling and phonics are interconnected because both rely on knowledge of the alphabetic system. Spelling instruction begins at the sound level, moves to the structure level (word endings, prefixes, suffixes), and finally moves to the meaning level (compound words, homophones, word origins).

Because Research Says

Grapheme-phoneme knowledge, also referred to as alphabetic knowledge, is essential for literacy acquisition to reach a mature state. It is important to include spelling as well as reading in this picture, because learning to read and learning to spell words in English depend on processes that are tightly interconnected. —(Ehri, 1992)

LANGUAGE ARTS

In Reading Street

Conventions Students learn a new grammar skill each week. The skill is introduced on Day 1 with the Grammar Transparency and tied to reading and writing activities throughout the week.

Because Research Says

The study of grammar will help people become better users of the language, that is, more effective as listeners and speakers, and especially as readers and writers. —(Weaver, 1996)

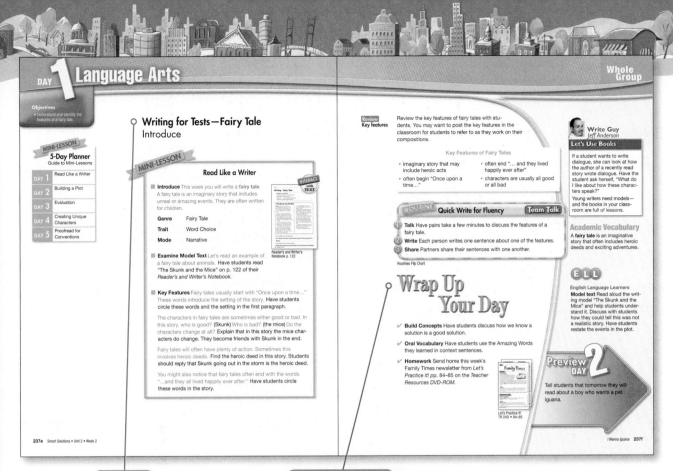

In Reading Street

Writing Each week, the writing lesson connects to the weekly concept and focuses on a product writing for tests. The writing lesson begins with a genre study, which includes key features of the genre and a close study of an exemplary writing model.

Because Research Says

The writing process is a series of interactive, recursive phases, in which various stages of writing build upon one another. The phases of prewriting, drafting, sharing, revising, editing, and publishing (or making your writing public in some way) are all interdependent and overlapping, more like a scaffold in which you move to a newer, higher step all the while pulling along the best from all preceding steps. —(Spandel, 2002)

In Reading Street

Wrap Up Your Day This end-of-the-day routine reviews the day's skill instruction, encourages discussion about shared literature and the week's concepts, and previews what's to come.

Because Research Says

For children to develop rich vocabularies, they need to have many interactions with adults. It is from these interactions that they will develop the words they need to negotiate their world. —(Stahl and Stahl, 2004)

Pages 238a–238b are based on the same research as pages 232j and 233a.

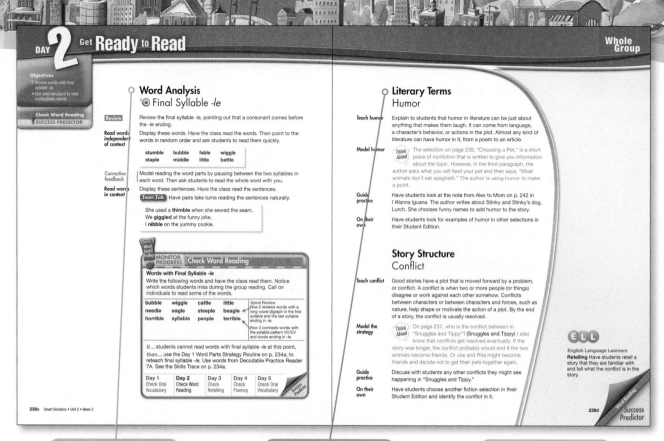

Word Analysis
Final Syllable -le

Review the final syllable -le, pointing out that a consonant comes before the -le ending.

Display these words. Have the class read the words. Then point to the words in random order and ask students to read them quickly.

stumble	bubble	fable	wiggle
staple	middle	little	battle

Model reading the word parts by pausing between the two syllables in each word. Then ask students to read the whole word with you.

Display these sentences. Have the class read the sentences.

Team Talk Have pairs take turns reading the sentences naturally.

She used a **thimble** when she sewed the seam.
We **giggled** at the funny joke.
I **nibble** on the yummy cookie.

MONITOR PROGRESS Check Word Reading

Words with Final Syllable -le
Write the following words and have the class read them. Notice which words students miss during the group reading. Call on individuals to read some of the words.

bubble	wiggle	cattle	little
needle	eagle	steeple	beagle
horrible	syllable	people	terrible

Spiral Review
Row 2 reviews words with a long vowel digraph in the first syllable and the last syllable ending in -le.
Row 3 contrasts words with the syllable pattern VC/CV and words ending in -le.

If... students cannot read words with final syllable -le at this point, then... use the Day 1 Word Parts Strategy Routine on p. 234a, to reteach final syllable -le. Use words from Decodable Practice Reader 7A. See the Skills Trace on p. 234a.

Day 1	Day 2	Day 3	Day 4	Day 5
Check Oral Vocabulary	Check Word Reading	Check Retelling	Check Fluency	Check Oral Vocabulary

Literary Terms
Humor

Explain to students that humor in literature can be just about anything that makes them laugh. It can come from language, a character's behavior, or actions in the plot. Almost any kind of literature can have humor in it, from a poem to an article.

Think Aloud The selection on page 239, "Choosing a Pet," is a short piece of nonfiction that is written to give you information about the topic. However, in the third paragraph, the author asks what you will feed your pet and then says, "Most animals don't eat spaghetti." The author is using humor to make a point.

Have students look at the note from Alex to Mom on p. 242 in *I Wanna Iguana*. The author writes about Stinky and Stinky's dog, Lurch. She chooses funny names to add humor to the story.

Have students look for examples of humor in other selections in their Student Edition.

Story Structure
Conflict

Good stories have a plot that is moved forward by a problem, or conflict. A conflict is when two or more people (or things) disagree or work against each other somehow. Conflicts between characters or between characters and forces, such as nature, help shape or motivate the action of a plot. By the end of a story, the conflict is usually resolved.

Think Aloud On page 237, who is the conflict between in "Snuggles and Tippy"? (Snuggles and Tippy) I also know that conflicts get resolved eventually. If the story was longer, the conflict probably would end if the two animals become friends. Or Joe and Rita might become friends and decide not to get their pets together again.

Discuss with students any other conflicts they might see happening in "Snuggles and Tippy."

Have students choose another fiction selection in their Student Edition and identify the conflict in it.

ELL

English Language Learners
Retelling Have students retell a story that they are familiar with and tell what the conflict is in the story.

238c Smart Solutions • Unit 2 • Week 2

238d Success Predictor

READING VOCABULARY

In Reading Street

Word Analysis Every week, word analysis instruction focuses on a specific skill pertaining to word structure.

Because Research Says

As part of vocabulary instruction, structural analysis of words can draw students' attention to the morphemes that compose a word, and from an analysis of the meanings of the individual morphemes, students are helped to understand the meaning of the whole word. —(Blachowicz and Fisher, 2002)

COMPREHENSION

In Reading Street

Literary Terms This instruction provides students the opportunity to analyze what they have read, focusing on text structure, literary concepts, and story elements.

Because Research Says

Comprehension improves when teachers design and implement activities that support the understanding of the texts that students will read in their classes. —(Pearson and Duke, 2002)

INFORMATIONAL TEXT

In Reading Street

Text Features Paired selections are used to introduce text features of informational texts, including headings/subheadings, insets, sidebars, captions, illustrations, photos, diagrams, charts and tables, labels, maps, and timelines. The teacher provides direct instruction in using the text features to access and understand content.

Because Research Says

To provide the knowledge needed to read informational texts with a "road map" in their heads, students need to have many experiences with informational text to develop an understanding of the structures most commonly used to organize these texts. Students who learn to use the internal (text structure) and external (text features) organization of informational text are more able to comprehend and retain key facts. —(Ogle and Blachowicz, 2002)

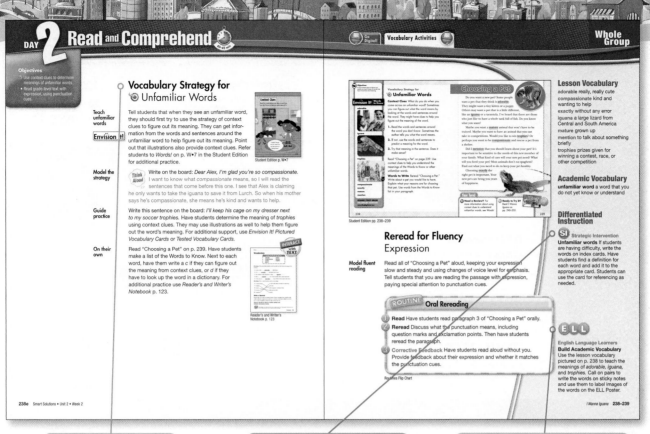

READING VOCABULARY

In Reading Street

Vocabulary Strategy Students' word knowledge is expanded by introducing them to word-learning strategies and concepts such as using a dictionary or glossary. Using words from the selection, the teacher explains the concept. Then students provide additional examples.

Because Research Says

Effective vocabulary teaching in the early years should make students curious about words. To be a good word learner, one must be hungry for words. Learning (and using) new words can be exciting because a new word not only is a sign of growing up, but it also is a sign of greater control and understanding about one's world. —(Stahl and Stahl, 2004)

DIFFERENTIATED INSTRUCTION

In Reading Street

Strategic Intervention Students who are struggling receive more explicit, intensive instruction, more scaffolding, more practice with critical skills, and more opportunities to respond.

Because Research Says

A consistent finding in meta-analyses examining effective instructional practices for students with reading and learning disabilities is that a combination of explicit and systematic instruction that provides modeling and feedback is associated with improved academic outcomes. —(Vaughn and Linan-Thompson, 2003)

ENGLISH LANGUAGE LEARNERS

In Reading Street

Support for English Language Learners English Learners receive extra support to allow them to successfully participate in and progress through the daily lessons of the basic program with their peers.

Because Research Says

Given the diversity in our society, it is imperative to recognize that students may differ considerably in their inventory of skills and abilities, and these differences should not be treated as reflecting deficiencies in ability. —(Wong Fillmore and Snow, 2002)

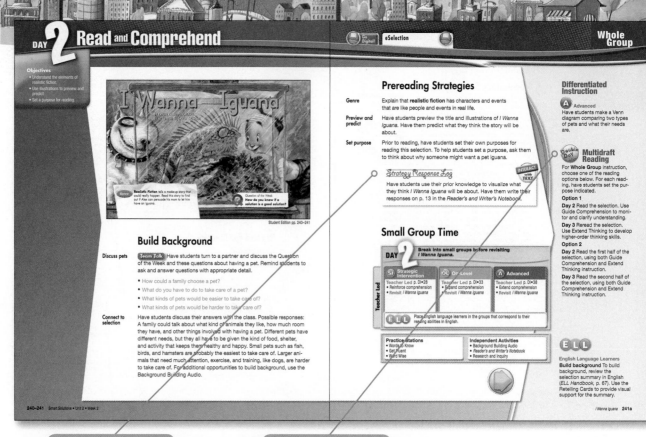

COMPREHENSION

In Reading Street

Strategy Response Log
Students keep a Strategy Response Log to record their use of a specific strategy and do a mid-selection self-check on their use of the strategy. The teacher monitors their progress on how and when they apply the strategy and coaches them as necessary. After reading, students do a Strategy Self-Check, looking back on how and when they applied the strategy. Students apply strategy to their independent reading.

Because Research Says

Comprehension processes instruction is about encouraging young readers to be cognitively active as they read, just the way that mature, excellent readers are active cognitively. —(Block and Pressley, 2003)

COMPREHENSION

In Reading Street

Multidraft Reading Students read the selection multiple times for different purposes. The purpose of the first reading is literal comprehension and understanding. Students respond to Guide Comprehension questions that address a target skill or strategy in context. The purpose of the second read is the application of higher-order thinking skills such as analysis, synthesis, and evaluation. When students reread a text for different purposes, they increase fluency, comprehension, and their ability to interpret the text.

Because Research Says

More effective teachers engage students in more higher-level responses to text (both in discussions and written assignments) as part of what the researchers labeled a framework of instruction promoting cognitive engagement during reading. —(Taylor, Pearson, Peterson, and Rodriguez, 2005)

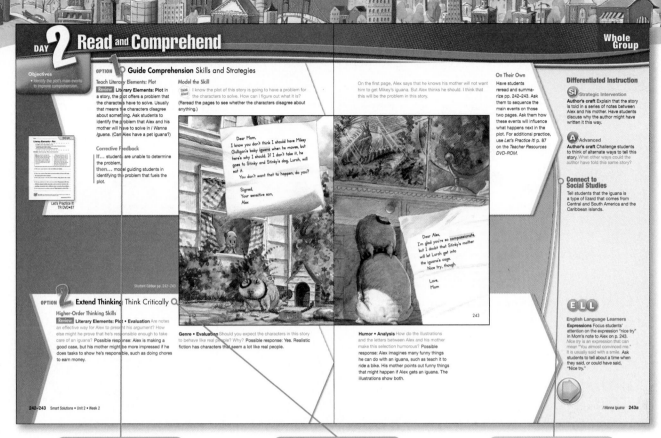

COMPREHENSION

In Reading Street

Guide Comprehension Each week students are introduced to a target skill and strategy. Using a "Think Aloud" approach, the teacher models the application of the target strategy in context. Through guided practice, students apply the strategy as they continue to read throughout the week.

Because Research Says

Good comprehenders have learned that they have control of the reading process. They actively construct meaning as they read by directing their own comprehension using basic strategies. They know reading works because they have knowledge about how sounds, letters, and print work; they know what strategies to use to help them understand; and they know when to use which strategies.
—(Blachowicz and Ogle, 2001)

COMPREHENSION

In Reading Street

Extend Thinking During reading students respond to questions requiring them to apply previously taught comprehension skills. These questions engage the higher-order thinking skills of analysis, synthesis, and evaluation.

Because Research Says

More effective teachers engage students in more higher-level responses to text (both in discussions and written assignments) as part of what the researchers labeled a framework of instruction promoting cognitive engagement during reading. —(Taylor, Pearson, Peterson, and Rodriguez, 2005)

INFORMATIONAL TEXT

In Reading Street

Connect to Social Studies Instruction is organized around unit themes that emphasize science and social studies concepts. As students read the selections, they have multiple opportunities to make connections to science and social studies concepts.

Because Research Says

When concept goals were prominent in reading, students focused on gaining meaning, building knowledge, and understanding deeply. Meaningful conceptual content in reading instruction increases motivation for reading and text comprehension. —(Guthrie, et al., 2004)

Pages 244–245 and 245a are based on the same research as pages 242–243 and 243a. Pages 246–247 and 247a are based on the same research as pages 242–243 and 243a. Pages 247b–247c are based on the same research as pages 237b and 237c–237d.

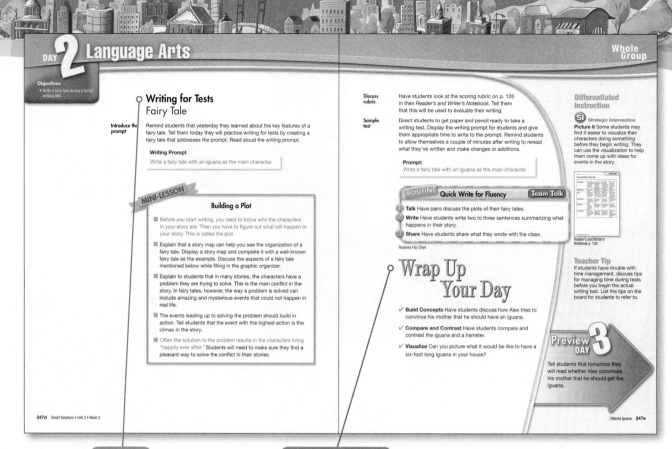

Objectives
• Write a fairy tale during a timed writing test.

Writing for Tests
Fairy Tale

Introduce the prompt
Remind students that yesterday they learned about the key features of a fairy tale. Tell them today they will practice writing for tests by creating a fairy tale that addresses the prompt. Read aloud the writing prompt.

Writing Prompt

Write a fairy tale with an iguana as the main character.

MINI-LESSON

Building a Plot

■ Before you start writing, you need to know who the characters in your story are. Then you have to figure out what will happen in your story. This is called the plot.

■ Explain that a story map can help you see the organization of a fairy tale. Display a story map and complete it with a well-known fairy tale as the example. Discuss the aspects of a fairy tale mentioned below while filling in the graphic organizer.

■ Explain to students that in many stories, the characters have a problem they are trying to solve. This is the main conflict in the story. In fairy tales, however, the way a problem is solved can include amazing and mysterious events that could not happen in real life.

■ The events leading up to solving the problem should build in action. Tell students that the event with the highest action is the climax in the story.

■ Often the solution to the problem results in the characters living "happily ever after." Students will need to make sure they find a pleasant way to solve the conflict in their stories.

Discuss rubric
Have students look at the scoring rubric on p. 126 in their *Reader's and Writer's Notebook*. Tell them that this will be used to evaluate their writing.

Sample test
Direct students to get paper and pencil ready to take a writing test. Display the writing prompt for students and give them appropriate time to write to the prompt. Remind students to allow themselves a couple of minutes after writing to reread what they've written and make changes or additions.

Prompt:

Write a fairy tale with an iguana as the main character.

ROUTINE Quick Write for Fluency **Team Talk**

① **Talk** Have pairs discuss the plots of their fairy tales.

② **Write** Have students write two to three sentences summarizing what happens in their story.

③ **Share** Have students share what they wrote with the class.

Routines Flip Chart

Wrap Up Your Day

✔ **Build Concepts** Have students discuss how Alex tries to convince his mother that he should have an iguana.

✔ **Compare and Contrast** Have students compare and contrast the iguana and a hamster.

✔ **Visualize** Can you picture what it would be like to have a six-foot long iguana in your house?

Differentiated Instruction

SI Strategic Intervention
Picture it Some students may find it easier to visualize their characters doing something before they begin writing. They can use the visualization to help them come up with ideas for events in the story.

Reader's and Writer's Notebook p. 126

Teacher Tip
If students have trouble with time management, discuss tips for managing time during tests before you begin the actual writing test. List the tips on the board for students to refer to.

Preview DAY 3
Tell students that tomorrow they will read whether Alex convinces his mother that he should get the iguana.

247d Smart Solutions • Unit 2 • Week 2

I Wanna Iguana 247e

WRITING

In Reading Street

Writing Prompts Teachers are provided with prompts that focus on the week's concept, oral vocabulary, grammar lesson, and featured writing trait.

Because Research Says

Learning to write should include composing staged across various phases of rumination, investigation, consultation with others, drafting, feedback, revision, and perfecting. —(National Writing Project and Nagin, 2003)

ORAL LANGUAGE

In Reading Street

Wrap Up Your Day This end-of-the-day routine reviews the day's skill instruction, encourages discussion about shared literature and the week's concepts, and previews what's to come.

Because Research Says

For children to develop rich vocabularies, they need to have many interactions with adults. It is from these interactions that they will develop the words they need to negotiate their world. —(Stahl and Stahl, 2004)

Pages 248a–248b are based on the same research as pages 232j and 233a. Pages 248c–248d are based on the same research as pages 234a and 235a.

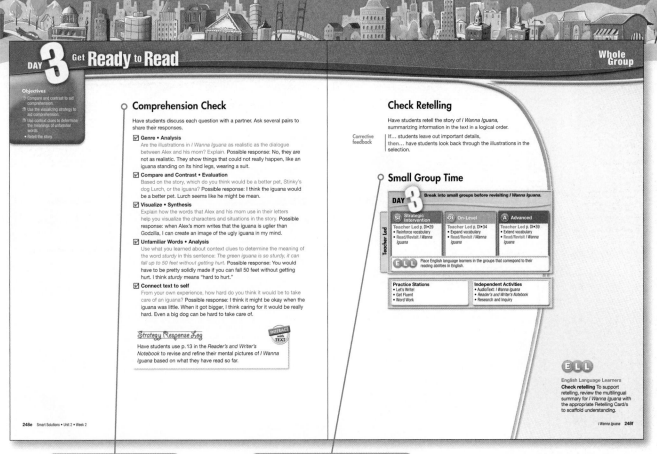

In Reading Street

COMPREHENSION

Comprehension Check Comprehension questions provide opportunities for discussion and skill application. Most questions require analysis, synthesis, or evaluation.

Because Research Says

The model of comprehension instruction best supported by research has five components: (1) an explicit description of the strategy/skill and when and how it should be used; (2) teacher modeling the strategy/skill in action, usually by thinking aloud; (3) collaborative use of the strategy/skill in action; (4) guided practice using the strategy/skill with gradual release of responsibility; and (5) independent use of the strategy/skill. —(Duke and Pearson, 2002)

In Reading Street

DIFFERENTIATED INSTRUCTION

Small Group Time Group instruction is based on the 3-Tier Reading Model developed at the University of Texas. At the start of the school year, teachers use the Baseline Group Test to make initial instructional and grouping decisions for Strategic Intervention, On-Level, and Advanced instruction.

Because Research Says

The components of effective reading instruction are the same whether the focus is prevention or intervention. By coordinating research evidence from effective classroom reading instruction with effective small-group and one-on-one reading instruction, teachers can meet the literacy needs of all students. —(Foorman and Torgesen, 2001)

Pages 248–249 and 249a are based on the same research as pages 242–243 and 243a. Pages 250–251 and 251a are based on the same research as pages 242–243 and 243a. Pages 252–253 and 253a are based on the same research as pages 242–243 and 243a. Pages 254–255 and 255a are based on the same research as pages 242–243 and 243a.

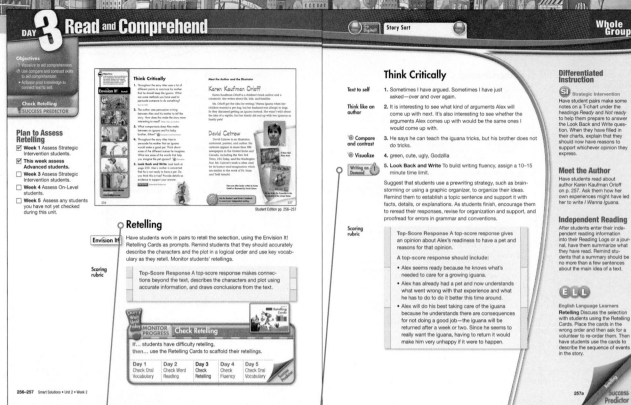

COMPREHENSION

In Reading Street

Retelling Using the Envision It! Retelling Cards as prompts, students retell narrative text or summarize expository text.

Because Research Says

▶ Oral retelling provides information as a process and a product. It allows teachers to assess what students remember about what they read without direct questioning or support from a teacher. —(Paratore and McCormack, 2005)

▶ Practice, guidance, and evaluation of stories retold and rewritten have been found to improve children's written and oral original stories. —(Morrow, 1996)

WRITING

In Reading Street

Writing on Demand Students respond to a question that sends them back into the selection and then write their response, focusing on either the skill or strategy or both. A scoring rubric serves as an assessment tool for the teacher.

Because Research Says

▶ Writing is a more complex activity; more than just a skill or talent, it is a means in inquiry and expression for learning in all grades and disciplines. —(National Writing Project and Nagin, 2003)

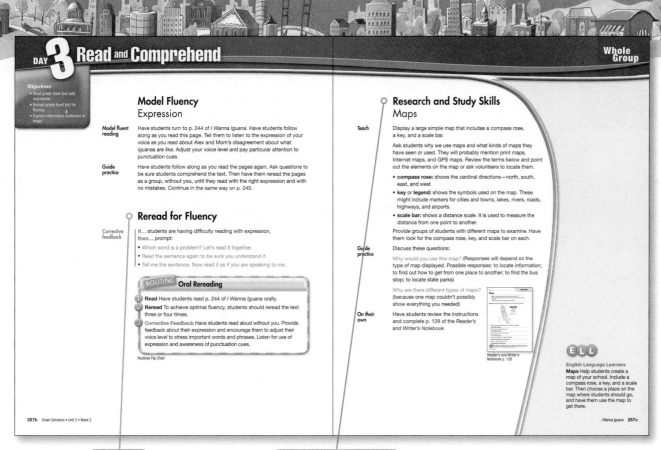

Objectives
- Read grade-level text with expression.
- Reread grade-level text for fluency.
- Explain information contained in maps.

Model Fluency
Expression

Model fluent reading Have students turn to p. 244 of *I Wanna Iguana*. Have students follow along as you read this page. Tell them to listen to the expression of your voice as you read about Alex and Mom's disagreement about what iguanas are like. Adjust your voice level and pay particular attention to punctuation cues.

Guide practice Have students follow along as you read the pages again. Ask questions to be sure students comprehend the text. Then have them reread the pages as a group, without you, until they read with the right expression and with no mistakes. Continue in the same way on p. 245.

Reread for Fluency

Corrective feedback If... students are having difficulty reading with expression, then... prompt:
- Which word is a problem? Let's read it together.
- Read the sentence again to be sure you understand it.
- Tell me the sentence. Now read it as if you are speaking to me.

ROUTINE Oral Rereading
1. **Read** Have students read p. 244 of *I Wanna Iguana* orally.
2. **Reread** To achieve optimal fluency, students should reread the text three or four times.
3. **Corrective Feedback** Have students read aloud without you. Provide feedback about their expression and encourage them to adjust their voice level to stress important words and phrases. Listen for use of expression and awareness of punctuation cues.

Routines Flip Chart

257b Smart Solutions • Unit 2 • Week 2

Research and Study Skills
Maps

Teach Display a large simple map that includes a compass rose, a key, and a scale bar.

Ask students why we use maps and what kinds of maps they have seen or used. They will probably mention print maps, Internet maps, and GPS maps. Review the terms below and point out the elements on the map or ask volunteers to locate them.

- **compass rose:** shows the cardinal directions—north, south, east, and west
- **key** or **legend:** shows the symbols used on the map. These might include markers for cities and towns, lakes, rivers, roads, highways, and airports.
- **scale bar:** shows a distance scale. It is used to measure the distance from one point to another.

Provide groups of students with different maps to examine. Have them look for the compass rose, key, and scale bar on each.

Discuss these questions:

Guide practice Why would you use this map? (Responses will depend on the type of map displayed. Possible responses: to locate information; to find out how to get from one place to another; to find the bus stop; to locate state parks)

Why are there different types of maps? (because one map couldn't possibly show everything you needed)

On their own Have students review the instructions and complete p. 128 of the *Reader's and Writer's Notebook*.

Reader's and Writer's Notebook p. 128

ELL

English Language Learners
Maps Help students create a map of your school. Include a compass rose, a key, and a scale bar. Then choose a place on the map where students should go, and have them use the map to get there.

I Wanna Iguana 257c

FLUENCY

In Reading Street

Reread for Fluency Students have opportunities to reread the same text orally several times throughout the week. After the teacher models an aspect of fluent reading, students engage in repeated oral reading as the teacher monitors fluency and provides guidance and feedback.

Because Research Says

Perhaps the best known of the strategies designed to support fluency development is that of repeated readings. Generally, the students involved in using this strategy enjoy seeing the gains they make through their tracking of the changes in their reading and experience gratification when making visible improvement over a short period of time. —(Kuhn, 2003)

INFORMATIONAL TEXT

In Reading Street

Research and Study Skills Each week, students learn a specific research, study, or technology skill. Instruction includes a review of terms related to the skill, a practice activity with questions that can be answered by students, and an additional activity that can be used to assess students' understanding. Students then apply the skill to their Research and Inquiry project that week.

Because Research Says

A key to good critical thinking and reading is checking sources of information and verifying ideas. —(McKee and Ogle, 2005)

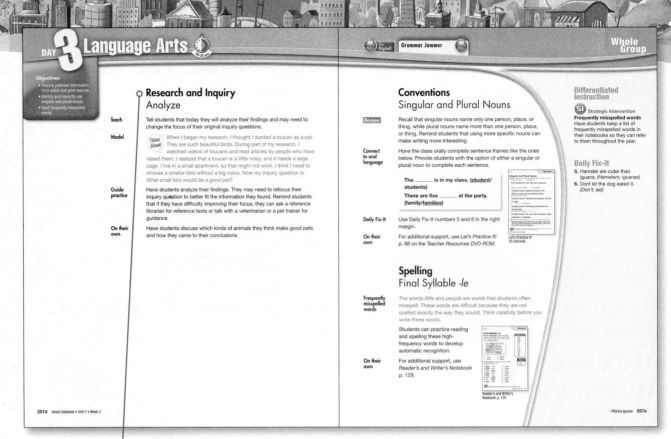

Objectives
- Analyze pertinent information from online and print sources.
- Identify and correctly use singular and plural nouns.
- Spell frequently misspelled words.

Research and Inquiry
Analyze

Teach Tell students that today they will analyze their findings and may need to change the focus of their original inquiry questions.

Model

Think Aloud When I began my research, I thought I wanted a toucan as a pet. They are such beautiful birds. During part of my research, I watched videos of toucans and read articles by people who have raised them. I realized that a toucan is a little noisy, and it needs a large cage. I live in a small apartment, so that might not work. I think I need to choose a smaller bird without a big voice. Now my inquiry question is *What small bird would be a good pet?*

Guide practice Have students analyze their findings. They may need to refocus their inquiry question to better fit the information they found. Remind students that if they have difficulty improving their focus, they can ask a reference librarian for reference texts or talk with a veterinarian or a pet trainer for guidance.

On their own Have students discuss which kinds of animals they think make good pets and how they came to their conclusions.

Conventions
Singular and Plural Nouns

Review Recall that singular nouns name only one person, place, or thing, while plural nouns name more than one person, place, or thing. Remind students that using more specific nouns can make writing more interesting.

Connect to oral language Have the class orally complete sentence frames like the ones below. Provide students with the option of either a singular or plural noun to complete each sentence.

The _____ is in my class. (**student**/students)

There are five _____ at the party. (family/**families**)

Daily Fix-It Use Daily Fix-It numbers 5 and 6 in the right margin.

On their own For additional support, use *Let's Practice It!* p. 88 on the *Teacher Resources DVD-ROM.*

*Let's Practice It!
TR DVD•88*

Spelling
Final Syllable -le

Frequently misspelled words The words *little* and *people* are words that students often misspell. These words are difficult because they are not spelled exactly the way they sound. Think carefully before you write these words.

Students can practice reading and spelling these high-frequency words to develop automatic recognition.

On their own For additional support, use *Reader's and Writer's Notebook* p. 129.

Reader's and Writer's Notebook p. 129

Differentiated Instruction

SI Strategic Intervention
Frequently misspelled words Have students keep a list of frequently misspelled words in their notebooks so they can refer to them throughout the year.

Daily Fix-It

5. Hamster are cuter than iguana. (*Hamsters; iguanas*)
6. Dont let the dog eated it. (*Don't; eat*)

21ST CENTURY SKILLS

In Reading Street

Research and Inquiry Much of student research is now done on the internet. Students learn skills, including navigating a student-friendly search engine, analyzing acquired information, synthesizing research, and communicating findings.

Because Research Says

The new literacies of the Internet include the skills necessary to successfully use and adapt to rapidly changing information and communication technologies and contexts. These skills allow us to use technology to identify important questions, locate information, critically evaluate the usefulness of that information, synthesize information to answer those questions, and then communicate the answers to others. —(Leu, Kinzer, Coiro, and Cammack, 2004)

DAY **3** **Language Arts**

Objectives
• Understand the criteria for writing an effective fairy tale.

Whole Group

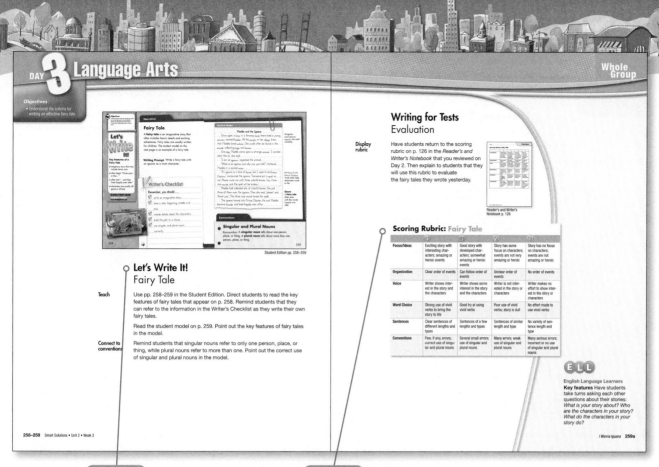

Student Edition pp. 258–259

Let's Write It!
Fairy Tale

Teach Use pp. 258–259 in the Student Edition. Direct students to read the key features of fairy tales that appear on p. 258. Remind students that they can refer to the information in the Writer's Checklist as they write their own fairy tales.

Read the student model on p. 259. Point out the key features of fairy tales in the model.

Connect to conventions Remind students that singular nouns refer to only one person, place, or thing, while plural nouns refer to more than one. Point out the correct use of singular and plural nouns in the model.

Writing for Tests
Evaluation

Display rubric Have students return to the scoring rubric on p. 126 in the *Reader's and Writer's Notebook* that you reviewed on Day 2. Then explain to students that they will use this rubric to evaluate the fairy tales they wrote yesterday.

Reader's and Writer's Notebook p. 126

Scoring Rubric: *Fairy Tale*

	4	3	2	1
Focus/Ideas	Exciting story with interesting characters; amazing or heroic events	Good story with developed characters; somewhat amazing or heroic events	Story has some focus on characters; events are not very amazing or heroic	Story has no focus on characters; events are not amazing or heroic
Organization	Clear order of events	Can follow order of events	Unclear order of events	No order of events
Voice	Writer shows interest in the story and the characters	Writer shows some interest in the story and the characters	Writer is not interested in the story or characters	Writer makes no effort to show interest in the story or characters
Word Choice	Strong use of vivid verbs to bring the story to life	Good try at using vivid verbs	Poor use of vivid verbs; story is dull	No effort made to use vivid verbs
Sentences	Clear sentences of different lengths and types	Sentences of a few lengths and types	Sentences of similar length and type	No variety of sentence length and type
Conventions	Few, if any, errors; correct use of singular and plural nouns	Several small errors; use of singular and plural nouns	Many errors; weak use of singular and plural nouns	Many serious errors; incorrect or no use of singular and plural nouns

ELL

English Language Learners
Key features Have students take turns asking each other questions about their stories: *What is your story about? Who are the characters in your story? What do the characters in your story do?*

WRITING

In Reading Street

Let's Write It Each week, children identify the key features—genre, conventions, and grammar—of a student writing model as the teacher reads it aloud. The teacher also provides direct instruction of a specific grammar skill.

Because Research Says

Students need to see models of good writing and practice identifying the conventions that make it ready for publication or readable for the intended audience. The model is shared and discussed during the writing process, not in isolation.
—(Anderson, 2007)

WRITING

In Reading Street

Scoring Rubric Rubrics allow teachers to judge students' written work based on the traits of good writing. Students can use the scoring rubric to understand expectations and as a checklist for self-evaluation.

Because Research Says

To know how well students are doing, teachers and administrators should use or consider 1) extended writing samples; 2) writing in multiple genres; 3) valid rubrics; 4) writing over time, across genres and content areas; and 5) student participation in developing assessment. —(National Writing Project and Nagin, 2003)

Pages 259b–259c are based on the same research as pages 258–259 and 259a. Pages 260a–260b are based on the same research as pages 232j and 233a. Pages 260c–260d are based on the same research as page 234a. Pages 260e–260f are based on the same research as page 235a.

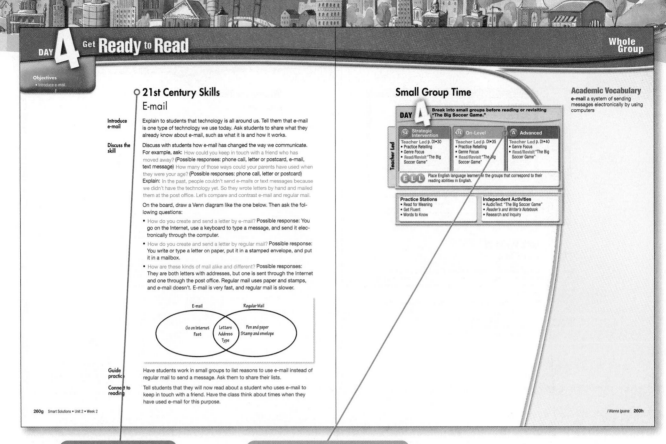

Objectives
• Introduce e-mail.

21st Century Skills
E-mail

Introduce e-mail
Explain to students that technology is all around us. Tell them that e-mail is one type of technology we use today. Ask students to share what they already know about e-mail, such as what it is and how it works.

Discuss the skill
Discuss with students how e-mail has changed the way we communicate. For example, ask: How could you keep in touch with a friend who has moved away? (Possible responses: phone call, letter or postcard, e-mail, text message) How many of those ways could your parents have used when they were your age? (Possible responses: phone call, letter or postcard) Explain: In the past, people couldn't send e-mails or text messages because we didn't have the technology yet. So they wrote letters by hand and mailed them at the post office. Let's compare and contrast e-mail and regular mail.

On the board, draw a Venn diagram like the one below. Then ask the following questions:

• How do you create and send a letter by e-mail? Possible response: You go on the Internet, use a keyboard to type a message, and send it electronically through the computer.

• How do you create and send a letter by regular mail? Possible response: You write or type a letter on paper, put it in a stamped envelope, and put it in a mailbox.

• How are these kinds of mail alike and different? Possible responses: They are both letters with addresses, but one is sent through the Internet and one through the post office. Regular mail uses paper and stamps, and e-mail doesn't. E-mail is very fast, and regular mail is slower.

E-mail — Go on Internet, Fast | **Letters, Address, Type** | **Regular Mail** — Pen and paper, Stamp and envelope

Guide practice
Have students work in small groups to list reasons to use e-mail instead of regular mail to send a message. Ask them to share their lists.

Connect to reading
Tell students that they will now read about a student who uses e-mail to keep in touch with a friend. Have the class think about times when they have used e-mail for this purpose.

260g Smart Solutions • Unit 2 • Week 2

Small Group Time

DAY 4 Break into small groups before reading or revisiting "The Big Soccer Game."

Teacher Led

Strategic Intervention	**On-Level**	**Advanced**
Teacher Led p. DI•30	Teacher Led p. DI•35	Teacher Led p. DI•40
• Practice Retelling	• Practice Retelling	• Genre Focus
• Genre Focus	• Genre Focus	• Read/Revisit "The Big
• Read/Revisit "The Big Soccer Game"	• Read/Revisit "The Big Soccer Game"	Soccer Game"

ELL Place English language learners in the groups that correspond to their reading abilities in English.

Practice Stations
• Read for Meaning
• Get Fluent
• Words to Know

Independent Activities
• AudioText: "The Big Soccer Game"
• Reader's and Writer's Notebook
• Research and Inquiry

I Wanna Iguana 260h

Academic Vocabulary
e-mail a system of sending messages electronically by using computers

---

21ST CENTURY SKILLS

In Reading Street

21st Century Skills Using reading skills and strategies in new contexts such as computer technology will become increasingly important. Paired selections focus on the skills and strategies students need to write, send, and respond to e-mail; access the Web; use a search engine; or use online directories and reference sources.

Because Research Says

The Internet has entered our classrooms faster than books, television, computers, the telephone, or any other technology for information and communications. Moreover, the Internet will be the vehicle for a host of new technologies that will continue to enter the classroom, regularly requiring new literacies from all of us. One of the more consistent findings from research in this area is that students are highly motivated and interested in these new literacies. —(Leu, 2002)

DIFFERENTIATED INSTRUCTION

In Reading Street

Advanced Instruction Daily advanced lessons enhance the skills taught in the core lesson, provide exposure to more challenging reading and vocabulary, and incorporate independent investigative work.

Because Research Says

Many talented readers read early and above grade level. They typically demonstrate enjoyment of reading, are capable of grasping complex ideas, and possess advanced language skills. Differentiated teaching strategies that address the needs of talented readers include curriculum compacting, acceleration, assigning reading material that is above their current grade level, and allowing independent reading choices.
—(Kaplan, 1999; Reis and Renzulli, 1989; VanTassel-Baska, 1996)

Pages 260–261 and 261a are based on the same research as pages 242–243 and 243a. Pages 262–263 and 263a are based on the same research as pages 242–243 and 243a.

Objectives
- Read with fluency and comprehension.
- Use context clues to figure out the meanings of unfamiliar words.
- Give a presentation.

Check Fluency WCPM
SUCCESS PREDICTOR

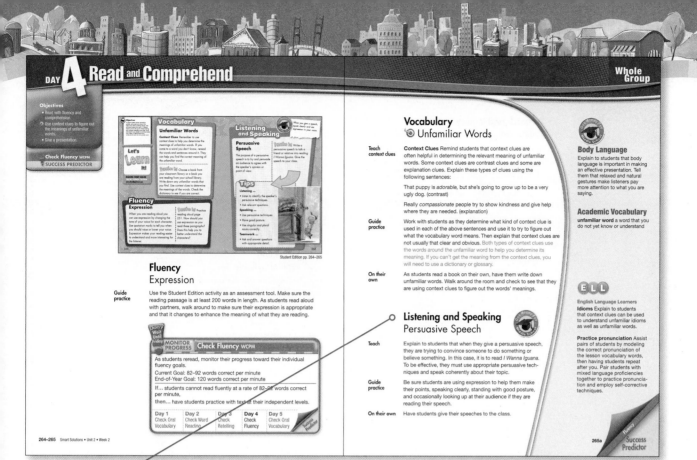

Student Edition pp. 264–265

Fluency
Expression

Guide practice — Use the Student Edition activity as an assessment tool. Make sure the reading passage is at least 200 words in length. As students read aloud with partners, walk around to make sure their expression is appropriate and that it changes to enhance the meaning of what they are reading.

MONITOR PROGRESS **Check Fluency WCPM**

As students reread, monitor their progress toward their individual fluency goals.
Current Goal: 82–92 words correct per minute
End-of-Year Goal: 120 words correct per minute
If... students cannot read fluently at a rate of 82–92 words correct per minute,
then... have students practice with text at their independent levels.

Day 1	Day 2	Day 3	Day 4	Day 5
Check Oral Vocabulary	Check Word Reading	Check Retelling	Check Fluency	Check Oral Vocabulary

Vocabulary
Unfamiliar Words

Teach context clues — **Context Clues** Remind students that context clues are often helpful in determining the relevant meaning of unfamiliar words. Some context clues are contrast clues and some are explanation clues. Explain these types of clues using the following sentences:

That puppy is *adorable*, but she's going to grow up to be a very ugly dog. (contrast)

Really *compassionate* people try to show kindness and give help where they are needed. (explanation)

Guide practice — Work with students as they determine what kind of context clue is used in each of the above sentences and use it to try to figure out what the vocabulary word means. Then explain that context clues are not usually that clear and obvious. Both types of context clues use the words around the unfamiliar word to help you determine its meaning. If you can't get the meaning from the context clues, you will need to use a dictionary or glossary.

On their own — As students read a book on their own, have them write down unfamiliar words. Walk around the room and check to see that they are using context clues to figure out the words' meanings.

Listening and Speaking
Persuasive Speech

Teach — Explain to students that when they give a persuasive speech, they are trying to convince someone to do something or believe something. In this case, it is to read *I Wanna Iguana*. To be effective, they must use appropriate persuasive techniques and speak coherently about their topic.

Guide practice — Be sure students are using expression to help them make their points, speaking clearly, standing with good posture, and occasionally looking up at their audience if they are reading their speech.

On their own — Have students give their speeches to the class.

Body Language
Explain to students that body language is important in making an effective presentation. Tell them that relaxed and natural gestures make listeners pay more attention to what you are saying.

Academic Vocabulary
unfamiliar word a word that you do not yet know or understand

ELL

English Language Learners
Idioms Explain to students that context clues can be used to understand unfamiliar idioms as well as unfamiliar words.

Practice pronunciation Assist pairs of students by modeling the correct pronunciation of the lesson vocabulary words, then having students repeat after you. Pair students with mixed language proficiencies together to practice pronunciation and employ self-corrective techniques.

265a **Success Predictor**

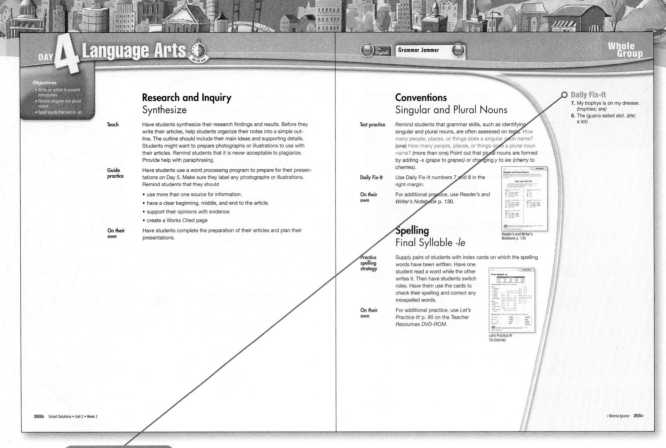

LANGUAGE ARTS

In Reading Street

Daily Fix-It Practice sentences provide opportunities for reviewing conventions, such as spelling, grammar, and punctuation. Each sentence contains errors in previously taught skills.

Because Research Says

Instead of formally teaching students grammar, we need to give them plenty of structured and unstructured opportunities to deal with language directly.
—(Weaver, 1979)

Pages 265d–265e are based on the same research as pages 258–259 and 259a.

30

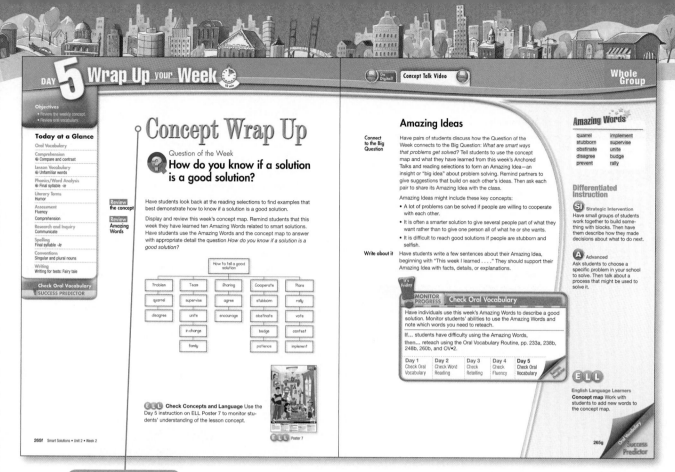

Concept Talk Video

Whole Group

Objectives
• Review the weekly concept.
• Review oral vocabulary.

Today at a Glance

Oral Vocabulary

Comprehension
✷ Compare and contrast

Lesson Vocabulary
✷ Unfamiliar words

Phonics/Word Analysis
✷ Final syllable -le

Literary Terms
Humor

Assessment
Fluency
Comprehension

Research and Inquiry
Communicate

Spelling
Final syllable -le

Conventions
Singular and plural nouns

Writing
Writing for tests: Fairy tale

Check Oral Vocabulary
⚡ SUCCESS PREDICTOR

Concept Wrap Up

Question of the Week
How do you know if a solution is a good solution?

Review the concept

Have students look back at the reading selections to find examples that best demonstrate how to know if a solution is a good solution.

Review Amazing Words

Display and review this week's concept map. Remind students that this week they have learned ten Amazing Words related to smart solutions. Have students use the Amazing Words and the concept map to answer with appropriate detail the question *How do you know if a solution is a good solution?*

How to tell a good solution

Problem — quarrel — disagree
Team — supervise — unite — in charge — family
Sharing — agree — encourage
Cooperate — stubborn — obstinate — budge — patience
Plans — rally — vote — contest — implement

ELL **Check Concepts and Language** Use the Day 5 instruction on ELL Poster 7 to monitor students' understanding of the lesson concept.

ELL Poster 7

265f Smart Solutions • Unit 2 • Week 2

Amazing Ideas

Connect to the Big Question

Have pairs of students discuss how the Question of the Week connects to the Big Question: *What are smart ways that problems get solved?* Tell students to use the concept map and what they have learned from this week's Anchored Talks and reading selections to form an Amazing Idea—an insight or "big idea" about problem solving. Remind partners to give suggestions that build on each other's ideas. Then ask each pair to share its Amazing Idea with the class.

Amazing Ideas might include these key concepts:

• A lot of problems can be solved if people are willing to cooperate with each other.

• It is often a smarter solution to give several people part of what they want rather than to give one person all of what he or she wants.

• It is difficult to reach good solutions if people are stubborn and selfish.

Write about it

Have students write a few sentences about their Amazing Idea, beginning with "This week I learned . . . ." They should support their Amazing Idea with facts, details, or explanations.

DAY 5 Friday

MONITOR PROGRESS **Check Oral Vocabulary**

Have individuals use this week's Amazing Words to describe a good solution. Monitor students' abilities to use the Amazing Words and note which words you need to reteach.

If... students have difficulty using the Amazing Words,
then... reteach using the Oral Vocabulary Routine, pp. 233a, 238b, 248b, 260b, and OV•2.

Day 1	Day 2	Day 3	Day 4	**Day 5**
Check Oral Vocabulary	Check Word Reading	Check Retelling	Check Fluency	**Check Oral Vocabulary**

Success Predictor

Amazing Words

quarrel   implement
stubborn   supervise
obstinate   unite
disagree   budge
prevent   rally

Differentiated Instruction

SI **Strategic Intervention**
Have small groups of students work together to build something with blocks. Then have them describe how they made decisions about what to do next.

A **Advanced**
Ask students to choose a specific problem in your school to solve. Then talk about a process that might be used to solve it.

ELL

English Language Learners
Concept map Work with students to add new words to the concept map.

265g   Oral Vocabulary   Success Predictor

ORAL VOCABULARY

In Reading Street

Concept Wrap Up In the Concept Wrap Up the class revisits the weekly concept and the Question of the Week using the week's concept web. Students apply the information they've learned and the Amazing Words to create Amazing Ideas related to the weekly concept.

Because Research Says

Making word meanings and relationships visible is another way to involve students actively in constructing word meaning. Semantic webs, maps, organizers, or other relational charts not only graphically display attributes of meanings, but also provide a memory organizer for later word use. —(Blachowicz and Fisher, 2002)

Page 265h is based on the same research as pages 236a and 238e. Page 265i is based on the same research as pages 238c–238d.

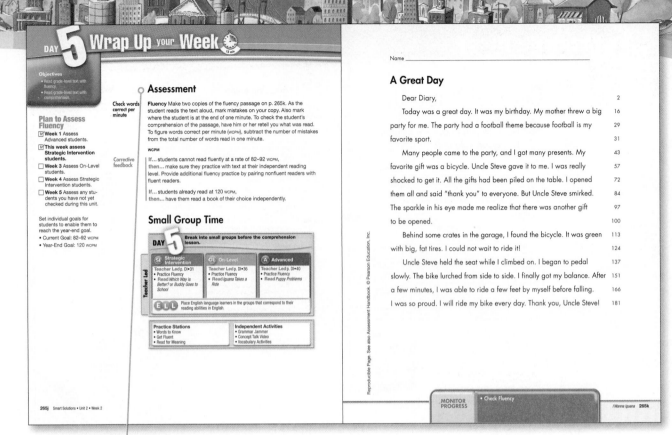

Objectives
• Read grade-level text with fluency.
• Read grade-level text with comprehension.

Plan to Assess Fluency
☑ **Week 1** Assess Advanced students.
☑ **This week assess Strategic Intervention students.**
☐ **Week 3** Assess On-Level students.
☐ **Week 4** Assess Strategic Intervention students.
☐ **Week 5** Assess any students you have not yet checked during this unit.

Set individual goals for students to enable them to reach the year-end goal.
• Current Goal: 82–92 WCPM
• Year-End Goal: 120 WCPM

Assessment

Check words correct per minute

Fluency Make two copies of the fluency passage on p. 265k. As the student reads the text aloud, mark mistakes on your copy. Also mark where the student is at the end of one minute. To check the student's comprehension of the passage, have him or her retell you what was read. To figure words correct per minute (WCPM), subtract the number of mistakes from the total number of words read in one minute.

WCPM

Corrective feedback

If… students cannot read fluently at a rate of 82–92 WCPM, then… make sure they practice with text at their independent reading level. Provide additional fluency practice by pairing nonfluent readers with fluent readers.

If… students already read at 120 WCPM, then… have them read a book of their choice independently.

Small Group Time

DAY 5 Break into small groups before the comprehension lesson.

Teacher Led

SI Strategic Intervention	**OL** On-Level	**A** Advanced
Teacher Led p. DI•31	Teacher Led p. DI•36	Teacher Led p. DI•40
• Practice Fluency	• Practice Fluency	• Practice Fluency
• Read *Which Way is Better?* or *Buddy Goes to School*	• Read *Iguana Takes a Ride*	• Read *Puppy Problems*

ELL Place English language learners in the groups that correspond to their reading abilities in English.

Practice Stations	**Independent Activities**
• Words to Know	• Grammar Jammer
• Get Fluent	• Concept Talk Video
• Read for Meaning	• Vocabulary Activities

Name _____

A Great Day

Dear Diary, 2

Today was a great day. It was my birthday. My mother threw a big 16

party for me. The party had a football theme because football is my 29

favorite sport. 31

Many people came to the party, and I got many presents. My 43

favorite gift was a bicycle. Uncle Steve gave it to me. I was really 57

shocked to get it. All the gifts had been piled on the table. I opened 72

them all and said "thank you" to everyone. But Uncle Steve smirked. 84

The sparkle in his eye made me realize that there was another gift 97

to be opened. 100

Behind some crates in the garage, I found the bicycle. It was green 113

with big, fat tires. I could not wait to ride it! 124

Uncle Steve held the seat while I climbed on. I began to pedal 137

slowly. The bike lurched from side to side. I finally got my balance. After 151

a few minutes, I was able to ride a few feet by myself before falling. 166

I was so proud. I will ride my bike every day. Thank you, Uncle Steve! 181

MONITOR PROGRESS • Check Fluency

I Wanna Iguana **265k**

SUCCESS PREDICTORS

In Reading Street

Assessment On Day 5, teachers administer assessments. A written assessment monitors progress in the week's target comprehension skill. To assess fluency, the teacher takes a timed sample of students' oral reading from reproducible pages. If students have difficulty reading the on-level fluency passage, the teacher provides additional opportunities for them to read text at their independent levels.

Because Research Says

Providing ongoing assessment of student reading progress may be one of the most valuable things teachers can do. The most valuable way to monitor student progress in fluency is to take timed measures of the number of words they read correctly in one minute. —(Vaughn and Linan-Thompson, 2004)

Pages 265l–265m are based on the same research as pages 265j–265k. Pages 265n–265o are based on the same research as pages 265b–265c. Pages 265p–265q are based on the same research as pages 258–259 and 259a.

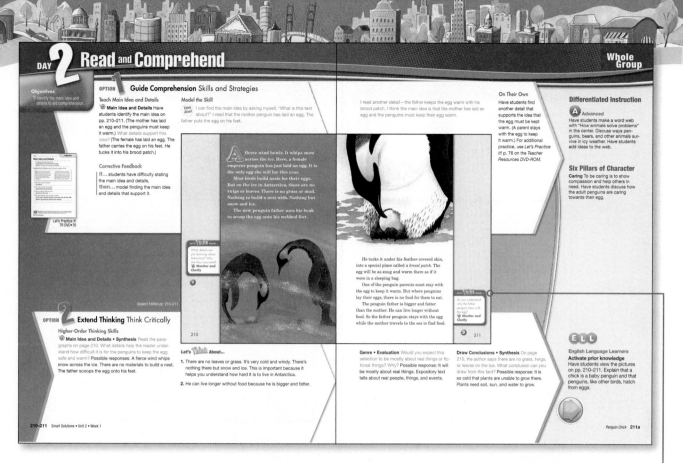

Read and Comprehend

Let's Think About It!

The first main selection of every unit, all of the second selections (except for 21st Century Skills lessons), and the first spread of each unit's Poetry Collection are annotated with thought-provoking Let's Think About It! questions. Main selection questions allow students to access the text by providing practice with the ten target strategies. Second selection questions guide students in identifying the elements of genre. Poetry Collection questions allow students to fully appreciate the poems by identifying the elements of poetry. All of these questions guide students in becoming strategic readers.

Research Says

"True comprehension goes beyond literal understanding and involves the reader's interaction with text. If students are to become thoughtful, insightful readers, they must merge their thinking with the text and extend their thinking beyond a superficial understanding." —(Harvey, Stephanie and Anne Goudvis. *Strategies That Work: Teaching Comprehension for Understanding and Engagement,* 2nd ed. Stenhouse Publishers, 2007.)

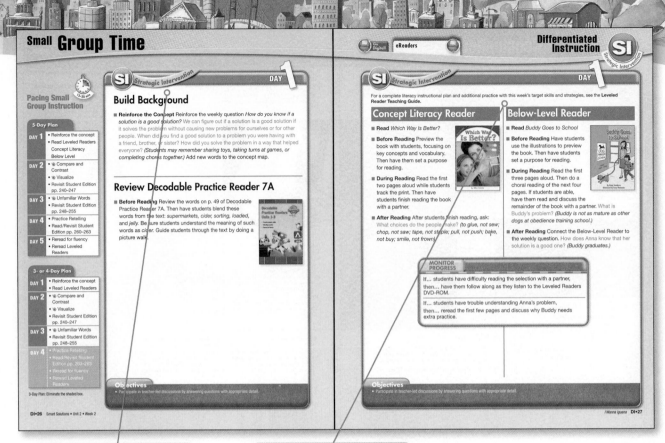

DIFFERENTIATED INSTRUCTION

In Reading Street

Strategic Intervention

Instruction Daily Small Group Time lessons provide struggling readers with more intensive instruction, more scaffolding, more practice with critical skills, and more opportunities to respond.

Because Research Says

A combination of explicit and systematic instruction with carefully scaffolded instruction that provides modeling and feedback is associated with improved academic outcomes for students with reading and learning disabilities. —(Vaughn and Linan-Thompson, 2003)

DIFFERENTIATED INSTRUCTION

In Reading Street

Leveled Readers Instructional-level fiction and nonfiction books are provided for readers at the Strategic Intervention, On-Level, and Advanced levels. These books relate to weekly concepts and offer students opportunities to read texts and practice targeted skills and strategies in small groups at their individual instructional levels. Teachers also use progress monitoring to move students along a continuum to independent reading.

Because Research Says

One of the five components of the model of explicit comprehension instruction best supported by research is guided practice with gradual release of responsibility. —(Duke and Pearson, 2002)

Pages DI•28–DI•31 are based on the same research as pages DI•26–DI•27.

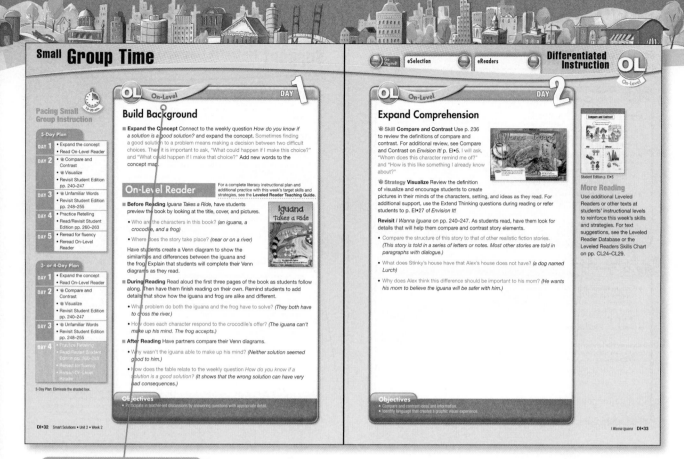

Pacing Small Group Instruction

5-Day Plan

DAY 1	• Expand the concept • Read On-Level Reader
DAY 2	• ⊛ Compare and Contrast • ⊛ Visualize • Revisit Student Edition pp. 240–247
DAY 3	• ⊛ Unfamiliar Words • Revisit Student Edition pp. 248–255
DAY 4	• Practice Retelling • Read/Revisit Student Edition pp. 260–263
DAY 5	• Reread for fluency • Reread On-Level Reader

3- or 4-Day Plan

DAY 1	• Expand the concept • Read On-Level Reader
DAY 2	• ⊛ Compare and Contrast • ⊛ Visualize • Revisit Student Edition pp. 240–247
DAY 3	• ⊛ Unfamiliar Words • Revisit Student Edition pp. 248–255
DAY 4	• Practice Retelling • Read/Revisit Student Edition pp. 260–263 • Reread for fluency • Reread On-Level Reader

3-Day Plan: Eliminate the shaded box.

OL On-Level — **DAY 1**

Build Background

■ **Expand the Concept** Connect to the weekly question *How do you know if a solution is a good solution?* and expand the concept. Sometimes finding a good solution to a problem means making a decision between two difficult choices. Then it is important to ask, "What could happen if I make this choice?" and "What could happen if I make that choice?" **Add new words to the concept map.**

On-Level Reader

For a complete literacy instructional plan and additional practice with this week's target skills and strategies, see the **Leveled Reader Teaching Guide.**

■ **Before Reading** *Iguana Takes a Ride,* have students preview the book by looking at the title, cover, and pictures.

• Who are the characters in this book? *(an iguana, a crocodile, and a frog)*

• Where does the story take place? *(near or on a river)*

Have students create a Venn diagram to show the similarities and differences between the iguana and the frog. Explain that students will complete their Venn diagrams as they read.

■ **During Reading** Read aloud the first three pages of the book as students follow along. Then have them finish reading on their own. Remind students to add details that show how the iguana and frog are alike and different.

• What problem do both the iguana and the frog have to solve? *(They both have to cross the river.)*

• How does each character respond to the crocodile's offer? *(The iguana can't make up his mind. The frog accepts.)*

■ **After Reading** Have partners compare their Venn diagrams.

• Why wasn't the iguana able to make up his mind? *(Neither solution seemed good to him.)*

• How does the fable relate to the weekly question *How do you know if a solution is a good solution?* *(It shows that the wrong solution can have very bad consequences.)*

Objectives
• Participate in teacher-led discussions by answering questions with appropriate detail.

DI•32 Smart Solutions • Unit 2 • Week 2

OL On-Level — **DAY 2**

Expand Comprehension

⊛ **Skill Compare and Contrast** Use p. 236 to review the definitions of compare and contrast. For additional review, see Compare and Contrast on *Envision It!* p. EI•5. I will ask, "Whom does this character remind me of?" and "How is this like something I already know about?"

⊛ **Strategy Visualize** Review the definition of visualize and encourage students to create pictures in their minds of the characters, setting, and ideas as they read. For additional support, use the Extend Thinking questions during reading or refer students to p. EI•27 of *Envision It!*

Revisit *I Wanna Iguana* on pp. 240–247. As students read, have them look for details that will help them compare and contrast story elements.

• Compare the structure of this story to that of other realistic fiction stories. *(This story is told in a series of letters or notes. Most other stories are told in paragraphs with dialogue.)*

• What does Stinky's house have that Alex's house does not have? *(a dog named Lurch)*

• Why does Alex think this difference should be important to his mom? *(He wants his mom to believe the iguana will be safer with him.)*

Objectives
• Compare and contrast ideas and information.
• Identify language that creates a graphic visual experience.

I Wanna Iguana DI•33

Student Edition p. EI•5

More Reading

Use additional Leveled Readers or other texts at students' instructional levels to reinforce this week's skills and strategies. For text suggestions, see the Leveled Reader Database or the Leveled Readers Skills Chart on pp. CL24–CL29.

DIFFERENTIATED INSTRUCTION

In Reading Street

On-Level Instruction Daily Small Group Time lessons focus on appropriate instructional strategies for students reading at grade level.

Because Research Says

Smaller group ratios increase the likelihood of academic success through student-teacher interactions, individualization of instruction, student on-task behavior, and teacher monitoring of student progress and feedback. —(Vaughn, et al., 2003)

Pages DI•34–DI•36 are based on the same research as pages DI•32–DI•33. Pages DI•37–DI•39 are based on the same research as page DI•40.

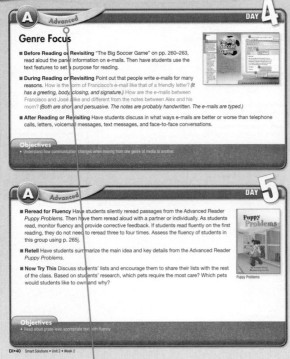

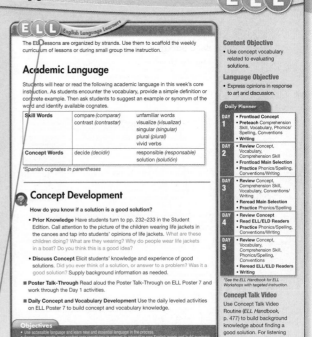

Pages DI•42–DI•47 are based on the same research as page DI•41.

DIFFERENTIATED INSTRUCTION

In Reading Street

Advanced Instruction Daily Small Group Time lessons for students reading above grade level enhance the skills taught in the core lesson, provide exposure to more challenging reading and vocabulary, and incorporate independent investigative work. Activities provide advanced readers additional opportunities to engage in critical and creative thinking, and to focus on problem-solving skills.

Because Research Says

In general, grouping academically talented students together for instruction has been found to produce positive achievement outcomes when the curriculum provided to students in different groups is appropriately differentiated. In other words, it is the instruction that occurs within groups that makes grouping an appropriate instructional strategy. —(Reis, et al., 2003)

ENGLISH LANGUAGE LEARNERS

In Reading Street

ELL Instruction English learners receive extra support to allow them to successfully participate in and progress through the daily lessons of the basic program with their peers.

Because Research Says

Given the diversity in our society, it is imperative to recognize that students may differ considerably in their inventory of skills and abilities, and these differences should not be treated as reflecting deficiencies in ability. —(Wong Fillmore and Snow, 2002)

ENGLISH LANGUAGE LEARNERS

In Reading Street

In the Comfort Zone Complex academic English instruction is made more accessible when English learners are comfortable in the classroom. Lessons for English language learners provide many strategies for increasing students' comfort level, including the use of visual supports in dramatizing, making personal and cultural connections, and total physical response.

Because Research Says

In second language acquisition, affective variables, such as motivation, self-confidence, and anxiety, play a role. Learners with high motivation and confidence and low anxiety are better equipped for success in the second language. A natural approach is to lower an affective barrier. —(Krashen and Terrell, 1983)

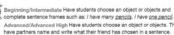

Comprehension
Mamá's Birthday Garden

- **Before Reading** Distribute copies of the ELL and ELD Readers, *Mamá's Birthday Garden*, to students at their reading level.

- **Preview** Read the title aloud with students: This is a realistic fiction story about a girl who wants to give her mother a special birthday gift. Invite students to look through the pictures and predict what they think will happen.

- **Set a Purpose for Reading** Let's read to find out how Paula solves her problem of what to get her mother.

1. Read the entire Reader aloud slowly.

2. Reread pp. 2–5, pausing to build background or model comprehension. Have Beginning students finger-point as you read. Use the questions in the chart to check students' comprehension.

3. Have students do a choral rereading of pp. 2–5.

4. Repeat steps 2–3 above for pp. 6–8 of the Reader.

- **During Reading** Follow the Reading Routine for both reading groups.

- **After Reading** Use the exercises on the inside back cover of each Reader and invite students to share their writing. In a whole-group discussion, ask students How does Paula solve her problem? Record their answers on the board and invite them to point to pictures in the book to support their answers.

ELD Reader Beginning/Intermediate

- **pp. 2–5** What does Paula want to give her mother for her birthday? (a garden)

- **p. 6** What does Paula get first? (plastic flowers) Read the sentences that tell you the answer. (bottom of p. 6)

- **p. 8** What does Paula do at the end? (plants seeds)

Writing What problem does Paula need to solve? Find the sentence in the book that tells her problem. Copy the sentence. Then read it aloud to your partner.

ELL Reader Advanced/Advanced High

- **pp. 2–3** What does Paula want to give her mother for her birthday? (a garden)

- **p. 6** What is Paula's problem? (She bought plastic flowers by accident.)

- **pp. 7–8** How does she solve her problem? (Mrs. Bailey helps her plant the flower seeds.)

Study Guide Distribute copies of the ELL Reader Study Guide (*ELL Handbook*, p. 70). Scaffold comprehension of story structure by helping students look back through the Reader in order to fill in the graphic organizer. Review their responses together. (See *ELL Handbook*, pp. 209–212.)

ELL English Language Learners

Conventions
Singular and Plural Nouns

- **Preteach** Point to an object in the classroom. That is one book. Point to several objects. Those are many books. Have students orally practice using singular and plural nouns.

- **Practice** Place several groups of objects on a table.

L/S Beginning/Intermediate Have students choose an object or objects and complete sentence frames such as: *I have many pencils. I have one pencil.*
Advanced/Advanced High Have students choose an object or objects. Then have partners name and write what their friend has chosen in a sentence.

- **Reteach** Display the following chart below and explain:
  - Add -s to most nouns to form the plural.
  - If the noun ends in -ch, -sh, -s, -ss, or -x, add -es.
  - If the noun ends in a consonant + y, change the y to i and add -es.

add -s	add -es	change y to i and add -es
pen/pens/ truck/trucks	box/boxes peach/peaches	berry/berries baby/babies

- **Practice** Use the chart above.

L/S Beginning/Intermediate Have students complete the following sentence frames with words from the chart orally or in writing:
There is one _____. There are two _____.
Advanced Have partners write a sentence for each word and edit each other's work.
Advanced High Have partners find more words to add to the chart, write them in the correct columns, and check a dictionary to make sure they added the plural ending correctly.

Content Objective
- Correctly form and use singular and plural nouns.

Language Objectives
- Speak using the pattern of singular and plural nouns.
- Write phrases and sentences with singular and plural nouns.

Transfer Skills
Plurals
- Spanish speakers use -s and -es endings for nouns.
- In some languages, including Chinese, Hmong, and Vietnamese, nouns do not have plural forms. Instead, the plural is indicated with an adjective.

Grammar Jammer
For more practice with nouns, use the Grammar Jammer Routine (*ELL Handbook*, p. 476).

ELL Workshop
Students may need extra practice using language structures heard during classroom interactions. Use Nouns in Your Speaking (*ELL Handbook*, pp. 424–425) provides extra support.

ENGLISH LANGUAGE LEARNERS

In Reading Street

ELL Leveled Support Teachers use a variety of instructional activities to support English language learners at different levels of proficiency. Different techniques can be chosen as the teacher observes which students need more support or more challenging language activities. At the beginning level, techniques include gesturing and having students draw. For more advanced levels, students are encouraged to speak in more complex sentences and use a wider range of vocabulary.

Because Research Says

Often beginning and intermediate English language learners may not understand what their classroom teachers say or read aloud in English. When it becomes clear from students' actions and responses that they understand what is being said, teachers can vary their strategies. —(García, 2010)

ENGLISH LANGUAGE LEARNERS

In Reading Street

Social Language Lessons provide teachers ways to engage English language learners in authentic use of social language. Students learn and use fixed English expressions such as *run away* and *throw it to* while teachers model language and correct their usage so that students' English sounds natural.

Because Research Says

The most effective activities provide English language learners ample opportunity to hear English and to use it productively in meaningful communication. Students must be able to participate to the extent possible in discussions with classmates who are more proficient in English, but only teachers can ensure that English language learners get access to the kind of language needed for literacy development. —(Wong Fillmore, 2010)

ENGLISH LANGUAGE LEARNERS

In Reading Street

Sheltered Reading Prompts and questions designed for English language learners help teachers guide students as they read and comprehend text. The prompts allow students at different English language levels to answer by pointing, with yes/no or single words, or with longer statements as they interact with text and pictures.

Because Research Says

Beginning and intermediate English language learners often do not understand what their classroom teachers say or read aloud, or what they read on their own in English. These students benefit when teachers shelter, or make comprehensible, their literacy instruction through a variety of sheltered techniques, including activities that integrate reading, writing, listening, and speaking. —(García, 2010)

Research Bibliography

Anderson, Jeff. *Mechanically Inclined: Building Grammar, Usage, and Style into Writer's Workshop.* Stenhouse Publishers, 2005.

Anderson, R., E. Hiebert, J. Scott, and I. Wilkinson. "The Report of the Commission on Reading." *Becoming a Nation of Readers.* The National Institute of Education, 1985.

Armbruster, B. B., F. Lehr and J. Osborn. *Put Reading First: The Research Building Blocks for Teaching Children to Read.* Partnership for Reading, 2001.

Beck, Isabel L., Margaret G. McKeown, Rebecca L. Hamilton, and Linda Kucan. *Bringing Words to Life: Robust Vocabulary Instruction.* The Guilford Press, 2002.

Blachowicz, Camille and Peter J. Fisher. *Teaching Vocabulary in All Classrooms,* 2nd ed. Merrill Prentice Hall, 2002.

Block, Cathy Collins and Michael Pressley. "Best Practices in Comprehension Instruction." *Best Practices in Literary Instruction.* The Guilford Press, 2003.

Coyne, Michael D., Deborah C. Simmons, and Edward J. Kame'enui. "Vocabulary Instruction for Young Children at Risk of Experiencing Reading Difficulties." *Vocabulary Instruction: Research to Practice.* The Guilford Press, 2004.

Cummins, Jim. "The Three Pillars of English Language Learning." *Pearson Scott Foresman EL Handbook Teacher's Manual,* 2010.

Duke, Nell K. and P. David Pearson. "Effective Practices for Developing Reading Comprehension." *What Research Has to Say About Reading Instruction,* 3rd ed. International Reading Association, 2002.

Duke, Nell K., V. Susan Bennett-Armistead, Ebony M. Roberts. "Bridging the Gap Between Learning to Read and Reading to Learn." *Literacy and Young Children: Research-Based Practices.* The Guilford Press, 2003.

Ehri, Linnea C. and Simone R. Nunes. "The Role of Phonemic Awareness in Learning to Read." *What Research Has to Say About Reading Instruction,* 3rd ed. International Reading Association, 2002.

Ehri, Linnea C., M. R., and S. A. Stahl. "Fluency: A Review of Developmental and Remedial Practices." *Journal of Educational Psychology,* vol. 95, 2003.

Ehri, Linnea C. "Grapheme-Phoneme Knowledge Is Essential for Learning to Read Words in English." *Word Recognition in Beginning Literacy.* Lawrence Erlbaum Associates, 1992.

Foorman, B. R., and J. Torgesen. "Critical Elements of Classroom and Small-Group Instruction Promote Reading Success in All Children." *Learning Disabilities Research and Practice,* vol. 16, November 2001.

Galda, Lee, and Richard Beach. "Response to Literature as a Cultural Activity." *Theoretical Models and Processes of Reading,* 5th ed. International Reading Association, 2004.

García, Georgia Earnest. "English Learners and Literacy: Best Practices." *Pearson Scott Foresman EL Handbook Teacher's Manual,* 2010.

Gaskins, Irene W. "A Multidimensional Approach to Beginning Literacy." *Literacy and Young Children: Research-Based Practices.* The Guilford Press, 2003.

Ivey, Gay. "Building Comprehension When They're Still Learning to Read the Words." *Comprehension Instruction: Research-Based Best Practices.* The Guilford Press, 2002.

Juel, Connie. "Impact of Early School Experiences," *Handbook of Early Literacy Research,* 2nd ed. The Guilford Press, 2005.

Kaplan, S. "Reading Strategies for Gifted Readers." *Teaching for High Potential,* vol. 1, no. 2, 1999.

Kuhn, M. R., and S. A. Stahl. "Fluency: A Review of Developmental and Remedial Practices." *Journal of Educational Psychology,* vol. 95, 2003.

Kuhn, Melanie. "How Can I Help Them Pull It All Together? A Guide to Fluent Reading Instruction." *Literacy and Young Children: Research-Based Practices.* The Guilford Press, 2003.

Krashen, Stephen D., and Tracy D. Terrell. *The Natural Approach: Language Acquisition in the Classroom.* Alemany Press, 1983.

Leu, D. J. Jr., C. K. Kinzer, J. Coiro, and D. Cammack. "Toward a Theory of New Literacies Emerging from the Internet and Other Information and Communication Technologies." *Theoretical Models and Processes of Reading,* 5th ed. International Reading Association, 2004.

Leu, Donald and Charles Kinzer. "The Convergence of Literary Instruction with Networked Technologies for Information and Communication." *Reading Research Quarterly,* vol. 35, no. 1, January/February/March 2000.

Leu, Donald. "The New Literacies: Research on Reading Instruction With the Internet." *What Research Has to Say About Reading Instruction,* 3rd ed., International Reading Association, 2002.

McKee, Judith and Donna Ogle. *Integrating Instruction, Literacy and Science.* The Guilford Press, 2005.

Morrow, Lesley Mandel and Linda Gambrell. "Literature-Based Instruction in the Early Years." *Handbook of Early Literacy Research.* The Guilford Press, 2002.

Morrow, L. M., "Story Retelling: A Discussion Strategy to Develop and Assess Comprehension." *Lively Discussions! Fostering Engaged Reading.* International Reading Association, 1996.

National Reading Panel. *Teaching Children to Read.* National Institute of Child Health and Human Development. 1999.

National Writing Project and Carl Nagin. *Because Writing Matters.* Jossey-Bass, 2003.

Noguchi, Rei R. *The English Record.* Winter, 2002.

Ogle, D. and C. L. Blachowicz. "Beyond Literature Circles: Helping Students Comprehend Informational Texts." *Comprehension Instruction: Research-Based Best Practices.* The Guilford Press, 2002.

Paratore, Jeanne and Rachel McCormack. *Teaching Literacy in Second Grade.* The Guilford Press, 2005.

Pearson, P. D., L. R. Roehler, J. A. Dole, and G. G. Duffy. "Developing Expertise in Reading Comprehension." *What Research Says About Reading Instruction,* 2nd ed. International Reading Association, 1992.

Pearson, P. David and Nell K. Duke. "Comprehension Instruction in the Primary Grades." *Comprehension Instruction: Research-Based Best Practices.* The Guilford Press, 2002.

Pressley, M., and C. C. Block. "Summing Up: What Comprehension Instruction Could Be." *Comprehension Instruction: Research-Based Best Practices.* The Guilford Press, 2002.

Pressley, M. "Metacognition and Self-Regulated Comprehension." *What Research Has to Say About Reading Instruction,* 3rd ed. International Reading Association, 2002.

Reis, Sally M., E. Jean Gubbins, Christine Briggs, Fredric J. Schreiber, Susannah Richards, Joan Jacobs, Rebecca D. Eckert, Joseph S. Renzulli, and Margaret Alexander. *Reading Instruction for Talented Readers: Case Studies Documenting Few Opportunities for Continuous Progress* (RM03184). The National Research Center on the Gifted and Talented, University of Connecticut, 2003.

Reis, Sally M., and Joseph S. Renzulli. "Developing Challenging Programs for Gifted Readers." *The Reading Instruction Journal,* vol. 32, 1989.

Samuels, S. J. "Reading Fluency: Its Development and Assessment." *What Research Has to Say About Reading Instruction,* 3rd ed. International Reading Association, 2002.

Seefeldt, Carol and Barbara A. Wasik. *Early Education: Three-, Four-, and Five-Year Olds Go to School,* 2nd ed. Pearson Merrill Prentice Hall, 2006.

Smith, Sylvia B., Deborah C. Simmons, and Edward J. Kame'enui. "Phonological Awareness: Instructional and Curricular Basics and Implications." *What Reading Research Tells Us About Children With Diverse Learning Needs: Bases and Basics.* Lawrence Erlbaum Associates, 1998.

Snow, Catherine E., M. Susan Burns, and Peg Griffin, eds. *Preventing Reading Difficulties in Young Children.* National Research Council, 1998.

Spandel, Vicki. "Assessing With Heart." National Staff Development Council, vol. 27, no. 3. Summer 2006.

_____. *Creating Writers Through 6-Trait Writing Assessment and Instruction.* 2nd ed. Merrill Prentice Hall, 2002.

_____. *Creating Writers Through 6-Trait Writing Assessment and Instruction.* 3rd ed. Addison Wesley Longman, 2001.

_____. *Creating Writers Through 6-Trait Writing Assessment and Instruction.* 4th ed. Allyn and Bacon, 2004.

Stahl, Steven A. and Katherine A. Dougherty Stahl. "Word Wizards All! Teaching Word Meanings in Preschool and Primary Education." *Vocabulary Instruction: Research to Practice.* The Guilford Press, 2004.

Tatum, Alfred. *Teaching Reading to Black Adolescent Males.* Stenhouse Publishers, 2005.

Taylor, Barbara M., P. David Pearson, Debra S. Peterson, and Michael C. Rodriguez. "The CIERA School Change Framework: An Evidence-Based Approach to Professional Development and School Reading Improvement." *Reading Research Quarterly,* vol. 40, no. 1, January/February/March 2005.

VanTassel–Baska, J. "Effective Curriculum and Instructional Models for Talented Students." *Gifted Child Quarterly,* vol. 30, 1996.

Vaughn, Sharon and Sylvia Linan–Thompson. *Research-Based Methods of Reading Instruction.* Association for Supervision and Curriculum Development, 2004.

_____. "Group Size and Time Allotted to Intervention: Effects for Students with Reading Difficulties." *Preventing and Remediating Reading Difficulties: Bringing Science to Scale.* Baltimore York Press, 2003.

Vaughn, Sharon, Sylvia Linan–Thompson, Kamiar Kouzekanani, Diane Pedrotty, Shirley Dickson, and Shelly Blozis. "Reading Instruction Grouping for Students with Reading Difficulties." *Remedial and Special Education,* vol. 24, no. 5, September/October 2003.

Weaver, Constance. *Grammar for Teachers: Perspectives and Definitions.* NCTE, 1979.

Wiggins, Grant and Jay McTighe. *Understanding by Design.* Pearson Education, Inc., 2006.

Wilkinson, L. C. and E. R. Silliman. "Classroom Language and Literacy Learning." *Handbook of Reading Research,* vol. III. Lawrence Erlbaum Associates, 2000.

Wong Fillmore, Lily and Catherine E. Snow. "What Teachers Need to Know About Language." *What Teachers Need to Know About Language.* The Center for Applied Linguistics and Delta Systems Co., Inc., 2002.

Wong Fillmore, Lily. "Preparing English Language Learners for Assessment." *Pearson Scott Foresman EL Handbook Teacher's Manual,* 2010.

Wray, David and Maureen Lewis. "But Bonsai Tress Don't Grow in Baskets: Young Children's Talk During Authentic Inquiry." *Lively Discussions! Fostering Engaged Reading.* International Reading Association, 1996.

Zevenenbergen, Andrea and Grover Whitehurst. *On Reading Books to Children: Parents and Teacher.* Lawrence Erlbaum Associates, 2003.

Guide to
Reading Street

Your third grade students are eager to be independent. You have an opportunity to channel their eagerness and launch them on future journeys, to fourth grade and beyond—to a lifelong love of reading. How do you meet the challenge that teaching third grade brings?

Section 2 guides you through *Reading Street*.
It gives suggestions for setting up your classroom and managing it effectively. Refer to this section when you need ideas and background information to teach these critical elements of literacy:

- Phonics

- Word Structure

- Fluency

- Vocabulary

- Comprehension

- Writing

The section ends with a visit with the renowned authors whose research is the foundation of *Scott Foresman Reading Street*, so they can answer some of your questions.

Setting Up Your Classroom

Students will look to you for guidance and support as they explore the world of third grade. You'll want to set up your classroom so that you have separate areas for different instructional activities.

How Should I Organize My Classroom?

Whole-Group Instruction

Use an open area from which all students can easily see the chalkboard and instructional materials. In many classrooms students will be seated at desks that may be arranged in groups. During the day students can also use their own desks for independent work.

Small Group Time

Small group work is best done at a table with convenient storage space for the leveled materials nearby. Choose a place where you can lead the group and monitor the rest of the class.

Practice Stations

Practice stations should be inviting areas where students can work independently, in pairs, or in small groups. The *Reading Street Practice Stations Kit* helps simplify the task of managing practice stations by providing ideas for setting up your stations, weekly activities, and suggested routines for each station. You will find weekly activities for vocabulary, writing, phonics, spelling, comprehension, fluency, and technology in your *Reading Street Teacher's Edition.*

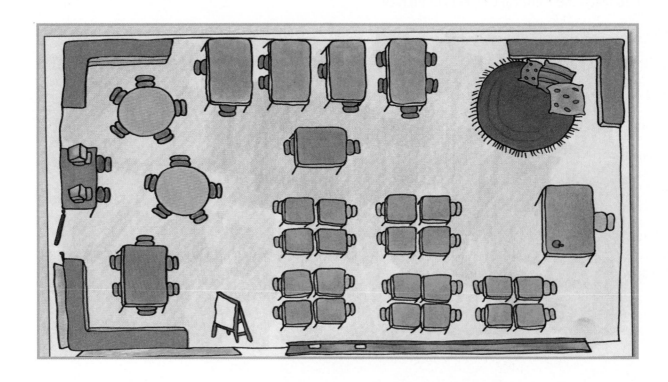

Effective Classroom Management

How Can I Teach Effectively?

Fast-Paced, High-Density Instruction Students should be on-task most of the time. Planning is a key to keeping students actively engaged in learning.

Explicit, Systematic Instruction Throughout *Reading Street*, you'll find routines that contain the language and steps you need to make instruction explicit. You'll also have built-in supports for incorporating these practices throughout each day.

- Connect to what students already know; build on their prior knowledge.
- Introduce a small amount of new information at a time.
- Always model a new skill before asking students to use it.
- "Front-load," or preteach, skills for English language learners.
- Provide ample practice, first guided, then independent.
- Encourage students to use language.
- Monitor students' progress regularly and provide corrective feedback.
- Use visuals and graphic organizers to clarify instruction.
- Provide a cumulative and spiraled review of previously learned skills.

Scaffold Students' Learning Offer modeling and prompts frequently as students learn new skills. For reading comprehension, thinking aloud is often the best way to model skills and strategies. It also supports English learners with needed academic language and literacy skills transfer opportunities. When you use Anchored Talk to provide explicit instruction, you are building valuable language skills.

Differentiate Instruction Group students according to their instructional levels. With students' abilities in mind, you can go on to plan either additional intensive instruction and practice or more challenging work for groups. Regroup when necessary and allow students to help model for their peers.

Establish Routines Students work best when they know what they're supposed to do, not just at one station, but at several. As students move routinely from one task to another, you will be able to devote more attention to small-group instruction.

Create High Expectations State your cognitive demands clearly, showing confidence that each student can meet them.

Reinforce Achievement Use praise to recognize improvement and specific goals students meet.

Encourage Self-Regulation Praise students often for making their own good decisions.

> Spiral Review
> In addition to teaching new skills each week, you review both new skills *and* those you taught before. The spiral review is systematic, so you spend the right amount of time reviewing each skill.

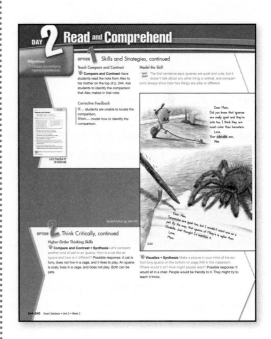

Phonics

Sounds and Symbols

Your third grade reading curriculum spans a broad set of skills. For a few students, you will provide phonemic awareness instruction. You will teach others to relate the sounds of spoken English to the symbols of the written language. They need the explicit and systematic phonics instruction provided in *Reading Street*.

Blending Sounds Leads to Decoding

Phonics instruction begins with introducing letter-sounds in isolation and moves students from recognizing sounds to blending sounds to decoding words. At each step, teaching routines make instruction explicit.

It's an exciting moment for students when they "crack the code" and read words with meanings they understand!

How Does Segmenting Sounds Lead to Writing?

To strengthen students' grasp of sound-spellings, ask them to segment sounds for spelling. To "write for sounds," students think about sounds, their sequence in a word, and the letters that stand for those sounds. This instruction must be explicit. Model this process when you write and engage students in structured writing activities.

Expecting Symbols to Make Sense

What is a new word? Is the new word a word you know? Does it make sense in the sentence?

Ask these questions to help students make sense of written symbols when they decode. As students respond to your feedback and questions, they reevaluate and adapt until they are successful. That "on my own" success encourages them to ask *themselves* the same questions when they read independently. You're teaching them an important lesson: they can expect written symbols to make sense.

Phonics: the relationship between sounds and letters

Teaching Routine

Sound-by-Sound Blending

1. **Display** Write the word *brought*.

2. **Segment** Put your hand under *b* and say /b/. Move your hand to *r* and say /r/. Move to *ough* and say /ö/. Move to *t* and say /t/.

3. **Blend** Then move your hand below the word from left to right. To blend, say the sounds sequentially, with no pause between letter-sounds, /b/ /r/ /o/ /t/.

4. **Read** Then pronounce the word *brought* normally.

5. **Repeat** Have students repeat the blending process for *brought*, first with you, and then as a group.

Teaching Routine

Segmenting

1. **Model** Say each word slowly and distinctly.

2. **Guide Practice** Have students segment, or listen for each sound.

3. **Guide Practice** Have students write what they hear, sound by sound.

Word Structure

Along with an awareness of letter-sound relationships, students must develop an awareness of morphemes. **Morphemes** are the smallest meaningful units of language and include word parts such as base words, prefixes, and suffixes. A morpheme may be the whole word, such as *carry*, or a part of a word such as *-est*. A word may be made up of one or more morphemes. *Friend* consists of one morpheme; *friendly*, two; *unfriendly*, three; *unfriendliest*, four.

How Does Word Structure Aid Decoding?

For morphemes to be useful to students, they must be taught explicitly, sequentially, and systematically. Instruction in Grade 3 includes inflected endings, such as *-s, -es, -ed, -ing*; compound words; the most common suffixes and prefixes; and spelling changes. Instructional routines for blending the syllables in multisyllabic words are provided in word structure lessons throughout *Scott Foresman Reading Street*.

Model how to read multisyllabic words.

- Examine a word for its word parts.
- Take off first any prefixes and then any endings or suffixes.
- Determine if the base word is known or can be decoded.
- Add back the prefixes, endings, and suffixes and pronounce the word in sequence, part by part.

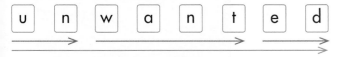

How Does Word Structure Give Clues to Meaning?

Since morphemes are meaningful units, instruction must include the meaning conveyed by each word part. For example, students should understand that *-s* or *-es* may convey "more than one," *-ed* signals an action that happened in the past, and *un-* means "not" or "the opposite of." Think about how you can group meaning-related words together as you teach. Then you can expect these positive outcomes:

- Students expand their vocabularies faster.
- They more quickly determine the meaning of new words.
- They read with greater comprehension.

---

morpheme the smallest meaningful unit of language, including base words, prefixes, and suffixes

morpheme awareness the ability to attend to the structure of words and to the word parts that convey meaning

---

The "Why" of Teaching Morphemes

Students, including English language learners, who learn to examine these important word parts gain a powerful strategy for identifying unfamiliar words as they read, for expanding their vocabularies, and for spelling.

---

sharp
sharply
sharper
sharpest

Fluency

What Is Fluency?

Fluency is the ability to read quickly and accurately. Fluency develops over time and with considerable practice. Fluent readers decode words automatically. This freedom from decoding allows them to concentrate on understanding their reading.

How Do I Help Students Become Fluent Readers?

You can develop students' fluency in two ways. First, **model key fluency skills.** Demonstrate how to read with accuracy, appropriate pace, attention to punctuation, and expression. Have students engage in **repeated oral reading.** Then monitor them and provide guidance and feedback.

Reading Street provides explicit instruction for each of the key fluency skills. Because students need ample opportunities and different ways to practice reading aloud, *Reading Street* offers a variety of methods. The lessons in the Teacher's Editions will help you establish fluency routines for oral rereading, paired reading, echo reading, choral reading, and Reader's Theater. Students can practice with you or an aide, other students, or even by themselves.

What Should Students Read to Develop Fluency?

It is important to have students reread a variety of short texts that are relatively easy. The texts should be at their independent reading level, that is, students should have a 95% success rate (misreading only about 1 in 20 words). When instructing students, you may use an instructional level text—a challenging but manageable text—with which students will have a 90% success rate (misreading only about 1 in 10 words). Text that is too difficult does not allow students to develop fluency or to experience success. *Reading Street* offers materials that can be used for fluency practice, including Student Editions, Decodable Readers, Leveled Readers, and Audio CDs.

How Do I Monitor Progress in Fluency?

To assess students' fluency formally, take timed samples of their oral reading, measure words read correctly per minute (WCPM), and set goals for progress. *Reading Street* provides weekly opportunities for fluency assessment, including benchmark goals for words correct per minute and a Fluency Assessment Plan that identifies which students to assess each week.

Why Is Fluency Important?

A **fluent reader** reads accurately and quickly with expressiveness, stress, and intonation. This reader can also interpret text. **Fluent readers** can comprehend and decode at the same time. Without fluency, students are unable to comprehend what they have read.

Vocabulary

Vocabulary knowledge has been strongly correlated with reading comprehension in many studies. Research shows that oral vocabulary and reading vocabulary can be learned both directly and indirectly. Vocabulary is learned **indirectly** when students hear books read aloud, when they take part in conversations, and when they read. **Direct instruction** involves systematic teaching of specific words. Studies show that direct instruction in vocabulary leads to gains in reading comprehension.

How Do I Help Students Increase Their Oral Vocabulary?

It is important to develop oral vocabulary. Students should be learning words and concepts that they will need as they progress in school.

In *Reading Street*, oral language is developed both directly and indirectly. A set of conceptually related "Amazing Words" is identified each week. These concept words are reviewed throughout the week, allowing students to encounter and use them frequently. An Oral Vocabulary Routine that includes multiple examples of each word's use is provided for direct instruction of these words.

Daily Anchored Talk provides opportunities for students to use and apply oral vocabulary when discussing weekly concepts and literature.

How Do I Help Students Increase Their Reading Vocabulary?

- **Teach** important selection words **prior to reading** and link them to students' reading. Encourage students to use the new vocabulary when they talk and write about the selection.
- Emphasize and model using **academic language.**
- Use **graphic organizers** to build concepts and vocabulary. Semantic webs are powerful ways to help students learn new words.
- Teach **word-learning strategies** so students will become independent word learners. Instruct them in how to use word parts, such as prefixes and suffixes, to determine word meanings and how to use context to figure out meanings of unfamiliar words.
- Provide ongoing opportunities for students to read **a wide variety of texts.** The more students read, the more vocabulary they learn.

"Students who receive rich, frequent vocabulary instruction demonstrate better understanding than students receive traditional definition-based instruction." (Beck, I., McKeown, M., Kucan, L., 2002)

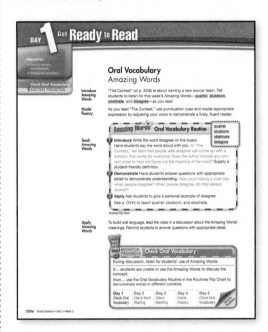

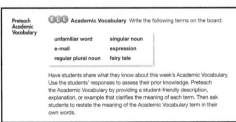

Comprehension

Comprehension is the process of making meaning from text. It involves not just reading words accurately, but drawing on prior knowledge, making inferences, making connections, and using strategies to make sense of text. Listening to texts read aloud leads to familiarity with text structures, a more enriched vocabulary, and an increased understanding of written texts. As your third grade students move through the year reading and listening to a wide variety of literature, the gap between their listening and reading comprehension closes, and they read more independently.

How Do Readers Use Skills and Strategies?

Most students need to learn key reading strategies through explicit instruction within the context of their reading. Strategy instruction has two critical components. First, students must **learn a strategy,** the procedure or set of steps to follow to comprehend text. Second, they must **learn to think consciously about when and how to apply the strategy.** *Reading Street* provides direct instruction for key comprehension strategies including:

- Using Prior Knowledge
- Previewing
- Predicting
- Identifying the Main Idea and Supporting Details
- Summarizing
- Making Inferences
- Distinguishing Fact and Opinion

Why Should Readers "Think about Thinking?"

Students can become aware of strategies by writing about their own reading process in a journal. The Strategy Response Log in *Reading Street* allows students to record what strategy they used, how they used it, whether they used it before, during, or after reading, and how the strategy worked for them. Self-assessment leads to students using strategies more automatically. However, until "thinking about thinking"

internalizes their use of strategies, students need frequent modeling, ample practice, and consistent feedback for their strategy use.

How Can I Help Students Develop Reading Comprehension?

Teachers who provide explicit comprehension instruction will see growth in students' progress and will increase students' enjoyment of reading. Effective instructional practices include

- **Direct, Explicit Teaching** Students must be taught what the skill or strategy is as well as when and how to use it.

- **Teacher Modeling and Demonstration** In *Reading Street*, this is accomplished in think-alouds that appear in comprehension skill and strategy lessons.

- **Guided and Independent Practice** Guided comprehension practice accompanies every Student Edition selection. Teacher modeling for skills and strategies occurs with most frequency early in the year. Student models help teachers scaffold instruction and move students toward skill independence. As the year progresses, students are expected to assume more responsibility for applying comprehension skills and strategies independently.

- **Frequent Application of the Skill or Strategy** When reading occurs in small groups, teachers can guide students' application of skills and strategies and provide feedback to individuals. In *Scott Foresman Reading Street*, students use a Strategy Response Log to apply and self-monitor their use of strategies.

- **Monitoring Progress** In third grade, perform this assessment by having students retell stories or summarize the main ideas of expository text using the Retelling Cards. Provide extra support as necessary. Don't wait until Friday!

"When skill and strategy complement each other, they can provide student readers with motivation and self-efficacy from both sources (I am good at this *and* I can work through the tough spots)."
(Afflerbach, P., Pearson, P., Paris, S., 2008)

Writing

Why Is Writing Instruction Valuable?

Writing and reading are closely connected. Teachers who spend time on focused writing instruction in third grade know that it plays a central role in early reading development.

How Can I Help Students Become Writers?

Just as with reading fluency, students need explicit and systematic instruction as well as considerable practice to become fluent writers. In *Reading Street* you will find daily writing instruction and culminating unit activities that take students through the writing process. Additionally, students will explore how to use research and technology skills for writing. As you teach using modeled and independent writing, your role gradually decreases as students apply writing skills and strategies on their own.

Weekly writing instruction features **mini-lessons** to help students learn about the key features of the product or form that is the weekly writing focus and the organizational patterns of that type of writing. Mini-lessons also focus on the writing traits and on writer's craft skills. Students learn through direct instruction and teacher-modeling. They then apply what they have learned in their own writing.

Helping students become fluent writers is an important part of the writing instruction in *Reading Street*. And the more students write, the better writers they become. A daily writing routine, **Quick Write for Fluency**, engages students in a short writing activity every day.

It is also important for students to learn the process of writing. Starting in Unit 1, there is a **writing process** lesson at the end of each unit. These lessons are carefully focused on teaching the process of writing: prewrite and plan, draft, revise, edit, and publish and present.

It's also important to prepare students for the future. In the middle of each unit, at the end of the first Teacher's Edition volume, you'll find a **21st Century Writing** project. These projects focus on new literacies and are dependent on the use of technology.

How Do I Monitor Progress in Writing?

A rubric is often the best way to assess students' writing. A rubric is a guide for assessing a writing assignment. It describes the qualities of a good, average, and poor product along a scaled continuum. *Reading Street* provides weekly rubrics that cover these writing traits: focus/ideas, word choice, organization, voice, sentences, and rules of grammar and punctuation.

How Can I Help Students Develop Good Writing Traits?

Each week, you'll focus on one of six writing traits in *Reading Street*. Your weekly instruction, which includes introducing the trait and providing modeling, strategies, and practice, is connected to the writing that students do during the Unit Writing Workshop. You can display models of writing genres from *Scott Foresman Reading Street Writing Transparencies* and discuss them in terms of the traits of good writing.

The Traits of Good Writing

Teach these writing traits to help students improve their writing.

1. **Focus** the writing on your main **ideas.**
2. **Organize** your ideas in the right order so your **paragraphs** make sense.
3. Show your **voice** in your writing. It's how you feel about your ideas.
4. **Choose words** that make your writing interesting.
5. Write so that your **sentences** make sense.
6. Use **conventions,** or correct rules of writing words and sentences.

"Students and teachers [need] to view grammar and mechanics as a creational facility rather than a correctional one." (Anderson, J., 2005).

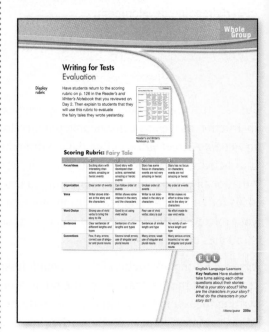

The *Reading Street* Authors answer the most Frequently Asked Questions

Here's "the scoop" on *Reading Street!*

1. **What's the underlying "story" of *Reading Street*?**
   Reading Street provides explicit, systematic, high-quality instruction focusing on the five critical elements of reading identified by research: phonemic awareness, phonics, fluency, vocabulary, and text comprehension, as well as an emphasis on concept and oral language development.

2. **How is *Reading Street* different from other basal programs?**
   Reading Street is built around the "Understanding by Design" model of instruction. Each unit focuses on a "big question" that connects reading, vocabulary, and writing for a full six weeks. Children expand their higher order thinking skills and conceptual understanding by exploring different aspects of the "big question" and a series of related sub-questions each week, creating a culture of engaging inquiry around ideas and texts.

3. **Is there a Spanish program? Are the same resources available in Spanish?**
   Calle de la Lectura is *Reading Street's* fully aligned Spanish literacy system. It provides parallel Spanish instruction, as well as integrated language and concept development.

4. **How are the Student and Teacher's editions organized?**
   Student Editions include six units of integrated reading, writing, skill, and vocabulary development organized under a unit concept. Weekly paired texts further develop each concept and are aligned to either Science or Social Studies.

   Our Teacher's Editions have a unique delivery system of 12 slim, manageable volumes, allowing for greater pacing flexibility while keeping the integrity of our validated scope and sequence. Teachers will find opportunities to customize grade level lesson plans to serve all learners for both reading and language arts instruction.

5. **Is *Reading Street* for all students? What about below and above level learners, English Language Learners, and other learners?**
   One of the key goals of *Reading Street* is to support and meet the individualized needs of all learners. Focused differentiated group work provides targeted and explicit instruction that helps all learners participate alongside their peers.

6. **Why is there a student book at Kindergarten?**
   Young children respond to lively, interactive print materials as they are building a sense of themselves as readers and learners. *My Skills Buddy*, designed to be a companion to the classroom content, serves as a handbook children can visit to apply and practice newly acquired skills.

7. **How does *Reading Street* help teachers assess students?**
   Reading Street's assessment plan helps teachers assess their students both formally and informally. Daily Success Predictors help teachers monitor priority skills by assessing predictors of reading success. Weekly Assessment Checkpoints provide a more formal way of identifying students' understanding of key concepts and skills.

8. **Are there digital resources that go with this program (or an online version)?**
   Reading Street provides a robust digital path that aligns with each week of instruction. Digital components such as animations, songs, videos, and interactive games support instruction and make the content relevant, motivating, and accessible to all learners.

9. **What other products and support materials come with the program?**
   Reading Street provides a wide array of text products, digital products, and interactive products that support the varying modalities and levels of all children.

Assessment
on Reading Street

As you travel with your third grade students on the path to literacy, you make frequent stops for rich instructional opportunities. When does the journey lead you to assessment?

On Reading Street assessment is not a destination. It's integrated all along the way to help you keep your students on the path to reading success.

Scott Foresman Reading Street makes sure you have assessment planning and tools at your fingertips. **Section 3** shows how you can use each type of assessment when you need it. You'll see at a glance how you can make decisions about the focus, pacing, and grouping for your instruction throughout the week, quarter, and year.

When you continue the assessment process throughout the year, you effectively build on the knowledge that your students had when they entered third grade. Then they're well on their way to becoming even more sophisticated readers.

Assessment and Grouping

What Makes Grouping and Assessment Effective?

Third graders have mastered many reading and language arts skills and strategies. They often demonstrate a firm foundation of vocabulary and comprehension. At the beginning of the year, you want know your students' interests, learning styles, and academic needs. When you use the right assessments at the right times, you get to know your students quickly. The next step, determining your groups for effective instruction, becomes easier. All along the way, you monitor students' progress and use that information to regroup students.

When and How Is It Best to Assess?

In order to know your students, you need critical information all through the year. This data comes through a 4-step process:

1. Diagnose and Differentiate
2. Monitor Progress
3. Assess and Regroup
4. Summative Assessment

❶ Diagnose and Differentiate

At the beginning of the year, it is important to diagnose students' instructional needs. Use the Baseline Group Test or another initial placement test such as the DIBELS. Then you can plan your groups.

Why Is Diagnosing a Critical Step?

Diagnosis gives you a picture of where each student is at that moment. When you diagnose early, you have data to identify who is at risk of failing and needs extra support. It also helps you determine which students have not mastered the previous year's standards. You also find out who is performing on level or above level.

How Do I Provide Differentiated Instruction for Different Abilities?

After you diagnose, you can turn to *Scott Foresman Reading Street* for lessons and pacing designed for three levels.

If students assess at the **SI** level, use the regular instruction and the daily **Strategic Intervention** small group lessons.

If students assess at the **OL** level, use the regular instruction and the daily **On Level** small group lessons.

If students assess at the **A** level, use the regular instruction and the daily **Advanced** small group lessons.

The lessons focus on target strategies and skills as they help you offer intensive, explicit, and advanced instructional approaches. When it's time for students to read, you can match them to a wide array of books at their instructional and independent reading levels. With leveled books, students are continually challenged and engaged.

For more support for struggling readers, you can also use the Strategic Intervention lessons in the Teacher's Edition and the Reading Street Intervention Kit for students who need intensive intervention.

❷ Monitor Progress

Each week you can assess at the lesson level by taking time to monitor targeted skills and strategy instruction. Using a variety of these "during-the-lesson" and weekly assessments, you are consistently aware of how students change and develop throughout the year. You are equipped with performance data so you can meet individual needs.

Scott Foresman Reading Street offers tools that allow you to pause for assessment at different critical points of instruction.

During lesson instruction, pause for spiral review and *if..., then...* suggestions. They help you quickly track students' understanding of key instruction. You can use Don't Wait Until Friday checklists to assess students' progress for word reading, retelling, fluency, and oral vocabulary. At various points during instruction, you can use Reader's and Writer's Notebook activities as assessment tools. When you determine that students are ready for comprehension and fluency assessment as they read new texts, assign Fresh Reads.

When you teach the weekly skills and strategies, you don't want to wait until the weekly tests on Friday, or even later, to find if your teaching has been effective for all students. An effective practice is to monitor students' progress at key times during the week. These informal assessments are guides that help you identify students who need extra support as well as those who will benefit from challenge activities.

③ Assess and Regroup

A clearer picture of each third grade student is coming into focus as a result of your assessment throughout the weekly lessons. The initial groups you formed were based on data from diagnosis at the beginning of the year. As students change and develop throughout third grade, you will need to regroup your students for differentiated instruction.

When Is It Best to Regroup?

Regrouping is a part of the assessment process, so you rely on assessments to help you determine new groups. Recommendations in *Scott Foresman Reading Street* guide teachers to begin by recording the results of the Weekly Assessments. Then they use the data from retelling, phonics, and fluency to track progress. *Reading Street's* Unit Benchmark Test results are important to include. This summative assessment reveals how students are achieving mastery of the unit skills.

Other assessments, such as DRA, may recommend regrouping at other times during the year.

These assessments keep the goal of mastery reachable for all students because you quickly identify students in need of additional practice or reteaching. Responsive individual or group instruction will return students to on-level learning. Begin to think about regrouping as you near the end of the second unit of instruction, and then regroup for subsequent units.

④ Summative Assessment

At fixed times, you need to check students' progress toward skills and standards. These assessments show the effectiveness of your instruction.

The Unit Benchmark Tests measure students' mastery of target skills taught throughout the unit.

The End-of-Year test measures students' mastery of target skills taught throughout the six units of the program.

Grouping Throughout the Year	
Initial Grouping	Diagnose using the Baseline Group Test. Use the same groups for Units 1 and 2.
Regroup	for Unit 3
Regroup	for Unit 4
Regroup	for Unit 5
Regroup	for Unit 6

Teacher Form

Narrative Retelling Chart

Unit _____ Selection Title _____

Name _____ Date _____

Retelling Criteria/Teacher Prompt	Teacher-Aided Response	Student-Generated Response	Rubric Score (Circle one)
Connections Has anything like this happened to you? How does this story remind you of other stories?			4 3 2 1
Author's Purpose Why do you think the author wrote this story? What was the author trying to tell us?			4 3 2 1
Characters Describe _____ (character's name) at the beginning and end of the story.			4 3 2 1
Setting Where and when did the story happen?			4 3 2 1
Plot Tell me what the story was about in a few sentences.			4 3 2 1

Summative Retelling Score   4   3   2   1

Comments _____

See also Assessment Handbook | © Pearson Education, Inc.

See also *Assessment Handbook* | © Pearson Education, Inc.

Teacher Form

Expository Summarizing Chart

Unit _____ Selection Title _____ Name _____ Date _____

Summarizing Criteria/Teacher Prompt	Teacher-Aided Response	Student-Generated Response	Rubric Score (Circle one.)			
Connections Did this selection make you think about something else you have read? What did you learn about as you read this selection?			4	3	2	1
Author's Purpose Why do you think the author wrote this selection?			4	3	2	1
Topic What was the selection mostly about?			4	3	2	1
Important Ideas What is important for me to know about _____ (topic)?			4	3	2	1
Conclusions What did you learn from reading this selection?			4	3	2	1

Summative Summarizing Score 4   3   2   1

Comments _____

57

Monitoring Fluency
How to Measure Words Correct Per Minute—WCPM

Ongoing assessment of student reading fluency is one of the most valuable measures we have of students' reading skills. One of the most effective ways to assess fluency is taking timed samples of students' oral reading and measuring the number of words correct per minute (WCPM).

Choose a Text Start by choosing the appropriate week's fluency passage from the Teacher's Edition. Make a copy of the text for yourself and have one for the student.

Timed reading of the text Tell the student: *As you read this aloud, I want you to do your best reading and to read as quickly as you can. That doesn't mean it's a race. Just do your best, fast reading. When I say* begin, *start reading.* As the student reads, follow along in your copy. Mark words that are read incorrectly.

<u>Incorrect</u>	<u>Correct</u>
• omissions	• self-corrections within 3 seconds
• substitutions	
• mispronunciations	• repeated words
• reversals	

After one minute At the end of one minute, draw a line after the last word that was read. Have the student finish reading but don't count any words beyond one minute. Arrive at the words correct per minute—WCPM—by counting the total number of words that the student read correctly in one minute.

FLUENCY GOALS
Grade 3 End-of-Year Goal = 120 WCPM
Target goals by unit

Unit 1 80 to 90 WCPM	**Unit 4** 95 to 105 WCPM
Unit 2 85 to 95 WCPM	**Unit 5** 102 to 112 WCPM
Unit 3 90 to 100 WCPM	**Unit 6** 110 to 120 WCPM

More frequent monitoring You may want to monitor some students more frequently because they are falling far below grade-level benchmarks or they have a result that doesn't seem to align with their previous performance. Follow the same steps above, but choose 2 or 3 additional texts at their independent reading level.

Fluency Progress Chart Copy the chart on the next page. Use it to record each student's progress across the year.

See also *Assessment Handbook* | © Pearson Education, Inc.

Fluency Progress Chart, Grade 3

Name _____

WCPM	1	2	3	4	5	6	7	8	9	10	11	12	13	14	15	16	17	18	19	20	21	22	23	24	25	26	27	28	29	30	31	32	33	34	35	36
145																																				
140																																				
135																																				
130																																				
125																																				
120																																				
115																																				
110																																				
105																																				
100																																				
95																																				
90																																				
85																																				
80																																				
75																																				
70																																				
65																																				
60																																				
55																																				
50																																				

Timed Reading/Week

Assessment Chart

Name _____   Date _____

WEEK		Day 3 Retelling Assessment		Day 5 Fluency Assessment		Day 5 Comprehension Assessment		Reteach	Teacher's Comments
		Benchmark Score	Actual Score	Benchmark WCPM	Actual Score	Benchmark Score	Actual Score		
1	**When Charlie McButton Lost Power** Character, Setting, and Theme	3–4		75–85		3–4		✔	
2	**What About Me?** Sequence	3–4		75–85		3–4			
3	**Kumak's Fish** Sequence	3–4		75–85		3–4			
4	**Supermarket** Compare and Contrast	3–4		75–85		3–4			
5	**My Rows and Piles of Coins** Author's Purpose	3–4		75–85		3–4			
	Unit 1 Test Score								

Benchmark Score reflects grade-level target.

- **RECORD SCORES** Use this chart to record scores for the Day 3 Retelling, Day 5 Fluency, Day 5 Comprehension, and Unit Test.

- **REGROUPING** Compare the student's actual score to the benchmark score and group flexibly or provide extra support as needed.

- **RETEACH** If a student is unable to complete any part of the assessment process, use the weekly Reteach lessons in the *First Stop* book for additional support. Record the lesson information in the space provided on the chart. After reteaching, you may want to reassess using the Unit Test.

Assessment Chart

Name _____ Date _____

	Day 3 Retelling Assessment		Day 5 Fluency Assessment		Day 5 Comprehension Assessment		Reteach	Teacher's Comments
Benchmark Score reflects grade-level target.	Benchmark Score	Actual Score	Benchmark WCPM	Actual Score	Benchmark Score	Actual Score	✔	
WEEK 1 *Penguin Chick* Main Idea and Details	3–4		82–92		3–4			
WEEK 2 *I Wanna Iguana* Compare and Contrast	3–4		82–92		3–4			
WEEK 3 *Prudy's Problem and How She Solved It* Draw Conclusions	3–4		82–92		3–4			
WEEK 4 *Tops & Bottoms* Author's Purpose	3–4		82–92		3–4			
WEEK 5 *Amazing Bird Nests* Main Idea and Details	3–4		82–92		3–4			
Unit 2 Test Score								

- **RECORD SCORES** Use this chart to record scores for the Day 3 Retelling, Day 5 Fluency, Day 5 Comprehension, and Unit Test.

- **REGROUPING** Compare the student's actual score to the benchmark score and group flexibly or provide extra support as needed.

- **RETEACH** If a student is unable to complete any part of the assessment process, use the weekly Reteach lessons in the *First Stop* book for additional support. Record the lesson information in the space provided on the chart. After reteaching, you may want to reassess using the Unit Test.

Assessment Chart

Name _____ Date _____

	Day 3 Retelling Assessment		Day 5 Fluency Assessment		Day 5 Comprehension Assessment		Reteach	Teacher's Comments
	Benchmark Score	Actual Score	Benchmark WCPM	Actual Score	Benchmark Score	Actual Score		
WEEK 1 *How Do You Raise a Raisin?* Draw Conclusions	3–4		90–100		3–4		✔	
WEEK 2 *Pushing Up the Sky* Character, Setting, and Plot	3–4		90–100		3–4			
WEEK 3 *Seeing Stars* Graphic Sources	3–4		90–100		3–4			
WEEK 4 *A Symphony of Whales* Generalize	3–4		90–100		3–4			
WEEK 5 *Around One Cactus* Cause and Effect	3–4		90–100		3–4			
Unit 3 Test Score								

Benchmark Score reflects grade-level target.

- **RECORD SCORES** Use this chart to record scores for the Day 3 Retelling, Day 5 Fluency, Day 5 Comprehension, and Unit Test.

- **REGROUPING** Compare the student's actual score to the benchmark score and group flexibly or provide extra support as needed.

- **RETEACH** If a student is unable to complete any part of the assessment process, use the weekly Reteach lessons in the *First Stop* book for additional support. Record the lesson information in the space provided on the chart. After reteaching, you may want to reassess using the Unit Test.

See also *Assessment Handbook* | © Pearson Education, Inc.

See also *Assessment Handbook* | © Pearson Education, Inc.

Assessment Chart

Name _____ Date _____

		Day 3 Retelling Assessment		Day 5 Fluency Assessment		Day 5 Comprehension Assessment		Reteach	Teacher's Comments
Benchmark Score reflects grade-level target.		Benchmark Score	Actual Score	Benchmark WCPM	Actual Score	Benchmark Score	Actual Score		
WEEK 1	*The Man Who Invented Basketball* Generalize	3–4		95–105		3–4		✔	
WEEK 2	*Hottest, Coldest, Highest, Deepest* Graphic Sources	3–4		95–105		3–4			
WEEK 3	*Rocks in His Head* Fact and Opinion	3–4		95–105		3–4			
WEEK 4	*America's Champion Swimmer: Gertrude Ederle* Fact and Opinion	3–4		95–105		3–4			
WEEK 5	*Fly, Eagle, Fly!* Cause and Effect	3–4		95–105		3–4			
	Unit 4 Test Score								

- **RECORD SCORES** Use this chart to record scores for the Day 3 Retelling, Day 5 Fluency, Day 5 Comprehension, and Unit Test.

- **REGROUPING** Compare the student's actual score to the benchmark score and group flexibly or provide extra support as needed.

- **RETEACH** If a student is unable to complete any part of the assessment process, use the weekly Reteach lessons in the *First Stop* book for additional support. Record the lesson information in the space provided on the chart. After reteaching, you may want to reassess using the Unit Test.

Assessment Chart

Name _____ Date _____

	Day 3 Retelling Assessment		Day 5 Fluency Assessment		Day 5 Comprehension Assessment		Reteach	Teacher's Comments
	Benchmark Score	Actual Score	Benchmark WCPM	Actual Score	Benchmark Score	Actual Score		
WEEK 1 *Suki's Kimono* Compare and Contrast	3–4		102–112		3–4		✔	
WEEK 2 *I Love Saturdays y domingos* Main Idea and Details	3–4		102–112		3–4			
WEEK 3 *Good-bye, 382 Shin Dang Dong* Sequence	3–4		102–112		3–4			
WEEK 4 *Jalapeño Bagels* Draw Conclusions	3–4		102–112		3–4			
WEEK 5 *Me and Uncle Romie* Author's Purpose	3–4		102–112		3–4			
Unit 5 Test Score								

Benchmark Score reflects grade-level target.

- **RECORD SCORES** Use this chart to record scores for the Day 3 Retelling, Day 5 Fluency, Day 5 Comprehension, and Unit Test.

- **REGROUPING** Compare the student's actual score to the benchmark score and group flexibly or provide extra support as needed.

- **RETEACH** If a student is unable to complete any part of the assessment process, use the weekly Reteach lessons in the *First Stop* book for additional support. Record the lesson information in the space provided on the chart. After reteaching, you may want to reassess using the Unit Test.

See also *Assessment Handbook* | © Pearson Education, Inc.

Assessment Chart

Name _____ Date _____

Benchmark Score reflects grade-level target.	Day 3 Retelling Assessment		Day 5 Fluency Assessment		Day 5 Comprehension Assessment		Reteach	Teacher's Comments
	Benchmark Score	Actual Score	Benchmark WCPM	Actual Score	Benchmark Score	Actual Score		
WEEK 1 *The Story of the Statue of Liberty* Fact and Opinion	3–4		110–120		3–4		✔	
WEEK 2 *Happy Birthday Mr. Kang* Cause and Effect	3–4		110–120		3–4			
WEEK 3 *Talking Walls: Art for the People* Graphic Sources	3–4		110–120		3–4			
WEEK 4 *Two Bad Ants* Plot and Theme	3–4		110–120		3–4			
WEEK 5 *Atlantis: Legend of a Lost City* Generalize	3–4		110–120		3–4			
Unit 6 Test Score								

- **RECORD SCORES** Use this chart to record scores for the Day 3 Retelling, Day 5 Fluency, Day 5 Comprehension, and Unit Test.

- **REGROUPING** Compare the student's actual score to the benchmark score and group flexibly or provide extra support as needed.

- **RETEACH** If a student is unable to complete any part of the assessment process, use the weekly Reteach lessons in the *First Stop* book for additional support. Record the lesson information in the space provided on the chart. After reteaching, you may want to reassess using the Unit Test.

Unit 1
Assess and Regroup

FYI In Grade 3 there are opportunities for regrouping every five weeks—at the end of Units 2, 3, 4, and 5. These options offer sensitivity to each student's progress although some teachers may prefer to regroup less frequently.

Assess Unit 1

Regrouping recommended at the end of Units 2, 3, 4, and 5. Record students' Unit 1 scores to inform regrouping decisions at the end of Unit 2. At that time, consider students' scores for
- Unit 1 Retelling
- Fluency (WCPM)
- Unit 1 Benchmark Test

Group Time

On-Level	Strategic Intervention	Advanced
Students' performance is On-Level if they	Students' performance is below level if they	Students' performance is Advanced if they
• score 3 or better on their cumulative unit rubric scores for Retelling	• score 2 or lower on their cumulative unit rubric scores for Retelling	• score 4 on their cumulative unit rubric scores for Retelling
• meet the current benchmark for fluency (80–90 WCPM), reading On-Level text such as Student Edition selections	• do not meet the current benchmark for fluency (80–90 WCPM)	• score 91% or better on the Unit 1 Benchmark Test
• score 66% or better on the Unit 1 Benchmark Test	• score below 66% on the Unit 1 Benchmark Test	• read above grade-level material (80–90 WCPM) with speed, accuracy, and expression. You may try them out on one of the Advanced leveled readers.
• are capable of working in the On-Level group based on teacher judgment	• are struggling to keep up with the On-Level group based on teacher judgment	• use expansive vocabulary and ease of language in retelling.
		• are capable of handling the problem solving and investigative work of the Advanced group based on teacher judgment

Questions to Consider

- What types of test questions did the student miss? Are they specific to a particular skill or strategy?
- Does the student have adequate background knowledge to understand the test passages or selections for retelling?
- Has the student's performance met expectations for daily lessons and assessments with little or no reteaching?
- Is the student performing more like students in another group?
- Does the student read for enjoyment, different purposes, and with varied interests?

Benchmark Fluency Scores
Mid-Year Goal: 80–90 WCPM
End-of-Year Goal: 120 WCPM

Unit 2
Assess and Regroup

FYI In Grade 3 there are opportunities for regrouping every five weeks—at the end of Units 2, 3, 4, and 5. These options offer sensitivity to each student's progress although some teachers may prefer to regroup less frequently.

Regroup at the End of Unit 2
To make regrouping decisions at the end of Unit 2, consider student's end-of-unit scores for
- Units 1 and 2 Retelling
- Fluency (WCPM)
- Units 1 and 2 Benchmark Tests

Group Time

On-Level	Strategic Intervention	Advanced
To continue On-Level or to move into the On-Level group, students should	Students would benefit from Strategic Intervention if they	To move to the Advanced group, students should
• score 3 or better on their cumulative unit rubric scores for Retelling	• score 2 or lower on their cumulative unit rubric scores for Retelling	• score 4 on their cumulative unit rubric scores for Retelling
• meet the current benchmark for fluency (85–95 WCPM), reading On-Level text such as Student Edition selections	• do not meet the current benchmark for fluency (85–95 WCPM)	• score 91% or better on the Units 1 and 2 Benchmark Tests
• score 66% or better on the Units 1 and 2 Benchmark Tests	• score below 66% on the Units 1 and 2 Benchmark Tests	• read above grade-level material (85–95 WCPM) with speed, accuracy, and expression. You may try them out on one of the Advanced leveled readers.
• are capable of working in the On-Level group based on teacher judgment	• are struggling to keep up with the On-Level group based on teacher judgment	• use expansive vocabulary and ease of language in retelling.
		• be capable of handling the problem solving and investigative work of the Advanced group based on teacher judgment

Questions to Consider
- What types of test questions did the student miss? Are they specific to a particular skill or strategy?
- Does the student have adequate background knowledge to understand the test passages or selections for retelling?
- Has the student's performance met expectations for daily lessons and assessments with little or no reteaching?
- Is the student performing more like students in another group?
- Does the student read for enjoyment, different purposes, and with varied interests?

Benchmark Fluency Scores
Mid-Year Goal: 85–95 WCPM
End-of-Year Goal: 120 WCPM

Unit 3
Assess and Regroup

FYI In Grade 3 there are opportunities for regrouping every five weeks—at the end of Units 2, 3, 4, and 5. These options offer sensitivity to each student's progress although some teachers may prefer to regroup less frequently.

Regroup at the End of Unit 3
To make regrouping decisions at the end of Unit 3, consider student's end-of-unit scores for
- Unit 3 Retelling
- Fluency (WCPM)
- Unit 3 Benchmark Test

Group Time

On-Level	Strategic Intervention	Advanced
To continue On-Level or to move into the On-Level group, students should	Students would benefit from Strategic Intervention if they	To move to the Advanced group, students should
• score 3 or better on their cumulative unit rubric scores for Retelling	• score 2 or lower on their cumulative unit rubric scores for Retelling	• score 4 on their cumulative unit rubric scores for Retelling
• meet the current benchmark for fluency (90–100 WCPM), reading On-Level text such as Student Edition selections	• do not meet the current benchmark for fluency (90–100 WCPM)	• score 91% or better on the Unit 3 Benchmark Test
• score 66% or better on the Unit 3 Benchmark Test	• score below 66% on the Unit 3 Benchmark Tests	• read above grade-level material (90–100 WCPM) with speed, accuracy, and expression. You may try them out on one of the Advanced leveled readers.
• be capable of working in the On-Level group based on teacher judgment	• are struggling to keep up with the On-Level group based on teacher judgment	• use expansive vocabulary and ease of language in retelling.
		• be capable of handling the problem solving and investigative work of the Advanced group based on teacher judgment

Questions to Consider
- What types of test questions did the student miss? Are they specific to a particular skill or strategy?
- Does the student have adequate background knowledge to understand the test passages or selections for retelling?
- Has the student's performance met expectations for daily lessons and assessments with little or no reteaching?
- Is the student performing more like students in another group?
- Does the student read for enjoyment, different purposes, and with varied interests?

Benchmark Fluency Scores
Mid-Year Goal: 90–100 WCPM
End-of-Year Goal: 120 WCPM

Unit 4
Assess and Regroup

FYI In Grade 3 there are opportunities for regrouping every five weeks—at the end of Units 2, 3, 4, and 5. These options offer sensitivity to each student's progress although some teachers may prefer to regroup less frequently.

Regroup at the End of Unit 4
To make regrouping decisions at the end of Unit 4, consider student's end-of-unit scores for
- Unit 4 Retelling
- Fluency (WCPM)
- Unit 4 Benchmark Test

Group Time

On-Level	Strategic Intervention	Advanced
To continue On-Level or to move into the On-Level group, students should	Students would benefit from Strategic Intervention if they	To move to the Advanced group, students should
• score 3 or better on their cumulative unit rubric scores for Retelling	• score 2 or lower on their cumulative unit rubric scores for Retelling	• score 4 on their cumulative unit rubric scores for Retelling
• meet the current benchmark for fluency (95–105 WCPM), reading On-Level text such as Student Edition selections	• do not meet the current benchmark for fluency (95–105 WCPM)	• score 91% or better on the Unit 4 Benchmark Test
• score 66% or better on the Unit 4 Benchmark Test	• score below 66% on the Unit 4 Benchmark Test	• read above grade-level material (95–105 WCPM) with speed, accuracy, and expression. You may try them out on one of the Advanced leveled readers.
• be capable of working in the On-Level group based on teacher judgment	• are struggling to keep up with the On-Level group based on teacher judgment	• use expansive vocabulary and ease of language in retelling.
		• be capable of handling the problem solving and investigative work of the Advanced group based on teacher judgment

Questions to Consider
- What types of test questions did the student miss? Are they specific to a particular skill or strategy?
- Does the student have adequate background knowledge to understand the test passages or selections for retelling?
- Has the student's performance met expectations for daily lessons and assessments with little or no reteaching?
- Is the student performing more like students in another group?
- Does the student read for enjoyment, different purposes, and with varied interests?

Benchmark Fluency Scores
Mid-Year Goal: 95–105 WCPM
End-of-Year Goal: 120 WCPM

Unit 5
Assess and Regroup

FYI In Grade 3 there are opportunities for regrouping every five weeks—at the end of Units 2, 3, 4, and 5. These options offer sensitivity to each student's progress although some teachers may prefer to regroup less frequently.

Regroup for Unit 6
To make regrouping decisions at the end of Unit 5, consider student's end-of-unit scores for
- Unit 5 Retelling
- Fluency (WCPM)
- Unit 5 Benchmark Test

Group Time

On-Level	Strategic Intervention	Advanced
To continue On-Level or to move into the On-Level group, children should	Children's performance is Below-Level if they	To move to the Advanced group, children should
• score 3 or better on their cumulative unit rubric scores for Retelling	• score 2 or lower on their cumulative unit rubric scores for Retelling	• score 4 on their cumulative unit rubric scores for Retelling
• meet the current benchmark for fluency (102–112 WCPM), reading On-Level text such as Student Edition selections	• do not meet the current benchmark for fluency (102–112 WCPM)	• score 91% or better on the Unit 5 Benchmark Test
• score 66% or better on the Unit 5 Benchmark Test	• score below 66% on the Unit 5 Benchmark Test	• read above grade-level material (102–112 WCPM) with speed, accuracy, and expression. You may try them out on one of the Advanced leveled readers.
• be capable of working in the On-Level group based on teacher judgment	• are struggling to keep up with the On-Level group based on teacher judgment	• use expansive vocabulary and ease of language in retelling.
		• be capable of handling the problem solving and investigative work of the Advanced group based on teacher judgment

Questions to Consider
- What types of test questions did the student miss? Are they specific to a particular skill or strategy?
- Does the student have adequate background knowledge to understand the test passages or selections for retelling?
- Has the student's performance met expectations for daily lessons and assessments with little or no reteaching?
- Is the student performing more like students in another group?
- Does the student read for enjoyment, different purposes, and with varied interests?

Benchmark Fluency Scores
Mid-Year Goal: 102–112 WCPM
End-of-Year Goal: 120 WCPM

Unit 6
Assess and Regroup

FYI In Grade 3 there are opportunities for regrouping every five weeks—at the end of Units 2, 3, 4, and 5. These options offer sensitivity to each student's progress although some teachers may prefer to regroup less frequently.

End-of-Year Performance
There is no need to regroup at the end of Unit 6. To assess students' end-of-year performance, consider their scores for
- Unit 5 Retelling
- Fluency (WCPM)
- Unit 5 Benchmark Test and/or End-of-Year Benchmark Test

Group Time

On-Level	Strategic Intervention	Advanced
To continue On-Level or to move into the On-Level group, students should	Students would benefit from Strategic Intervention if they	To move to the Advanced group, students should
• score 3 or better on their cumulative unit rubric scores for Retelling	• score 2 or lower on their cumulative unit rubric scores for Retelling	• score 4 on their cumulative unit rubric scores for Retelling
• meet the current benchmark for fluency (110–120 WCPM), reading On-Level text such as Student Edition selections	• do not meet the current benchmark for fluency (110–120 WCPM)	• score 91% or better on the Unit 5 Benchmark Test
• score 66% or better on the Unit 6 Benchmark Test	• score below 66% on the Unit 6 Benchmark Test	• read above grade-level material (110–120 WCPM) with speed, accuracy, and expression. You may try them out on one of the Advanced leveled readers.
• are capable of working in the On-Level group based on teacher judgment	• are struggling to keep up with the On-Level group based on teacher judgment	• use expansive vocabulary and ease of language in retelling.
		• are capable of handling the problem solving and investigative work of the Advanced group based on teacher judgment

Questions to Consider

- What types of test questions did the student miss? Are they specific to a particular skill or strategy?
- Does the student have adequate background knowledge to understand the test passages or selections for retelling?

- Has the student's performance met expectations for daily lessons and assessments with little or no reteaching?
- Is the student performing more like students in another group?
- Does the student read for enjoyment, different purposes, and with varied interests?

Benchmark Fluency Scores
Mid-Year Goal: 110–120 WCPM
End-of-Year Goal: 120 WCPM

Writing
on Reading Street

Students in third grade are learning to communicate now—in a century that continually sends messages in new ways. **Section 4** provides ways that you can help students write their messages in a variety of forms and for purposes that reflect the world they'll grow into.

You can customize your writing with approaches that are infused throughout *Scott Foresman Reading Street*. You'll discover effective ways to lead Writer's Workshops and to conference with them about their writing. You'll also find how to evaluate students' writing using the Writing Rubrics and Anchor Papers.

When students delight in stories and feel a sense of wonder from nonfiction, they want to communicate these reactions. As you guide them on the bridge from reading to writing, they will write about it all.

Writing on *Reading Street*

Writing instruction on *Reading Street* emphasizes the reciprocal nature of reading and writing. Writing instruction integrates the skills and knowledge that students learn and practice as they read and helps students apply those skills and that knowledge in their writing. The instruction is also designed to give the teacher as much support as possible for teaching writing.

Read Like a Writer

Mentor Text The wonderful literature in the Student Editions is used as mentor text in the writing instruction. Not only do students examine the literature for the key features of the genre, but they also look at how the authors choose words and construct sentences. Mentor text is a cornerstone of the writing instruction on *Reading Street*.

Interact with Text In addition to examining mentor text, students also interact with model text. These models exemplify the features of good writing. Students might be asked to find and circle the time and order words in a piece of model text. Or they might be asked to highlight the main idea and number the supporting details. This interaction with text gives students a hands-on learning experience.

Weekly Writing

Writing Forms and Patterns In their weekly writing, students focus on a different product each week. Instruction focuses on the organizational patterns of that product or writing form. For example:
Writing Product/Form: Instructions
Organizational Pattern: Sequence

Mini-Lessons Daily 10-minute mini-lessons help students learn about the craft of writing and writing traits. Each weekly lesson focuses on one writing trait and one or two aspects of the writer's craft.

Writing Process

Six writing process lessons provide structure to help students learn the process of writing. These lessons are designed for flexible use by the teacher. For example, if a teacher likes to organize writing time as a Writing Workshop, the writing process lessons will work with the Writing Workshop approach. Also, 1-week and 2-week pacing plans allow teachers to customize the lessons to fit the needs of their own classrooms.

21st Century Writing Projects

Structured as collaborative writing process lessons, students write, process, and organize information using the Internet and other electronic resources. The 21st Century Writing Projects

- integrate traditional literacies and new literacies.
- foster authentic communication.
- focus critical thinking on real-life applications.
- encourage creativity and innovation.

There are six 21st Century Writing Projects in each grade. The third-grade projects are:

- Electronic Pen Pals—students exchange e-mails with another third-grade class.
- Story Exchange—from a story starter, students create a class story.
- Photo Writing—students create an online photo journal.
- Classroom Profile—students create and publish a classroom profile that encompasses multiple genre and includes photos and illustrations.
- E-Newsletter—students create an electronic newsletter about places they have visited.
- Discussion Forum—students use a wiki, or other safe site, to conduct an online discussion group.

Internet Guy
Don Leu

New Literacies

New literacies are especially important to the effective use of content area information on the Internet. They allow us to identify important questions, navigate complex information networks to locate appropriate information, critically evaluate that information, synthesize it to address those questions, and then communicate the answers to others. These five functions help define the new literacies that your students need to be successful with the Internet and other information and communication technologies.

Teacher Conferencing

Conferencing with students is an important part of writing instruction. The writing conference gives you the opportunity to assess how each student's writing is progressing. This program encourages teachers to conference with students on a regular basis. We do understand that conferencing is difficult to manage when you have a whole classroom full of students.

Managing Writing Conferences It is certainly beneficial to conference with every student every week, but that's not very realistic, is it? These tips can help manage writing conferences in your classroom.

- **Individual Conferences** Limit the time of each writing conference to three to five minutes and keep it positive. Try to meet with a few students every day. Ask questions that prompt students to talk to you about their writing. For example:

    Tell me about what you have written.
    What part is your favorite?
    What do you need help with?
    What else can you say about this part?
    I really liked the part where you . . .

- **Fishbowl Conference** When you can't confer with every student, a "fishbowl conference" with one willing student can allow others to observe, listen, and explore how to appropriately respond to others' writing. It's important to focus on what the student is doing well and how a draft might be revised and improved.

Write Guy
Jeff Anderson

Conferencing Is Listening

Conferring about children's writing is more about teachers *listening* than teachers speaking. What is the student thinking or trying to say? What help does he or she need? We can ask questions to keep kids speaking. "What do you want your reader to know? Wow, how did you think of this vivid phrase?"

Peer Conferencing

Peer conferencing is an important part of the writing process. It gets students actively involved in their own writing and the writing of others. In this program, we encourage weekly peer conferencing; however, it is very important to take time to teach students how to respond.

- The Fishbowl Conference, where you as the teacher model a conference with a student, is a good way to model a meaningful conversation about writing.

- To get Peer Conferences started, have the students pair up and exchange papers. Have Student 1 read Student 2's paper aloud. Then have Student 1 respond.

- When Student 1 is responding to Student 2's writing, Student 1 should focus on two things:
  Compliments—What did you really like about what your friend wrote? Why did you like it?
  Questions—What would you like to ask the writer?

- Give Student 2 a chance to respond to any questions asked by Student 1 and to ask additional questions to clarify or focus the comments on the writing.

- Then switch.

Remember that peer conferencing is difficult for students. They may not feel confident in their ability to respond to their peers. They may not be able to accept feedback from their peers gracefully. That's why it is really important that you teach and model for students how to conference on writing.

Write Guy
Jeff Anderson

The Sunny Side

I like to look for what's *right* in children's writing rather than focusing on things that need to be edited or fixed. It's important that as we teach children how to peer conference, we also encourage them to focus on the positive. Most children don't write flawlessly—who does? However, they will learn what they are doing well if we point it out.

Evaluating Writing

Reading Street provides tools to help as you evaluate students' writing. A well-done evaluation of student writing:

- provides feedback to students about the strengths of what they have written.
- provides guidance on areas for improvement.
- puts primary emphasis on the content and structure of the writing, while not ignoring conventions and mechanics.

Writing Rubrics Each writing lesson includes a rubric to help you evaluate student writing based on writing traits. The rubrics are intended to help you discern the differences between different levels of writing.

Writing Rubrics and Anchor Papers This product provides four student models for each of the writing process lessons in third grade. Models are written by real third-grade students. Each writing model is evaluated using the writing rubric from the lesson. Narrative is provided to explain how the score was decided for each anchor paper.

In addition, this product includes additional writing rubrics, so if you use a 6-point, 5-point, or 3-point evaluation system, we have rubrics for you to use to evaluate all student writing.

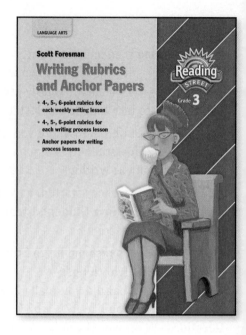

Differentiate Instruction on Reading Street

You probably have some students who seem to know every word before you teach it. In the same classroom, other students need to expand their vocabulary greatly. Whatever literacy skills or strategies you teach, you know your students have different needs.

Section 5 explains how *Scott Foresman Reading Street* supports you in addressing those needs. This section provides multiple options for differentiating instruction at the following levels:

- Strategic Intervention

- On-Level

- Advanced

- English Language Learners

Academic success depends on learning to read well. In turn, learning to read well depends on rich language knowledge. In this section, you'll see how the program's plans for small groups are carefully designed so that all students reach high and experience an increasingly rich language environment.

Differentiated Instruction

SI Strategic Intervention

Author's craft Work with students to set a purpose for reading, or if time permits, have students work with partners to set purposes.

 ELL

English Language Learners

Build background To build background, review the selection summary in English (*ELL Handbook*, p. 67). Use the Retelling Cards to provide visual support for the summary.

Differentiated Instruction for Group Time

How Can I Use Flexible Groups for Instruction?

The Baseline Group Test, published by Scott Foresman, will help identify students's needs at the beginning of the year. Throughout the year, use the results of regular progress monitoring to make regrouping decisions.

Reading Street provides weekly plans and daily lessons for these types of small group instruction: Strategic Intervention, On-Level, Advanced, and English Language Learners.

SI Strategic Intervention

OL On-Level

A Advanced

ELL English Language Learners

Reading Street follows the Response to Intervention model (RTI) to help you reach your goal of meeting the instructional needs of all students. It offers a process that monitors students's progress throughout the year so you can support on-level and advanced students and identify struggling readers early. More support is in the Response to Intervention Kit, which addresses the five core areas of reading instruction: phonemic awareness, phonics, fluency, vocabulary, and comprehension. As you work with struggling readers in small groups, you can use the kit for additional teacher modeling, more scaffolding, and multiple opportunities for practice. You have the strategies and tools you need to prevent these students from falling behind.

How Do I Use Practice Stations to Manage Small Groups?

During group time, students will need independent literacy activities to complete while you meet with small groups. Paired reading for fluency practice, journal writing, and activities at practice stations are all good activities for this time. The weekly Differentiated Instruction pages in each Teacher's Edition tell you where to find instruction for each group and provides *If . . . Then . . .* activities to support individual students.

Spend time at the beginning of the year coaching students on how to take responsibility for completing their independent work. Establish expectations, routines, and rules. Discuss rules with students and post them. Make sure students know what to do if they run out of materials or finish early. Support them in solving problems that may arise during this time.

The Scott Foresman Reading Street Practice Stations Kit contains grade level Practice Stations Flipcharts and a Management Handbook that includes lesson-specific reproducible work plans for students.

The Practice Stations Kit provides suggestions for six practice stations each week. The station activities support the week's skills and expand the week's concepts. Informal, ongoing assessments are an important means of guiding classroom instruction, and station activities provide excellent opportunities for ongoing assessments. Rubrics, portfolios, and other informal observation ideas are included in the Practice Stations Kit.

Differentiated Instruction for Strategic Intervention

Identifying your third grade students who need intervention is essential. Reading accomplishments in third grade set the stage for much of the learning that follows. Observe students who are at risk of problems in learning to read and plan early for intervention. These students will exhibit one or more of these characteristics:

- **Difficulties in mapping speech to print.** Students may struggle when applying sound-spelling meanings to printed words. Providing students with intensive, systematic, explicit instruction in word analysis along with additional practice and teacher feedback are essential components of *Reading Street*.

- **Lack of fluency in reading connected text.** Poor decoding skills lead to an inability to read accurately, fluently, and with expression. Repeated reading and other methods for improving fluency are especially important for struggling readers.

- **Lack of word knowledge and concepts** Deficiencies in understanding language and basic concepts affect students' abilities to comprehend and make meaning from text. Providing students with explicit, systematic instruction in vocabulary, both oral and reading vocabulary, is essential to helping them become better readers.

How Can I Help Students with a Very Low Reading Ability?

Some students come to third grade reading at a lower level than other students in the Strategic Intervention group. To provide them additional support in skills and concepts, the Small Group Instruction lessons for Strategic Intervention include the Concept Literacy Leveled Readers. Each book is written at a lower level than the Below-Level Reader for the week. The books align with the weekly concepts in each unit and provide struggling readers with a way to practice independent reading as they build understanding and develop concept knowledge. The Concept Literacy Readers play a role in the instruction for the Strategic Intervention group, but they can be used for independent reading practice for any struggling reader.

As necessary, use a variety of approaches and equipment aids in your classroom. They'll allow all students to succeed using *Reading Street.*

What Is Strategic Intervention?

Scott Foresman Reading Street integrates into the core program daily extra support strategies for strategic intervention—the differentiated instruction that students who are struggling need. You have comprehensive guidance and effective, efficient, and explicit instruction for readers who struggle. This extra support includes

- materials to reinforce and extend the daily lessons.

- instructional opportunities to increase background knowledge and reteach prerequisite skills.

- preteaching and reteaching of lesson skills.

- additional practice in key skills and strategies taught in the lesson.

- additional opportunities for vocabulary and concept development.

- more frequent opportunities to read and respond with teacher feedback.

- additional opportunities for checking understanding.

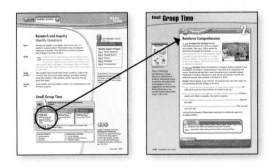

Differentiated Instruction for Advanced Learners

How Do Advanced Learners Differ from Other Learners?

Research suggests that advanced learners learn faster, identify and solve problems more easily, and understand and make connections among abstract concepts. Advanced readers show these characteristics:

- They enjoy reading. They read for knowledge and seek depth and complexity in their reading. They tend to prefer nonfiction and pursue interest-based reading opportunities.

- They read early and above-level. These learners read at least one-and-a-half to two grade levels above their chronological grade placement.

- They have advanced processing skills in reading. They retain large amounts of information and analyze and synthesize ideas quickly.

- They have advanced language skills. They enjoy the subtleties of language and use an expansive vocabulary.

Reading Street integrates daily instruction for advanced learners into the core program. The Advanced lessons include these strategies to meet advanced learners' needs:

- acceleration of the curriculum to provide more advanced work

- replacement of regular reading material with more advanced selections

- creative or critical thinking activities and advanced inquiry projects

- opportunities for independent study

- recommendations for advanced trade books on the week's theme

- interest-based reading opportunities

- small group instruction

All students should have opportunities to participate in appropriately challenging learning experiences. Advanced lessons will ensure that all learners make continuous progress in reading.

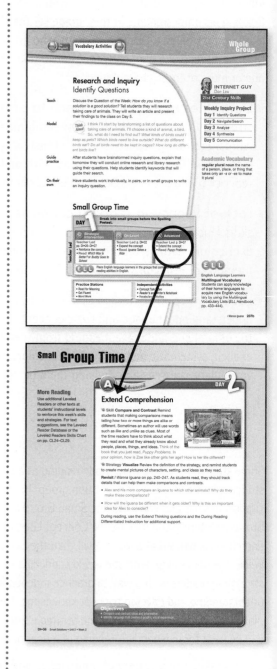

Differentiated Instruction for English Language Learners

How Do English Language Learners Differ from Other Learners?

Academic success depends on learning to read well. Learning to read well depends on rich language knowledge—which presents unique challenges for English language learners and others who have not acquired academic English.

A lack of reading and language skills should not be taken as a sign that students have a language or reading deficit, but rather that their language experiences haven't included sufficient academic instruction. In order for English language learners to participate fully in reading/language arts instruction and thrive as readers and writers, these language needs must be provided for.

How Do I Meet the Needs of English Language Learners?

Daily support for English language learners can be found in the Differentiated Instruction feature in the *Reading Street* Teacher's Edition, as well as daily lessons for your ELL group. They offer pacing suggestions for the week and scaffolded instruction for the week's target skills and strategies.

English language learner support is designed to enable you to "front-load," or preteach, the core instruction. It is also beneficial to students as reteaching. Activities address various levels of proficiency of English language learners, writing, science and history-social science, vocabulary, and transfer skills.

Support for English Language Learners on *Reading Street* includes

ELL Posters

- Large-format posters that support tested vocabulary and weekly concepts
- Daily structured talk for practice of speaking and listening skills

ELL/ELD Readers

- Weekly accessible readers specifically developed to support English language learners
- Readers that reinforce the weekly concept and vocabulary while building language and fluency

ELL Handbook

- Additional materials including grammar and phonics lessons, transference notes, reproducible pages for additional practice, language activities, and articles by notable experts in the English language learner community

Differentiated Instruction for On-Level Learners

The main instruction in *Reading Street* is designed for students who need instruction right at the third-grade level. While your small groups for Strategic Intervention, Advanced, and English Language Learners are engaged at their levels, your on-level students will benefit from small-group instruction that expands their knowledge of skills and strategies and provides on-level reading opportunities.

Reading Street integrates daily instruction for on-level students into the core program. On-level students are ready to expand what they learned in whole group lesson. The On-Level lessons provide multiple opportunities for students to talk and explore concepts in more depth.

- They expand their background knowledge of literature selections.
- They expand their understanding of the weekly concept by connecting it to a weekly question.
- They expand comprehension through focused activities.
- They expand their knowledge of vocabulary and word structure.

The On-Level daily lessons also offer

- opportunities for in-depth review of skills and strategies.
- on-level readers with practice for skills and strategies.
- multiple opportunities for retelling and fluency practice.
- writing response activities that extend reading skills and strategies.

Use the on-level lessons and choose from 5-Day and 3- or 4-Day pacing plans as a guide to ensure success.

How Do I Support Students with Different Needs in the Groups?

To form groups, it's necessary to give them labels. But never lose awareness that each student within a group is an individual with unique abilities and challenges. Small group time presents teachers the opportunity to become aware of students' needs and how best to support those needs. You can gain insight into students with special needs who may be in an advanced, on-level, or strategic intervention group. For these students, you can also use *Reading Street* materials to help them express their abilities and demonstrate their competence. These and many other activities can be used for students with different special needs:

Dyslexia—Guide the student's hand in forming letters or writing legibly.

Hearing Impairment—Pair students with others who can repeat explicit instructions.

Physical Disabilities—Suggest procedural or equipment modifications, such as modified computers, keyboards, scanners, and spell checkers.

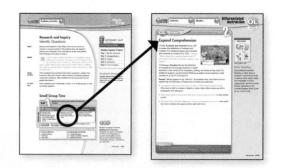

English Language Learners on Reading Street

Some of the most challenging—and rewarding—students to teach are those who are new to the United States or to English-language instruction. You can help these students acquire academic skills using specifically designed extra support.

Go to **Section 6** when you need ELL support in *Scott Foresman Reading Street.* The program provides multiple options to help you work with the English language learners in your classroom. The overview explains why it's important to support instruction for ELLs and how you can use the wide array of English language learning resources in *Scott Foresman Reading Street.*

Here, you'll find the essential, research-based instruction and methods you need. Renowned ELL researchers work alongside you through these materials, and you'll learn more about their expertise, findings, and practical tips here. Use them as you guide your English learners to success on *Reading Street.*

Essentials of ELL Instruction in Scott Foresman Reading Street

Identify and Communicate Content Objectives and Language Objectives

Frontload the Lesson

Provide Comprehensible Input

Enable Language Production

Assess for Content and Language Understanding

Overview of English Language Learners

The English language learners in your classroom come from diverse language backgrounds. What level of challenge should you expect of English learners to keep them learning and engaged? They may communicate well in English on the playground, so it's easy to think they are fluent English speakers. However, they may still be in the beginning stages of using English for learning purposes. Research proves that it takes at least five years of exposure to academic English to catch up with native-speaker proficiency in school.

How Do English Language Learners Differ from Other Learners?

ELLs face challenges because they have not acquired academic English. Students' reading and language skills may seem deficient because their language experiences have lacked academic instruction. ELLs need targeted instruction in order for them to fully participate in reading/language arts lessons with their peers. Helping ELL students achieve academically is critically important because they must meet the same state and federal grade-level standards as other students. Their academic success depends on learning to read well. Learning to read well depends on rich language knowledge.

> ### Academic Language
> is the language of classroom talk. It's used for academic purposes, not social or personal ones.

How Do I Meet the Needs of English Language Learners?

These five essential practices take into account language and academic needs of English language learners. They are incorporated into *Scott Foresman Reading Street* as common-sense, everyday strategies that help you build a positive, effective learning relationship between you and your ELL students.

Essentials of ELL Instruction

Identify and Communicate Content Objectives and Language Objectives
Your ELL students need instruction for the same grade-level skills and strategies as students whose first language is English. Deliver your instruction with clear, simple language. Provide extra support for academic vocabulary. Provide direct instruction for the academic language such as *compare, contrast,* and *solution,* that students need to use to successfully complete classroom tasks.

Frontload the Lesson
When new information arrives as a blur to ELL students, they are lost at beginning of a lesson. Taking time to frontload, or preteach, lesson elements will bring them into mainstream instruction. Activating prior knowledge, building background, previewing, and setting a purpose for reading are frontloading methods that remove learning obstacles. Asking students to make personal connections helps them see relationships and gives you insight into their experiences and backgrounds.

Provide Comprehensible Input
The instruction and content you present to ELL students is input that may be unclear because of language barriers. Using visual supports, multimedia, examples of real items, and demonstrations are a few ways to provide comprehensible input when teaching. In some cases, communicating through non-linguistic methods is an effective approach. These include gestures, props, dramatization, and others. Hands-on activities and multiple exposures to new concepts lessen confusion.

Enable Language Production
The listening, speaking, reading, and writing ELLs do for school is different from the language they use in everyday conversation. In school, ELLs need ample opportunities to demonstrate their use of English and the skills they are learning. Two critical methods for enabling students' English language production are direct instruction and modeling the use of a skill in a comprehensible way. Throughout lessons, create scaffolds so that students read and hear English language patterns and build on them to express their own thoughts. Paraphrasing, restatements, cloze sentences, writing prompts, and templated forms for note-taking are other useful supports. When you respond to students' strengths and needs by modifying instruction, you give students the opportunity they need to express themselves in an academic setting and gain proficiency in English.

Assess for Content and Language Understanding
Since ELLs are required to achieve the same high standards as mainstream students, you need assessment tools that help you plan how to support ELLs' strengths and address their challenges. Keep in mind that students are at different stages for learning English and for learning the literacy skills you are teaching. Asking these questions frequently and using assessments will help you determine how to modify your instruction for different proficiency levels.

- Where are ELLs students in their **acquisition of English** language proficiency?
- Where are they in their **acquisition of literacy** skills?

Just as for all students, you will rely on diagnostic, formative, and summative assessments for ELLs. When you consistently integrate informal assessment into your lessons, you can target specific problem areas for learning, adapt your instruction, and intervene earlier rather than later.

You can modify both formal and informal assessments so that ELLs show their proficiency in literacy skills with a minimal amount of negative impact due to being at a lower stage of learning English. These modifications include time extensions, use of bilingual dictionaries and glossaries, repeated readings of listening passages, use of dual-language assessments, and allowing written responses in the first language.

To meet ELLs at their own level of English acquisition, teachers use instructional supports and tools. Through scaffolding and modifying instruction you can lead ELLs to achieve the same instructional goals that mainstream students do. The ELL strategies and supports in *Scott Foresman Reading Street* have the five essential principles of ELL as their foundation. Use them throughout your instruction to modify or scaffold core instruction. With ELL Leveled Support activities, you meet students where they are—from beginning to advanced levels of English proficiency. The features provide on-the-spot information for vocabulary, writing, and language transfer information.

Other English language learner resources include:

Student Edition The third-grade student edition builds every student's reading and language skills.

Teacher's Edition The teacher's edition has ELL instructional strategies built into the lesson plans. The ELL weekly lessons have pacing plans to help you carefully integrate instruction. The lessons guide you in using sheltered techniques and routines for teaching academic vocabulary, listening comprehension, phonics, vocabulary, comprehension, and writing.

ELL Readers ELL readers develop English learners' vocabulary and comprehension skills.

ELL Posters ELL posters contain high-quality illustrations and five days of activities supporting key oral vocabulary, selection vocabulary, and lesson concepts.

English Language Support These supports are all provided as reproducible masters: English Language Support resource books with comprehension skill practice, selection vocabulary word cards, multilingual summaries of Student Edition literature, study guides for ELL Readers, and multilingual vocabulary charts. The English selection summaries and vocabulary charts are accompanied by translations in Spanish and in several other languages.

Ten Important Sentences The Ten Important Sentences reproducibles help students focus on comprehension while they expand their English proficiency.

ELL Handbook The ELL Handbook supports teachers' professional development and students' transition to advanced levels of proficiency.

ELL Teaching Guide This guide features lesson planners to accompany the core lessons in *Scott Foresman Reading Street*. The teaching strategies target ELL instruction for vocabulary, comprehension, conventions, and writing.

Tips for Providing Comprehensible Input

- Face students when speaking.
- Use vocabulary-rich visuals like ELL Posters.
- Use teaching techniques that involve the senses.
- Use ELL Readers and other materials with ELL supports.

The Three Pillars of English Language Learning

Dr. Jim Cummins, the University of Toronto

In order to understand how English learners develop second-language literacy and reading comprehension, we must distinguish between three different aspects of language proficiency:

Conversational fluency This dimension of proficiency represents the ability to carry on a conversation in face-to-face situations. Most native speakers of English have developed conversational fluency by age 5. This fluency involves use of high-frequency words and simple grammatical constructions. English learners generally develop fluency in conversational English within a year or two of intensive exposure to the language in school or in their neighborhood environments.

Discrete language skills These skills reflect specific phonological, literacy, and grammatical knowledge that students can acquire in two ways—through direct instruction and through immersion in a literacy-rich and language-rich environment in home or in school. The discrete language skills acquired early include:

- knowledge of the letters of the alphabet
- knowledge of the sounds represented by individual letters and combinations of letters
- the ability to decode written words

Students can learn these specific language skills concurrently with their development of basic English vocabulary and conversational fluency.

Academic language proficiency This dimension of proficiency includes knowledge of the less frequent vocabulary of English as well as the ability to interpret and produce increasingly complex written language. As students progress through the grades, they encounter:

- far more low-frequency words, primarily from Greek and Latin sources
- complex syntax (for example, sentences in passive voice)
- abstract expressions

Acquiring academic language is challenging. Schools spend at least 12 years trying to teach all students the complex language associated with academic success. It is hardly surprising that research has repeatedly shown that English language learners, on average, require *at least* 5 years of exposure to academic English to catch up to native-speaker norms.

Effective instruction for English language learners is built on three fundamental pillars.

English Learners

Activate Prior Knowledge/ Build Background	Access Content	Extend Language

Activate Prior Knowledge/ Build Background

No learner is a blank slate. Each person's prior experience provides the foundation for interpreting new information. In reading, we construct meaning by bringing our prior knowledge of language and of the world to the text. The more we already know about the topic in the text, the more of the text we can understand. Our prior knowledge enables us to make inferences about the meaning of words and expressions that we may not have come across before. Furthermore, the more of the text we understand, the more new knowledge we can acquire. This expands our knowledge base (what cognitive psychologists call *schemata*, or underlying patterns of concepts). Such comprehension, in turn, enables us to understand even more concepts and vocabulary.

It is important to *activate* students' prior knowledge because students may not realize what they know about a particular topic or issue. Their knowledge may not facilitate learning unless that knowledge is brought to consciousness.

Teachers can use a variety of strategies to activate students' prior knowledge:	
Brainstorming/Discussion	Visual stimuli
Direct experience	Student writing
Dramatization	Drawing

When students don't already have knowledge about a topic, it is important to help them acquire that knowledge. For example, in order to comprehened texts such as *The Midnight Ride of Paul Revere*, students need to have background knowledge about the origin of the United States.

Access Content

How can teachers make complex academic English comprehensible for students who are still in the process of learning English?

We can *scaffold* students' learning by modifying the input itself. Here are a variety of ways of modifying the presentation of academic content to students so that they can more effectively gain access to the meaning.

Using Visuals Visuals enable students to "see" the basic concepts we are trying to teach much more effectively than if we rely only on words. Among the visuals we can use are:

- *pictures/diagrams*
- *vocabulary cards*
- *real objects*
- *graphic organizers*
- *maps*

Dramatization/Acting Out For beginning English learners, *Total Physical Response*, in which they follow commands such as "Turn around," can be highly effective. The meanings of words can be demonstrated through *gestures* and *pantomime*.

Language Clarification This category of teaching methods includes language-oriented activities that clarify the meaning of new words and concepts. *Use of dictionaries*, either bilingual or English-only, is still the most direct method of getting access to meaning.

Making Personal and Cultural Connections We should constantly search for ways to link academic content with what students already know or what is familiar to them from their family or cultural experiences. This not only validates students' sense of identity, but it also makes the learning more meaningful.

Extend Language

A systematic exploration of language is essential if students are to develop a curiosity about language and deepen their understanding of how words work. Students should become *language detectives* who investigate the mysteries of language and how it has been used throughout history to shape and change society.

Students also can explore the building blocks of language. A large percentage of the less frequently heard academic vocabulary of English derives from Latin and Greek roots. Word formation follows predictable patterns. These patterns are very similar in English and Spanish.

When students know rules or conventions of how words are formed, it gives them an edge in extending vocabulary. It helps them figure out the meanings of words and how to form different parts of speech from words. The exploration of language can focus on meaning, form, or use:

Focus on meaning Categories that can be explored within a focus on meaning include:

- *home language equivalents or cognates*
- *synonyms, antonyms, and homonyms*
- *meanings of prefixes, roots, and suffixes*

Focus on form Categories that can be explored within a focus on form include:

- *word families*
- *grammatical patterns*
- *words with same prefixes, roots, or suffixes*

Focus on use Categories that can be explored within a focus on use include:

- *general uses*
- *idioms*
- *metaphorical use*
- *proverbs*
- *advertisements*
- *puns and jokes*

The Three Pillars

- Activate Prior Knowledge/ Build Background
- Access Content
- Extend Language

The Three Pillars establish a solid structure for the effective instruction of English language learners.

English Learners and Literacy: Best Practices

Dr. Georgia Earnest García, the University of Illinois at Urbana-Champaign

Like other students, English language learners come to school with much oral language knowledge and experience. Their knowledge and experience in languages other than English provide skills and world knowledge that teachers can build on.

Making literacy instruction comprehensible to English language learners is essential. Many of the teaching strategies developed for students who are proficient in English can be adapted for English learners, and many strategies from an English as a Second Language curriculum are also useful in "mainstream" reading education.

Building on Students' Knowledge

It is vital to learn about each student's literacy development and proficiency in the home language. School personnel should ask parents:

- How many years of school instruction has the student received in the home language?
- Can the student read and write in that language?
- Can the student read in any other language?

Students can transfer aspects of home-language literacy to their English literacy development, such as phonological awareness and reading (or listening) comprehension strategies. If they already know key concepts and vocabulary in their home languages, then they can transfer that knowledge to English. For the vocabulary concepts they already know in their home languages, they only need to learn the English labels. Not all English learners automatically transfer what they have learned in the home language to their reading in English. Teachers can help facilitate relevant transfer by explicitly asking English learners to think about what they have learned about a topic in the home language.

A teacher need not speak each student's home language to encourage English language learners to work together and benefit from one another's knowledge. Students can communicate in their home languages and English, building the content knowledge, confidence, and English skills that they need to participate fully in learning. Devising activities in which students who share home languages can work together also allows a school to pool resources, such as bilingual dictionaries and other books, as well as home-language tutors or aides.

Sheltering Instruction in English

Often, beginning and intermediate English language learners may not understand what their classroom teachers say or read aloud in English. These students benefit when teachers shelter, or make comprehensible, their literacy instruction.

Sheltered techniques include using:

- consistent, simplified, clearly enunciated, and slower-paced oral language to explain literacy concepts or activities
- gestures, photos, illustrations, drawings, real objects, dramatization, and/or physical action to illustrate important concepts and vocabulary
- activities that integrate reading, writing, listening, and speaking, so students see, hear, read, and write new vocabulary, sentence structures, and content

When it is clear from students' actions and responses that they understand what is being said, teachers can vary their strategies. As students' comprehension expands, teachers can gradually curtail their use of adapted oral language and of gestures, illustrations, and dramatizations.

Adapting Literacy Activities

Teachers can use many instructional activities developed for native English speakers with English language learners. For example, teacher read-alouds, shared reading, and paired reading can allow an English learner to follow the text during a reading. Such techniques greatly improve students' learning skills and comprehension.

Similarly, interactive journal writing, in which the teacher and student take turns writing entries, allows students to explore topics and ask questions. It also allows teachers to engage in ongoing authentic assessment of student proficiency and to pinpoint areas of misunderstanding.

Small group instruction and discussion also are helpful. Beginning English language learners benefit from the repeated readings of predictable texts with illustrations, especially when the teacher has provided a brief preview of each text to introduce the topic of the story and preview new vocabulary.

Repeated reading aloud of such predictable, patterned, illustrated texts provides English language learners with multiple opportunities to match the text they read with the words they hear. When students participate in shared reading and echo the spoken text or read the words aloud chorally, anxiety about pronunciation or decoding errors is reduced. When teachers choose texts that are culturally familiar and ask English language learners personal questions related to the text, the result is a lower-risk learning environment and an increased opportunity for students to make accurate inferences.

Examples of Teaching Strategies

Before students read content material, provide them with hands-on or visual experience directly related to the content. Then, have them use a graphic organizer to map what they have learned or seen about the topic. Let pairs or small groups of students brainstorm for words that are related to the concept. Then introduce other related words, including vocabulary from the reading. Illustrate new concepts or vocabulary with drawings, photographs, or artifacts that represent the concepts. The hands-on experience and graphic organizer that precede the reading help introduce students to new concepts. Students will thus be familiar with the selection's subject before they begin to read.

Semantic Mapping Working with graphic organizers can help teach vocabulary and concepts in subject areas.

For example, before a reading on the subject of baby animals, have students help you to complete a semantic map showing pictures of animals and the names of baby animals. Ask them to volunteer the names for animal babies in their home language and transcribe their responses. Then, show students examples of the different forms of writing. Ask students to meet in small groups to identify the examples. They may do this in English or their home language. If they use the home language, the teacher needs to write the English labels on the board for each form of writing. Then, students need to enter the words for the different forms of writing, with drawings or home language equivalents, into a vocabulary notebook.

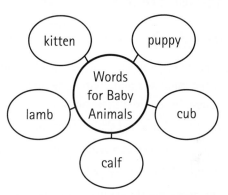

Summarizing After reading, students can dictate what they remember from their reading to the teacher. Students can then illustrate their summaries, and label the illustrations with vocabulary from the reading.

Preparing English Language Learners for Assessment

Dr. Lily Wong Fillmore, the University of California, Berkeley

Under federal and state law, all students—including English learners—must be assessed annually on their progress toward mastery of academic standards in reading, math, and science. Many questions arise when such assessments are used with ELLs, because their test scores are never easy to interpret when they are assessed in English. The most critical question is this: What do test scores mean when they are based on instruction and assessments given in a language students have not yet mastered? Although difficult to interpret, these assessments are required of all students, so we must consider how to help ELLs perform as well as possible.

Addressed in this essay

- What can teachers do to fast-track their ELL students' mastery of the language and content needed to perform as well as possible in required assessments?
- What language and literacy skills are needed?
- What learning strategies can teachers promote to facilitate language and literacy development?

Three types of assessments are vital to reading instruction for all students, including ELLs.

1. Ongoing informal assessments

The assessments that provide teachers the most useful and important information about English learners are those used as part of the instructional process. How well do children understand the materials they are working with, and what needs adjustment or modification in instruction? These are built into these instructional materials and help teachers keep an ongoing record of student progress over time. Such assessments do not need to

be elaborate. Asking students what they think is happening in a text can reveal how well they comprehend what they are reading. Asking children what they think words or phrases mean can show whether they are trying to make sense of text. These types of questions are highly useful to teachers since they allow them to monitor participation levels and help them discover who understands the materials and who needs more attention and support.

2. Diagnostic assessments

A second type of assessment that some ELLs may require is diagnostic, and it is needed when individuals are not making the progress expected of them. The school must determine where student problems lie (e.g., skill development, perception or awareness of English sounds, vocabulary, or grammar) before teachers can provide the corrective help needed.

3. Standardized assessments

The type of assessments that cause teachers of ELLs the greatest concern are the standards-based tests of English Language Arts and content area tests (especially in Math). These state tests are required of all students and are recognized as "high stakes" tests for students and for schools. They are often used to evaluate the effectiveness of a curriculum, the teacher, or the instructional approach used.

What's involved in reading?

Reading skills are built on several types of knowledge: linguistic, symbolic, experiential, and strategic. Each is crucial and is linked with the others. *Language is fundamental*; it is the medium through which meaning—information, story, knowledge, poetry, and thought—is communicated from writer to reader. Unlike speech, what is communicated by written language is indirect and *encoded in symbols* that must be deciphered before access to meaning is possible.

But reading goes beyond mere decoding. Texts call for readers to apply what they know about how language is used to convey thought and ideas to interpret what they are reading. Having *experienced reading as a sense-making activity*, readers will seek meaning as they learn to read. This calls for *special strategies:* they look for meaning if they assume it is to be found in texts. If they do not know the language in which the texts are written, they will recognize that learning the code is the key to unlocking meaning. They will pay attention to the language, and ask: What is this saying? What does this mean? How does this relate to what I already know about the way the language works?

English learners have an easier time learning to read in English if they have already learned to read in their first language. Without question, a language barrier makes learning to read a more difficult task. But if students have already learned to read in their primary language, they know what is involved, what to expect, and thus, they are in a better position to deal with learning to read in the new language in order to access meaning.

Can students learn to read in a language before they are fully proficient in that language?

Can they in fact learn the language through reading? *Yes, but only with ample instructional assistance that supports the development of both.* Ideally, reading instruction in English comes after ELLs have gained some familiarity with the sounds and patterns of spoken English. Students need to hear the sounds of the new language before they can connect symbols to those sounds. For example, in order for children to gain confidence relating the many vowel sounds of English to the 5 vowel symbols used to "spell them" they need help hearing them and differentiating them in words.

Similarly, many ELLs need help dealing with the ways consonants pile up at the beginning and at the ends of syllables and words in English, which may be quite different than the way consonants are used in their primary language. Most crucially, ELLs need help in connecting the words they are learning to decode from the text to their referents. Using pictures, demonstrations, diagrams, gestures, and enactments, teachers can help ELLs see how the words, phrases, and sentences in the reading selections have meaning that can be accessed through the language they are learning.

Helping ELLs become successful readers

The most important way to help ELLs perform well in mandated reading assessments is by giving them the instructional support they need to become successful readers. This involves help in:

- Learning English
- Discovering the purpose of reading
- Becoming active learners
- Gaining access to academic language

Learning English

The more proficient students are in the language they are reading, the more readily they learn to read. For ELLs, support for learning English is support for learning to read. The most effective kind of help comes in content-focused language instruction, where learners are engaged in grade-level-appropriate instructional activities and their participation is scaffolded and supported as needed.

The most effective activities provide ELLs ample opportunity to hear English and to use it productively in meaningful communication. Teachers play a vital role in creating a supportive classroom environment. ELLs must be able to participate to the extent possible (again, with as much support as needed) in discussions with classmates who are more proficient in English. Peers can offer practice and support, but only teachers can ensure that ELLs get access to the kind of language needed for literacy development.

Purpose of reading

The greatest dangers ELLs face in learning to read in English before they are proficient in that language is that the effort involved in decoding takes precedence in their minds over all else. Connections between words and referents, between words and structures, and between text and meaning are overlooked when children focus on sounding out, figuring out symbols, and figuring out sounds. This is especially likely to happen when there is too little emphasis placed on reading as a sense-making activity in instructional programs. If meaning—no matter how difficult it is to come by—is not constantly emphasized in reading instruction, children end up believing that decoding is reading, and that there is nothing missing when they read without understanding. Decoding

becomes an end in itself, and the real purpose of reading is lost. Unfortunately, this is the outcome for many ELLs, who even after having learned English do not perform well in reading assessments.

Literacy in English begins as deciphering for ELLs—they must first figure out how the code in which the text is written works. It is not until the reader engages in an interpretive process in which the thoughts, information,

concepts, situations, and relations encoded in the texts are manifested as meanings that there is real reading. This is true for both ELLs and for native English speakers. ELLs, however, will need a lot of guidance and instructional support from teachers to do that. Once students have gained enough familiarity with English to participate even at a rudimentary level in discussions about reading selections and content, they begin to learn that the materials they are reading have something to say to them and that hearing what they have to say is the real purpose of learning to read.

Active readers

Helping students become active learners of English and users of the literacy skills they are acquiring is a key to their becoming successful students and performing well in the assessments they have to take. This is accomplished by encouraging students to take an active role in instructional activities, asking questions, seeking answers, and trying to make sense of what they are studying in school.

Both teachers and students can have many preconceived ideas about the roles they play as teachers and learners. Students sometimes come to school believing that learning is something that will be done to them, rather than something they must take an active role in doing. In their view, the role of the teacher is active and the role they play as learners is passive. When teachers share that belief, there is little likelihood of active or independent learning. Instruction is most effective when teachers are knowledgeable about the subject matter they are teaching and they create a classroom environment in which learners can take an active role in discovering how things work, what things mean, and how to get and make sense of information.

Academic English

Teachers are aware that the language used in written texts is sufficiently different from everyday spoken language to constitute a barrier to students who are not already familiar with it. Academic English is not just another name for "standard English." It is, instead, the special forms of standard English used in academic discourse and in written texts. It makes use of grammatical constructions, words, and rhetorical conventions that are not often used in everyday spoken language.

Paradoxically, academic language is both a prerequisite for full literacy and the outcome of it. Some students arrive at school with a running start in acquiring it. Students who come from homes where family members engage in frequent discussions of books and ideas are already familiar with it, and thus have an advantage learning to read.

It should be noted that the language used at home does *not* have to be English for children to benefit from such experiences. Teachers can provide their students, irrespective of background, experiences with academic language by reading to them and discussing readings, instructional activities, and experiences. By drawing students into instructional conversations focused on the language they encounter in their school texts and other materials, teachers get students to notice language itself and to figure out how it works.

Supporting language and literacy development for ELLs

Teachers support language development by engaging children as active participants in making sense of the texts they are working on. They do it by drawing the English learners into discussions relating to the texts. Even relative newcomers are able to participate in these discussions as long as ample scaffolding is provided:

It says here, "Her teacher picked up the paper and studied it carefully."

Hector, what does the text tell us Vashti's teacher did first?

Yes, she picked up the paper first.

Take a look at the picture. Marta, can you show us, which part of the sentence tells us what the teacher is doing?

Can you tell us what she is doing?

Yes! She is studying the paper carefully.

Teachers draw attention to words, phrases, and sentences, asking: "Let's see if we can figure out what that means!" By relating language to meaning, they help students gain access to meaning by demonstrating, referring to illustrations and diagrams, and by paraphrasing in simpler language.

Instructional conversations about the texts they are reading are as essential for newcomers as they are for ELLs who have already gained some proficiency in English. It is vital to their literacy development to realize that what they are "reading" can be understood, even if its meaning is not immediately available to them as it would be to readers who are fully proficient in English. Without such help, ELLs sometimes come to believe that decoding without access to meaning is an empty exercise one does in school, and except for that, it has little relevance to their lives.

Teachers can help students discover how the language works and how to extract meaning from texts by considering how the language they encounter can convey information, ideas, stories, feelings, and images. This cannot wait until the learners are fully proficient in the language they are reading. It can enhance language development if done from the start, as soon as ELLs are introduced to English reading.

Strategies for supporting language and literacy development and preparing ELLs for assessment

The most effective support comes in the form of instructional conversations in which ELLs are drawn into discussions of reading selections and content. By hearing their teachers and other classmates discuss the materials they are reading, they gradually learn how the language works in texts and in conversation.

- Draw attention to the language used in reading selections and other text materials—words, phrases, and sentences— and relate them to meaning that is discussed and commented on, both locally and globally, to help ELLs learn how to get at meaning in texts.

- Provide students ample opportunity to use the language of texts in speaking (during discussions of the reading selections, for example) and in writing (in response to writing prompts).

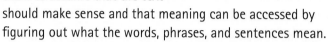

- Teach English learners to be strategic readers by guiding them to assume that the text should make sense and that meaning can be accessed by figuring out what the words, phrases, and sentences mean.

- Teach students to ask questions about meaning as it unfolds in the text. Help them recognize that some parts of texts provide background knowledge while other parts reveal new information.

- Teach students how to relate new information presented in a text to what is already known. Train students to make inferences about meaning based on the words and phrases used in a text.

- Expect ELLs to make progress, and then ensure it by providing ample grade level discussion of content. At the same time, recognize that it takes time to learn English, and that learners may differ in the amount and kind of help they need in order to make progress.

- Recognize that the most crucial kind of preparation for assessment is in helping children develop the **language and literacy skills** that are essential to successful performance in tests and for academic progress itself.

- Call students' attention to words, phrases, and constructions that often figure in text items. For example, words such as *both, not,* and *best* may not seem to be noteworthy, but their uses in test questions prove otherwise. ELLs need help in seeing how such words frame and constrain the ideas expressed in sentences in which they appear.

- Teach students the logic of test questions. Use released test items or models of test items (both of which are likely to be available online from your state department of education or district web sites). Show students, for example, that the question, "Which of the following is NOT a sentence?" entails that all of the listed options except one *are* sentences.

- Teach students to read carefully. Students who are fully proficient in English may occasionally benefit from test-taking strategies such as reading the test question and answer options first and then skimming the test passage to find information that will aid in the selection of the

correct answer to the question. This tactic does not serve English learners well. They need to read and understand the passage carefully, and then consider how to answer the questions asked.

- Teach students when the text calls for activation of prior knowledge. All children have such knowledge, but English learners need help in deciding where it is called for and how they should bring what they already know to interpret the texts they are reading.

- Expand students' horizons by reading them texts that may be too difficult to handle on their own. Help them make sense of such materials by commenting on meaning, drawing attention to how language is used in them, and engaging students in discussions about aspects of the texts.

The texts that are read to students, and the ones they read themselves, provide reliable access to the academic language they need for literacy and for assessment, provided teachers call their attention to language, and help children see how it works. Teachers do this by identifying interesting (not just new) phrases and commenting on them, inviting students to try using the phrases, and providing scaffolds as needed; they model the uses of language from texts in subsequent instructional activities; they encourage students to remember and keep records of words they learn from texts; they remind them when words and phrases encountered earlier show up again in different contexts.

The Concept of Transfer

Dr. Elena Izquierdo, the University of Texas at El Paso

Research continues to support the critical role of the student's first language (L1) in literacy development and its effect on literacy in (L2) English. Strong (L1) literacy skills facilitate the *transfer* into English literacy, and students ultimately progress rapidly into learning in English. In reality, the concept of transfer refers to the student's facility in appropriating knowledge from one language to the other. *Students do not know they know, but they know.* They are constantly and indirectly, unconsciously and automatically, constructing the knowledge that is inherent in the contexts for which each of these languages can function. The effective transfer of skills transpires as students develop their metalinguistic and metacognitive skills and as they engage in a contrastive analysis of the two languages (Cummins, 2007).

Matters of transfer occur within essentials of language that are (1) *common* to L1 and L2; (2) *similar*, but not exact in both languages; and (3) *specific* to each language and not applicable to the other language. In essence, children develop a special awareness of language and its function; learn that some sounds are the same in both languages; and also learn that there are certain boundaries for specific sounds depending on the language.

Students who have developed an awareness for phonemes, phonics, vocabulary building, and reading comprehension skills, can transfer these skills to English. They develop an enhanced awareness of the relationship between their L1 and English, which leads them to successfully appropriate strategies of transfer in similar types of word recognition processing; searching for cognates; making reference to prior knowledge, inferencing, questioning, and monitoring. Facilitating these cognitive skills in students will support their success in English literacy and their learning in English.

Introduction to Linguistics
How People Speak

All languages have both consonants and vowels. Consonants are made with some obstruction of the vocal tract, either a complete stoppage of air or enough constriction to create friction. Vowels are produced with the vocal tract more open, with no constriction that might cause friction.

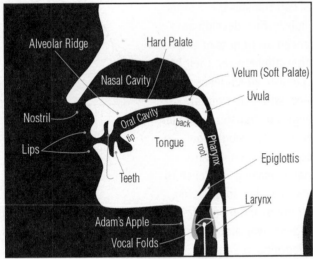

Figure 1: The human vocal tract makes the sounds of speech.

Consonants

Every consonant can be described by noting three characteristics: voicing, place of articulation, and manner of articulation.

Voicing Many sounds of language, including all vowels, employ vibration of the vocal folds in the larynx. This creates more resonance and energy for the sound. All speech sounds are characterized as either voiced (with vocal fold vibration) or voiceless (with no vocal fold vibration). Feeling the vibration around the Adam's apple can help you understand this difference. If you say "sssss" and then "zzzzz," you can feel the distinction: /s/ is voiceless and /z/ is voiced.

Place of Articulation This is the location in the vocal tract where the air stream may be constricted. The /s/ sound, for example, is made with the tongue tip close to the alveolar ridge (see Figure 1).

> **Place of Articulation Terms**
> **Alveolar:** tongue tip and ridge behind teeth
> **Bilabial:** using both lips
> **Glottal:** produced at the larynx
> **Interdental:** tongue tip between upper and lower teeth
> **Labio-dental:** upper teeth and lower lip
> **Labio-velar:** rounding of lips; tongue body raised toward velum
> **Palatal:** body of tongue and high part of palate
> **Palato-alveolar:** tongue tip and palate behind alveolar ridge
> **Velar:** body of tongue and velum (soft palate)

Manner of Articulation This is the type or degree of constriction that occurs in an articulation. For example, the /t/ sound completely stops the airflow with the tongue tip at the alveolar ridge, but /s/ allows air to pass noisily through a small opening.

> **Manner of Articulation Terms**
> **Affricate:** complete constriction followed by slow separation of the articulators resulting in friction
> **Approximant:** close constriction, but not enough for friction
> **Fricative:** narrow constriction; turbulent airflow causing friction
> **Glottal:** produced at the larynx
> **Lateral:** air passes over sides of tongue
> **Nasal:** lowered velum to let air escape through the nose
> **Stop:** complete constriction, closure so that air cannot escape through the oral cavity
> **Tap:** brief contact between tongue tip and alveolar ridge

Vowels

Vowels are open, sonorous sounds. Each vowel can be uniquely described by noting the position of the tongue, the tension of the vocal tract, and the position of the lips. Vowels are described by *height,* where the tongue is relative to the roof of the mouth. They can be high, mid, or low. Tongue backness tells if the tongue articulation is in the front or back of the mouth. Tense vowels are more common around the world. In English, they are longer and include an expansion of the throat at the pharynx. Lax vowels are shorter with a more neutral pharynx. An example is the tense long e as in *meet* versus the lax short *i* as in *mitt.* The lips either can be in a spread or neutral position, or they can be rounded and protrude slightly.

Speaking English

English is the third most widely spoken native language in the world, after Mandarin and Spanish. There are about 330 million native speakers of English and 600 million who speak it as a foreign language.

English Consonant Sounds

The following chart gives the International Phonetic Alphabet (IPA) symbol for each English consonant along with its voicing, place, and manner of articulation. This information can be used to understand and help identify problems that non-native speakers may encounter when learning to speak English.

Consonants of English		
IPA	**Articulation**	**Example**
p	voiceless bilabial stop	pit
b	voiced bilabial stop	bit
m	voiced bilabial nasal stop	man
w	voiced labio-velar approximant	win
f	voiceless labio-dental fricative	fun
v	voiced labio-dental fricative	very
θ	voiceless interdental fricative	thing
ð	voiced interdental fricative	there
t	voiceless alveolar stop	time
d	voiced alveolar stop	dime
n	voiced alveolar nasal stop	name
s	voiceless alveolar fricative	soy
z	voiced alveolar fricative	zeal
ɾ	voiced alveolar tap	butter
l	voiced alveolar lateral approximant	loop
ɹ	voiced alveolar central approximant	red
ʃ	voiceless palato-alveolar fricative	shallow
ʒ	voiced palato-alveolar fricative	vision
ʧ	voiceless palato-alveolar affricate	chirp
ʤ	voiced palato-alveolar affricate	joy
j	voiced palatal approximant	you
k	voiceless velar stop	kite
g	voiced velar stop	goat
ŋ	voiced velar nasal stop	king
h	voiceless glottal fricative	hope

English Vowel Sounds

Most languages in the world have around five vowel sounds. English has 13 common vowel sounds, which means that many students of English must learn more vowel distinctions than there are in their native language. The lax vowels are most difficult. Some vowels are diphthongs, meaning the tongue is in one position at the beginning of the sound, and it moves to another position by the end of it.

Vowels of English		
IPA	**Sound**	**Example**
i	ē	beat
ɪ	ĭ	bit
e	ā	bait
ɛ	ĕ	bet
æ	ă	bat
u	ōō	boot
ʊ	ŏŏ	could
o	ō	boat
ɔ	aw	law
ɑ	ŏ	hot
ə	ə	about
ʌ	ŭ	cut
ɝ	er	bird
ɑ ʊ	ow	house
ɔ ɪ	oy	boy
ɑ ɪ	ī	bite

Figure 2 is a schematic of the mouth. The left is the front of the mouth; the right is the back. The top is the roof of the mouth and the bottom is the floor. Placement of the vowel shows where the tongue reaches its maximum in the English articulation.

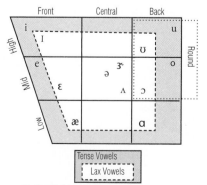

Figure 2: English vowel sounds

Transference

Pronunciation

All languages build on the same fundamentals. All languages contrast voiced and voiceless sound, and have stops and fricatives. Many languages use the same places of articulation for consonants as well. The majority of sounds will easily transfer from another language to English.

However, there will always be some sounds that are not found in a person's native language that can pose a challenge to the English language learner. English has a few relatively rare sounds, such as the interdental sounds spelled with *th*, /θ/ and /ð/. The /r/ sound in English is also a very rare type of sound. Most other languages use a tap or trill articulation for an /r/ sound.

In some languages, the /l/ and /r/ sounds belong to one psychological category. This means that they count as the same sound in that language. In this case, it is not the articulation that is difficult, but the perception of the difference and consistent use of one versus the other in any word context. This type of psychological category is called a *phoneme*, and multiple speech sounds all can be categorized as the same phoneme in that language.

This is true for English as well, where, for example, the alveolar lateral /l/ as in *lob* and the velarized lateral /ɫ/ as in *ball* are both counted as the same sound—an **l**—to native speakers of English. It is important to keep in mind that both the phonetic articulation of a sound and its psychological, phonemic category factor into the learning of a new language.

Grammar

Pronouncing English is not the only stumbling block for English learners. The grammar and usage, or syntax, of English may present distinctions that are unique to the language. For example, English syntax requires adjectives to precede the nouns they modify, as in *the tall girl*. In other languages, such as Spanish, Hmong, and Vietnamese, adjectives follow nouns, as in *la chica alta* (literally *the girl tall* in Spanish). This may cause word-order problems, particularly for less advanced English learners.

Other syntactic differences are less obvious and may cause problems even for advanced learners. For example, many East Asian languages (such as Mandarin, Cantonese, and Korean) do not mark agreement between subject and verb. Speakers of these languages may therefore leave out agreement markers such as the *-s* in *The girl like cats*.

The use of articles varies across languages. For instance, Spanish uses the definite article more often than English, while Mandarin and Cantonese do not have articles. A Spanish-speaking English learner might say *The girl likes the cats* instead of *The girl likes cats*, and a Mandarin or Cantonese speaker might say *Girl like cat*.

Plural marking is another potential trouble spot: Vietnamese, Filipino, Cantonese, and Mandarin do not add plural markers to nouns. Learners speaking these languages may have difficulty with English plurals, saying *cat* instead of *cats*.

Grammar Hot Spots

Look for Grammar Hot Spots on the following pages for tips on the most common syntax errors by speakers of languages other than English.

Common First Languages

In the Common First Languages section, you will find details of some common non-English languages spoken in the United States. They are:

- Spanish
- Vietnamese
- Cantonese
- Hmong
- Filipino
- Korean
- Mandarin

You can use the fundamentals of speech articulation already covered to help you understand where the languages differ from English. Differences in the spoken language and in the writing systems are explored as well. These sections pinpoint common trouble spots specific to learners of English.

> **Culture Clues**
>
> Look to Culture Clues for insights into the cultural differences of each language learner as well as ideas for ways to embrace students' diversity.

Linguistic Contrastive Analysis

The Linguistic Contrastive Analysis Charts provide a quick reference for comparing English sounds with those of other languages. The charts allow you to check at a glance which sounds have equivalents in other languages. For those sounds that don't have equivalents, you can find the closest sound used as a substitute and suggestions for helping someone gain a native English articulation.

In these charts, the sounds are notated using the International Phonetic Alphabet (IPA). This is the most widely recognized and used standard for representing speech sounds in any language. A guiding principle of the IPA across all languages is that each sound is uniquely represented by one symbol, and each symbol represents only one sound.

The chart has columns for each native language with rows corresponding to each English phoneme. Each cell in the chart gives an example word using that sound in the native language, a definition in parenthesis, and transference tips below. If there is no sound equivalent to English, a common substitution used by speakers of that language may be provided.

> **Transference Tips**
>
> Transference Tips give you ideas of how the sound will be produced by the learner. Cells in bold note where the English learner will have particular difficulty with the English sound.

Common First Languages
Spanish

Background Spanish is the second most widely spoken language in the world. There are more than 400 million native Spanish speakers in 20-plus countries on three continents. Spanish vocabulary and pronunciation differ from country to country. While most dialect differences in English are in vowel sounds, Spanish dialects differ in their consonants.

Spoken Spanish sounds are similar to those found in English, so there is a strong foundation for the native Spanish speaker learning English. However, there are three key differences between English and Spanish consonants:

1. Most of the alveolar sounds in English, such as /t/, /d/, and /n/ are produced farther forward in the mouth in Spanish. Instead of the tongue touching the alveolar ridge as in English, in Spanish it touches the back of the teeth.

2. Another difference is that the /r/ sound in English is not found in Spanish. There are two /r/ sounds in Spanish. One is the tap /ɾ/, which occurs in English as the quick sound in the middle of the name *Betty*. Psychologically, this tap sound is a kind of /t/ or /d/ sound in English, while in Spanish it is perceived as an /r/. The other /r/ sound in Spanish is a trill, or series of tongue taps on the alveolar ridge. This does not occur in English.

3. The third key difference between English and Spanish can be found in the English production of the voiceless stops /p/, /t/, and /k/. In English these sounds are aspirated, with an extra puff of air at the end, when the sound occurs at the beginning of a word or stressed syllable. So, /p/ is aspirated in *pit*. Learners can add a puff of air to such sounds to sound more like native English speakers.

There are five vowels in Spanish, which are a subset of the English vowels. Spanish vowels include tense vowel sounds /a/ /e/ /i/ /o/ /u/. Lax vowel sounds in English are the problematic ones for native Spanish speakers.

Written Like English, written Spanish uses the Roman alphabet, so both writing systems are similar. There are a few orthographic differences to note, however:

- The letter *h* in Spanish is silent, but the sound /h/ is written as *j* or *g*.

- A single letter *r* in Spanish represents a tap, while the double *rr* represents a trill.

- Accents are used to show the stress on a syllable when the stress is different from the usual rules. In some cases, words change meaning according to the accents. For example, *el* means *the* while *él* means *he*.

Written Spanish vowels are pronounced like the symbols in the IPA. So, the Spanish "i" is pronounced with the long ē as in the word *beat*. The IPA and Spanish symbol for this letter is the same: i.

Vietnamese

Background Approximately eighty million people in Vietnam speak Vietnamese. The northern dialect is the standard, though central and southern dialects also exist. Most Vietnamese speakers in the United States are from southern Vietnam and speak the southern dialect.

Spoken Vietnamese is a tonal language, so each syllable is pronounced with a distinctive tone that affects meaning. Vietnamese has a complex vowel system of 12 vowels and 26 diphthongs. Its consonants are simpler, but Vietnamese syllable structure allows few possibilities for final consonants.

> **Culture Clues**
> In traditional Vietnamese education, there is a strict division between the roles of student and teacher. Students may be confused if asked to direct a part of their own study, so encourage group work.

Students may need help noticing and learning to reproduce final consonant sounds in English words and syllables. Vietnamese syllable structure allows for limited combinations of initial consonants. Students also may need help with the more complex initial consonant clusters of English words and syllables.

Written Since the 1600s, Vietnamese has used a Romanized alphabet. Many characters written in Vietnamese have sounds different from their English counterparts, such as *d, x, ch, nh, kh, g, tr, r,* and *e.*

> **Grammar Hot Spots**
> - Like English, Vietnamese uses Subject-Verb-Object (SVO) syntax, or word order.
> - Vietnamese does not use affixes; instead, syntax expresses number, case, and tense.

Cantonese

Background Cantonese is one of the seven major Chinese languages, not all of which are mutually intelligible. Cantonese is mostly spoken in China's southern provinces, Hong Kong, and Macau by about 66 million people. It is a tonal language, and the same sequence of letters can have different meanings depending on their pitch.

Spoken Cantonese has six stops, aspirated and non-aspirated /p/, /t/, /k/; three fricatives /f/, /s/, /h/, and two affricates /ts/, /tsʰ/. Some sounds which do not exist in Cantonese can be difficult for the English language learner. The /v/ often gets pronounced as /f/ or /w/; the /z/ is often said as /s/; the sounds spelled with *th* are often said as /t/, /d/, or /f/. Cantonese speakers have difficulty distinguishing between /l/ and /r/, since /r/ is not present in their language. They tend to produce an /l/-like sound for both English sounds in words such as *ride* and *lied*.

Cantonese has 11 vowels and 10 diphthongs. One of the major problems for Cantonese speakers is distinguishing between English tense and lax vowels, because the distribution of Cantonese short and long vowels is determined by the sound context.

Syllables in Cantonese don't have consonant clusters. English consonant clusters are often deleted or broken up by vowel insertion (e.g., *list* becomes *lis*). This may be especially problematic when producing English past tense (e.g., *baked*).

Written Cantonese is written with standard Chinese characters known as *Hànzi* where each character represents a syllable and has a meaning. Additional Cantonese-specific characters were also added. Cantonese speakers may have difficulty with sound-letter correspondences in English.

> **Grammar Hot Spots**
> - English articles and prepositions are difficult for Cantonese speakers. *In, on,* and *at,* for instance, can be translated as the same pronoun in Cantonese.
> - Plurals, tenses, and gerund endings are difficult for Cantonese speakers to transfer to English.

Common First Languages

Hmong

Background Hmong is a group of approximately 18 languages within the Hmong-Mien family. There are roughly four million speakers of Hmong, including 200,000 in the United States. They are mainly from two groups with mutually intelligible dialects—Hmong Daw and Mong Leng.

Spoken Hmong vowels are few and simple, but its consonants are complex and differ from those of English. Notable features of Hmong phonology absent from English include consonantal pre-nasalization (the /m/n/ŋ/ sound before a consonant) and the contrast between nasalized and non-nasalized vowels. Hmong is tonal. Each syllable is pronounced with a distinctive pitch.

Written The Romanized Popular Alphabet (RPA), developed in the 1950s, is the usual way of transcribing Hmong. Syllable-final consonants are absent in pronunciation but are used to represent orthographically the tonal value of a given syllable. Students may need particular help in identifying and learning to reproduce the final consonant sounds of English words and syllables.

> **Culture Clues**
>
> In traditional Hmong culture, learning takes place through hands-on experience. Students may find it difficult to adjust to the use of graphics or print media. Competition, personal achievement, and self-directed instruction may be unfamiliar concepts, so students may prefer group work.

> **Grammar Hot Spots**
>
> - Like English, Hmong is an SVO language. Personal pronouns are marked for number, including inflection for singular, dual, and plural, though they are not marked for case.
> - Because Hmong and English prepositions often have different semantic qualities, students may need help mastering uses of English prepositions. For example, it is correct to say "think <u>about</u> [something]" rather than "think <u>on</u> [something]."

Filipino

Background Filipino and English are the official languages of the Philippines, where 175 languages are spoken. There are about 24 million native speakers of Filipino, and more than 50 million people speak Filipino as a second language. You may hear the terms Filipino and Tagalog being used interchangeably.

Spoken Filipino has many similar speech sounds to English. The notable exceptions are the lack of the consonant sounds /f/, /v/, and those spelled with *th*. Of these, the English /f/ and /v/ cause the most difficulty for learners. The distinction between long *e* (as in *beat*) and short *i* (as in *bit*) is also a trouble spot. Filipino does not allow consonant clusters at the end of syllables, so *detect* may be simplified to just one final consonant (*detec*).

Written The Filipino alphabet has 28 letters and is based on the Spanish alphabet, so the English writing system poses little problem.

> **Culture Clues**
>
> Most people from the Philippines can speak Filipino, but for many it is not their first language. Ask Filipino students about other languages they speak. Because English is used alongside Filipino as the language of instruction in the Philippines, most Filipinos are familiar with English.

> **Grammar Hot Spots**
>
> - Filipino word order is Verb-Subject-Object (VSO), which does not transfer well to English.
> - Inflectional verb endings, such as *-s, -en, -ed,* and *-ing* do not exist in Filipino, so it is common to leave out the third person singular verb marker (*"He walk,"* not *"He walks"*).

Korean

Background Korean is spoken by 71 million people in North and South Korea. Standard Korean is based on the speech in and around Seoul.

Spoken Korean does not have corresponding sounds for English /f/, /v/, /θ/, /ð/, and /dʒ/. In word-initial position, all Korean stops are voiceless. Voiced stops /b/, /d/, and /g/ are only produced between two vowels. Korean speakers may have difficulty producing /s/, /ʃ/, and /z/ in some contexts, in addition to English /r/ and /l/ sounds (e.g., *rock* and *lock*). They may have problems in producing English consonant clusters (e.g., *str-*, *sk-*). These problems can often be eliminated by vowel insertion or consonant deletion. In addition, the distinction between English tense and lax vowels (e.g., /i/ as in *beat* vs. /ɪ/ as in *bit*) may be problematic for Korean speakers.

> **Culture Clues**
>
> Korean uses a complex system of honorifics, so it is unusual for Korean students to use the pronoun *you* or call their teachers by their first name.

Written Modern Korean uses the Korean alphabet *(Hangul)* or a mixed script of *Hangul* and Chinese. *Hangul* is an alphabetic script organized into syllabic blocks.

> **Grammar Hot Spots**
>
> - In contrast to English, Korean word order is Subject-Object-Verb (SOV). The verb always comes at the end of a sentence.
> - Korean syllable stress is different, so learners may have difficulties with the rhythm of English.

Mandarin

Background Chinese encompasses a wide range of dialects and is the native language of two-thirds of China. There are approximately 870 million Mandarin speakers worldwide. North Mandarin, as found in Beijing, is the basis of the modern standard language.

Spoken Mandarin Chinese and English differ substantially in their sound structure. Mandarin lacks voiced obstruent consonants (/b/, /d/, /g/, /dʒ/), causing difficulty for speakers in perceiving and producing English voiced consonants (e.g., *buy* may be pronounced and perceived as *pie*). The sounds spelled with th are not present in Mandarin, so they are often substituted with /s/ or /t/ causing, for example, *fourth* to be pronounced as *fours*. Mandarin Chinese has five vowels. Due to the relatively small vowel inventory and contextual effects on vowels in Mandarin, many English vowels and tense/lax distinctions present problems for speakers of Mandarin Chinese. Mandarin allows only a very simple syllable structure, causing problems in producing consonant clusters in English. Speakers may drop consonants or insert vowels between them (e.g., film may become /filəm/). The use of tones in Mandarin may result in the rising and falling of pitch when speaking English.

Written Chinese is written with characters known as Hànzi. Each character represents a syllable and also has a meaning. A Romanized alphabet called Pinyin marks pronunciation of characters. Chinese speakers may have problems mastering letter-sound correspondences in written English, especially for sounds that are not present in Mandarin.

> **Grammar Hot Spots**
>
> - The non-inflected nature of Chinese causes Mandarin speakers to have problems with plurals, past-tense markers, and gerund forms *(-s, -ed, -ing)*.
> - Mastering English tenses and passive is difficult. Students should be familiarized with correct lexical and syntactic features as well as appropriate situations for the use of various tenses and passives.

Linguistic Contrastive Analysis Char
The Consonants of English

IPA	ENGLISH	SPANISH	VIETNAMESE	CANTONESE
p	*pit* Aspirated at the start of a word or stressed syllable	*pato* (duck) Never aspirated	*pin* (battery)	*pʰa (to lie prone)* Always aspirated
b	*bit*	*barco* (boat) Substitute voiced bilabial fricative /ɒ/ in between vowels	*ba* (three) Implosive (air moves into the mouth during articulation)	NO EQUIVALENT Substitute /p/
m	*man*	*mundo* (world)	*mot* (one)	*ma* (mother)
w	*win*	*agua* (water)	NO EQUIVALENT Substitute word-initial /u/	*wa* (frog)
f	*fun*	*flor* (flower)	*phuꞌoꞌng* (phoenix) Substitute sound made with both lips, rather than with the lower lip and the teeth like English /f/	*fa* (flower) Only occurs at the beginning of syllables
v	*very*	NO EQUIVALENT Learners can use correct sound	*Viẹt Nam* (Vietnam)	NO EQUIVALENT Substitute /f/
θ	*thing* Rare in other languages. When done correctly, the tongue will stick out between the teeth.	NO EQUIVALENT Learners can use correct sound	NO EQUIVALENT Substitute /tʰ/ or /f/	NO EQUIVALENT Substitute /tʰ/ or /f/
ð	*there* Rare in other languages. When done correctly, the tongue will stick out between the teeth.	*cada* (every) Sound exists in Spanish only between vowels; sometimes substitute voiceless θ.	NO EQUIVALENT Substitute /d/	NO EQUIVALENT Substitute /t/ or /f/
t	*time* Aspirated at the start of a word or stressed syllable English tongue-touch. Is a little farther back in the mouth than the other languages.	*tocar* (touch) Never aspirated	*tám* (eight) Distinguishes aspirated and non-aspirated	*tʰa (he/she)* Distinguishes aspirated and non-aspirated
d	*dime* English tongue-touch is a little farther back in the mouth than the other languages.	*dos* (two)	*Đōng* (Dong = unit of currency) Vietnamese /d/ is implosive (air moves into the mouth during articulation)	NO EQUIVALENT Substitute /t/
n	*name* English tongue-touch is a little farther back in the mouth than the other languages.	*nube* (cloud)	*nam* (south)	*na* (take)
s	*soy*	*seco* (dry)	*xem* (to see)	*sa* (sand) Substitute *sh-* sound before /u/ Difficult at ends of syllables and words
z	*zeal*	NO EQUIVALENT Learners can use correct sound	*ròi* (already) In northern dialect only Southern dialect, substitute /y/	NO EQUIVALENT Substitute /s/
ɾ	*butter* Written 't' and 'd' are pronounced with a quick tongue-tip tap.	*rana* (toad) Written as single *r* and thought of as an /r/ sound.	NO EQUIVALENT Substitute /t/	NO EQUIVALENT Substitute /t/
l	*loop* English tongue-touch is a little farther back in the mouth than the other languages. At the ends of syllables, the /l/ bunches up the back of the tongue, becoming velarized /ɫ/ or dark-l as in the word *ball*.	*libro* (book)	*cú lao* (island) /l/ does not occur at the ends of syllables	*lau* (angry) /l/ does not occur at the ends of syllables

HMONG	FILIPINO	KOREAN	MANDARIN
*p*eb (we/us/our) Distinguishes aspirated and non-aspirated	*p*aalam (goodbye) Never aspirated	*p*al (sucking)	*p*ʰei (cape) Always aspirated
NO EQUIVALENT Substitute /p/	*b*aka (beef)	NO EQUIVALENT /b/ said between vowels Substitute /p/ elsewhere	NO EQUIVALENT
*m*us (to go)	*m*abuti (good)	*m*al (horse)	*m*ei (rose)
NO EQUIVALENT Substitute word-initial /*u*/	*w*alo *(eight)*	*gw*e (box)	*w*en (mosquito)
*f*aib (to divide)	NO EQUIVALENT Substitute /p/	NO EQUIVALENT Substitute /p/	*f*a (issue)
*V*aj ('Vang' clan name)	NO EQUIVALENT Substitute /b/	NO EQUIVALENT Substitute /b/	NO EQUIVALENT Substitute /w/ or /f/
NO EQUIVALENT Substitute /tʰ/ or /f/	NO EQUIVALENT Learners can use correct sound, but sometimes mispronounce voiced /ð/.	NO EQUIVALENT Substitute /t/	NO EQUIVALENT Substitute /t/ or /s/
NO EQUIVALENT Substitute /d/	NO EQUIVALENT Learners can use correct sound	NO EQUIVALENT Substitute /d/	NO EQUIVALENT Substitute /t/ or /s/
*th*em (to pay) Distinguishes aspirated and non-aspirated	*t*akbo (run) Never aspirated	*t*al (daughter)	*t*a (wet) Distinguishes aspirated and non-aspirated
*d*ev (dog)	*d*eretso (straight)	NO EQUIVALENT Substitute /d/ when said between vowels and /t/ elsewhere.	NO EQUIVALENT Substitute /t/
*n*oj (to eat)	*n*aman (too)	*n*al (day)	*n*i (you) May be confused with /l/
*x*a (to send)	*s*ila (they)	*s*al (rice) Substitute *shi–* sound before /i/ and /z/ after a nasal consonant	*s*an (three)
NO EQUIVALENT Learners can use correct sound	NO EQUIVALENT Learners can use correct sound	NO EQUIVALENT Learners can use correct sound	NO EQUIVALENT Substitute /ts/ or /tsʰ/
NO EQUIVALENT Substitute /t/	*r*in/*d*in (too) Variant of the /d/ sound	Only occurs between two vowels Considered an /l/ sound	NO EQUIVALENT
*l*os (to come) /l/ does not occur at the ends of syllables	sa*l*amat (thank you)	ba*l*am (wind)	*l*an (blue) Can be confused and substituted with /r/

The Consonants of English (*continued*)

IPA	ENGLISH	SPANISH	VIETNAMESE	CANTONESE
ɹ	*red* Rare sound in the world Includes lip-rounding	NO EQUIVALENT Substitute /r/ sound such as the tap /ɾ/ or the trilled /r/	NO EQUIVALENT Substitute /l/	NO EQUIVALENT Substitute /l/
ʃ	*sha*llow Often said with lip-rounding	NO EQUIVALENT Substitute /s/ or /tʃ/	*sieu th*ị (supermarket) Southern dialect only	NO EQUIVALENT Substitute /s/
ʒ	*vi*sion Rare sound in English	NO EQUIVALENT Substitute /z/ or /dʒ/	NO EQUIVALENT Substitute /s/	NO EQUIVALENT Substitute /s/
tʃ	*chi*rp	*chi*co (boy)	*chí*nh phủ (government) Pronounced harder than English *ch*	NO EQUIVALENT Substitute /ts/
dʒ	*j*oy	NO EQUIVALENT Sometimes substituted with /ʃ/ sound Some dialects have this sound for the *ll* spelling as in *llamar*	NO EQUIVALENT Substitute /c/, the equivalent sound, but voiceless	NO EQUIVALENT Substitute /ts/ Only occurs at beginnings of syllables
j	*y*ou	*ci*elo (sky) Often substitute /dʒ/	*y*eu (to love)	*j*au (worry)
k	*k*ite Aspirated at the start of a word or stressed syllable	*ca*sa (house) Never aspirated	*c*om (rice) Never aspirated	*kʰ*a (family) Distinguishes aspirated and non-aspirated
g	*g*oat	*ga*to (cat)	NO EQUIVALENT Substitute /k/	NO EQUIVALENT Substitute /k/
ŋ	ki*ng*	ma*ng*o (mango)	*Ng*ūyen (proper last name)	pha*ŋ* (to cook)
h	*h*ope	*ge*nte (people) Sometimes substitute sound with friction higher in the vocal tract as velar /x/ or uvular /χ/	*h*oa (flower)	*h*a (shrimp)

HMONG	FILIPINO	KOREAN	MANDARIN
NO EQUIVALENT Substitute /l/	**NO EQUIVALENT** Substitute the tap /ɾ/	**NO EQUIVALENT** Substitute the tap or /l/ confused with /l/	*r*an (caterpillar) Tongue tip curled further backward than for English /r/
*s*au (to write)	*s*iya (s/he)	Only occurs before /i/; Considered an /s/ sound	*sh*i (wet)
*z*os village)	**NO EQUIVALENT** Learners can use correct sound	**NO EQUIVALENT**	**NO EQUIVALENT** Substitute palatal affricate /tɕ/
*ch*eb (to sweep)	*ts*a (tea)	*c*ʰal (kicking)	*ch*eng (red)
NO EQUIVALENT Substitute *ch* sound	*D*ios (God)	**NO EQUIVALENT** Substitute *ch* sound	**NO EQUIVALENT** Substitute /ts/
*Y*aj (Yang, clan name)	ta*y*o (we)	je:*z*an (budget)	*y*an (eye)
*K*oo (Kong, clan name) Distinguishes aspirated and non-aspirated	*k*alian (when) Never aspirated	*k*al (spreading)	*k*e (nest) Distinguishes aspirated and non-aspirated
NO EQUIVALENT Substitute /k/	*g*ulay (vegetable)	**NO EQUIVALENT** Substitute /k/ Learners use correct sound between two vowels	**NO EQUIVALENT** Substitute /k/
*g*us (goose)	an*g*aw (one million)	ba*ŋ* (room)	tan*g* (gong) Sometimes add /k/ sound to the end
*h*ais (to speak)	*h*indi (no)	*h*al (doing)	**NO EQUIVALENT** Substitute velar fricative /x/

Linguistic Contrastive Analysis Cha[rt]
The Vowels of English

IPA	ENGLISH	SPANISH	VIETNAMESE	CANTONESE
i	*beat*	*hijo* (son)	*di* (to go)	*si* (silk)
ɪ	*bit* Rare in other languages Usually confused with /i/ (*meat* vs. *mit*)	**NO EQUIVALENT** Substitute /ē/	**NO EQUIVALENT** Substitute /ē/	*sik* (color) Only occurs before velars Substitute /ē/
e	*bait* End of vowel diphthongized—tongue moves up to /ē/ or short *e* position	*eco* (echo)	*kê* (millet)	*se* (to lend)
ɛ	*bet* Rare in other languages Learners may have difficulty distinguishing /ā/ and /e/ (short *e*): *pain* vs. *pen*	**NO EQUIVALENT** Substitute /ā/	**NO EQUIVALENT** Substitute /ā/	*seŋ* (sound) Only occurs before velars; difficult to distinguish from /ā/ in all positions
æ	*bat* Rare in other languages Learners may have trouble getting the tongue farther forward in the mouth	**NO EQUIVALENT** Substitute mid central /u/ (short *u*) or low front tense /o/ (short *o*)	*ghe* (boat)	**NO EQUIVALENT** Hard to distinguish between /æ/ and /ā/
u	*boot*	*uva* (grape)	*mua* (to buy)	*fu* (husband)
ʊ	*could* Rare in other languages Learners may have difficulty distinguishing the vowel sounds in *wooed* vs. *wood*	**NO EQUIVALENT** Substitute long *u*	**NO EQUIVALENT** Substitute long *u* (high back unrounded)	*suk* (uncle) Only occurs before velars Difficult to distinguish from long *u* in all positions
o	*boat* End of vowel diphthongized—tongue moves up to long *u* or ʊ position	*ojo* (eye)	*cô* (aunt)	*so* (comb)
ɔ	*law*	**NO EQUIVALENT** Substitute long *o* or short *o* Substituting long *o* will cause confusion (*low* vs. *law*); substituting short *o* will not	*cá* (fish)	*hok* (shell) Only occurs before velars Difficult to distinguish from long *o* in all positions
ɑ	*hot*	*mal* (bad)	*con* (child)	*sa* (sand)
ɑ ʊ	*house* Diphthong	*pauta*	*dao* (knife)	*sau* (basket)
ɔ ɪ	*boy* Diphthong	*hoy* (today)	*rồi* (already)	*soi* (grill)
ɑ ɪ	*bite* Diphthong	*baile* (dance)	*hai* (two)	*sai* (to waste)
ə	*about* Most common vowel in English; only in unstressed syllables Learners may have difficulty keeping it very short	**NO EQUIVALENT** Substitute short *u* or the full vowel from the word's spelling	*mua* (to buy)	**NO EQUIVALENT**
ʌ	*cut* Similar to schwa /ə/	**NO EQUIVALENT** Substitute short *o*	*giờ* (time)	*san* (new)
ɝ	*bird* Difficult articulation, unusual in the world but common in American English Learners must bunch the tongue and constrict the throat	**NO EQUIVALENT** Substitute short *u* or /er/ with trill	**NO EQUIVALENT** Substitute /i̇/	*hæ* (boot)

HMONG	FILIPINO	KOREAN	MANDARIN
ib (one)	*ikaw* (you) This vowel is interchangeable with /ɪ/; hard for speakers to distinguish these	ʑɯːʃaŋ (market)	*ti* (ladder) Sometimes English /i/ can be produced shorter
NO EQUIVALENT Substitute /ē/	*limampu* (fifty) This vowel is interchangeable with /ē/; hard for speakers to distinguish these	**NO EQUIVALENT** Substitute /ē/	**NO EQUIVALENT**
tes (hand)	*sero* (zero)	*be:da* (to cut)	*te* (nervous) Sometimes substitute English schwa /ə/
NO EQUIVALENT Substitute /ā/	*sero* (zero) This vowel interchanges with /ā/ like *bait*; not difficult for speakers to learn	*thɛ:do* (attitude)	**NO EQUIVALENT**
NO EQUIVALENT Substitute short *e*	**NO EQUIVALENT** Substitute short *o* as in *hot*	**NO EQUIVALENT**	**NO EQUIVALENT** Substitute /ə/ or short *u*
kub (hot or gold)	*tunay* (actual) This vowel interchanges with vowel in *could*; not difficult for speakers to learn	*zu:bag* (watermelon)	*lu* (hut) Sometimes English long *u* can be produced shorter
NO EQUIVALENT Substitute a sound like long *e* (mid central with lips slightly rounded)	*gumawa* (act) This vowel interchanges with long *u* like *boot*; not difficult for speakers to learn	**NO EQUIVALENT**	**NO EQUIVALENT**
NO EQUIVALENT	*ubo* (cough)	*bo:zu* (salary)	*mo* (sword) This vowel is a little lower than English vowel
Yaj (Yang clan name)	**NO EQUIVALENT** Spoken as short *o*, as in *hot*	**NO EQUIVALENT**	**NO EQUIVALENT** Substitute long *o*
mov (cooked rice)	*talim* (blade)	*ma:l* (speech)	*ta* (he/she) Sometimes substitute back long *o* or *u*
plaub (four)	*ikaw* (you)	**NO EQUIVALENT**	**NO EQUIVALENT**
NO EQUIVALENT	*apoy* (fire)	**NO EQUIVALENT**	**NO EQUIVALENT**
qaib (chicken)	*himatay* (faint)	**NO EQUIVALENT**	**NO EQUIVALENT**
NO EQUIVALENT	**NO EQUIVALENT** Spoken as short *o*, as in *hot*	**NO EQUIVALENT** Difficult sound for learners	**NO EQUIVALENT**
NO EQUIVALENT	**NO EQUIVALENT** Spoken as short *o*, as in *hot*	**NO EQUIVALENT**	**NO EQUIVALENT**
NO EQUIVALENT Substitute diphthong /əɨ/	**NO EQUIVALENT** Spoken as many different vowels (depending on English spelling) plus tongue tap /ɾ/	**NO EQUIVALENT**	**NO EQUIVALENT**

Comparative Oral Language Proficiency Chart

Levels of Proficiency	Level 1 Entering Beginning **Beginning**	Level II Beginning Early Intermediate	Level III Developing Intermediate **Intermediate**	Level IV Expanding Early Advanced **Advanced**	Level V Bridging Advanced **Advanced High**
Characteristics of the English Language Learner	• Minimal comprehension • May be very shy • No verbal production • Non-English speaker • Silent period (10 hours to 3 months) • Uses gestures and actions to communicate	• Limited comprehension • Gives one- or two-word responses • May use two- or three-word phrases • Stage may last 6 months to 2 years	• Comprehension increases • Errors still occur in speech • Simple sentences • Stage may last 2 to 4 years	• Good comprehension • Sentences become more complex • Engages in conversation • Errors in speech are more complex	• Few errors in speech • Orally proficient • Near-native vocabulary • Lacks writing skill • Uses complex sentences
What They Can Do: Performance Indicators	• Listen • Point • Illustrate • Match • Choose	• Name • List and group • Categorize • Label • Demonstrate	• Compare and contrast • Recall and retell • Summarize • Explain	• Higher-order thinking skills • Analyze, debate, justify	• All performance indicators
Instructional Ideas for Teachers	• Visual cues • Tape passages • Pair students • Total Physical Response activities • Concrete objects • Graphic organizers	• Short homework assignments • Short-answer quizzes • Open-ended sentences	• Graphs • Tables • Group discussions • Student-created books • Cloze activities	• Group panels • Paraphrasing • Defending and debating	• Lessons on writing mechanics • Free reading of appropriate books • Cooperative learning groups

Customize Literacy
on Reading Street

Customizing your literacy program is a creative and rewarding way to teach. Like many teachers, you want to use different approaches as you develop your students' strengths and support their needs. At the same time, you carefully balance your plan to build in required skills.

Section 7 shows how *Scott Foresman Reading Street* provides just what you need to organize and carry out your customized literacy program. You'll find planning guides and instructional lessons to help you plan and implement your lessons. You can select from a rich array of readers to match texts to your third graders.

Keep your expectations high as you customize your literacy program. *Reading Street* is here to help!

What Are Goals for Customizing a Literacy Program?

When you customize literacy, you create a program that balances direct skill instruction with a variety of approaches to meet students' needs. Your goal is to allow students to be increasingly in charge of their own learning, so you use flexible grouping and organize your literacy materials and practice stations in specific ways. The decisions you make about setting up your classroom and your use of a variety of assessments support the overall goals you've set. You want to know the most effective ways to:

- assess students to determine their strengths and learning needs.
- meet state standards for reading, writing, speaking, and listening.
- plan lessons to focus on areas of instructional need, based on assessment.
- match books to meet readers at their instructional level.
- build a community of learners.

How Can You Customize Literacy with *Reading Street*?

Lesson plans can be thought out in broad strokes in advance. Yet, if instruction is to be truly effective, lesson plans need to be revised constantly to accommodate new assessment information, and lessons need to be customized to suit the learning needs of individual students. At the same time, your plan must include district and state standards.

How Should You Group Your Students for Reading Instruction?

As you conduct a variety of assessments, you learn about your students as individuals. You come to know a great deal about their achievement levels, their interests, and their ability to interact with other students. The results of these observations and performance-based assessments help you determine your students' instructional needs and make grouping decisions. Your flexible groups will vary depending on the different instructional purpose you want to address for each. You may address DRA2 Level instruction, strategy and skill instruction, students' interests, or their social abilities. Your guided reading groups may be based on specific areas of need from the DRA2 continuum and Focus for Instruction.

Grouping to Meet Students' Needs	
Grouping Pattern	**Instructional Purpose**
Strategy/Skill Instruction	To work with students who need instruction on a specific reading strategy
Interest	To provide an opportunity for students with the same interests to learn together
Social Skills	To give students an opportunity to build and practice skills for collaboration and cooperation

How Do I Connect with DRA2 Results When I Customize Literacy?

As you customize your literacy program, detailed planning is needed for grouping students based on DRA2 Levels or strategy and skill instruction. For DRA2 Levels, use the chart that begins on the following page to determine the DRA2 instructional strand you plan to teach. The accompanying Focus for Instruction is shown along with the DRA benchmark levels. You'll also want to use lessons in *Reading Street* and leveled readers for practicing the key skills. Those materials are listed for you as well.

What Tools Help Me Teach Skills and Strategies?

For other groups, you may want to teach based on comprehension skill and strategy instruction. The chart that begins on the next page will help you choose leveled readers based on comprehension skill and strategy instruction for these groups. This chart also shows the Fountas and Pinnell leveling criteria, the corresponding DRA benchmark levels, and the genres and content connections of the leveled readers available on *Reading Street*.

The Customize Literacy section in the *Reading Street* Teacher's Edition provides strategies and support as you plan groups, pacing, and the purpose of your instruction. You'll always be able to match your third grade readers with the right books. To be assured you are providing consistent instruction, you can incorporate the routines from the Teacher Edition in your customized lessons. The flexibility of *Reading Street* resources provides the structure you need when you customize your literacy program. Overall, you're in the driver's seat, always doing your own thinking and planning.

A Rich Array of Leveled Text Sets

You choose the texts when you customize your literacy program. Select from Below-Level, On-Level, and Advanced Readers in *Reading Street*. Specific text sets are also available for your ELD and ELL groups. For struggling readers who need to practice independent reading as they build understanding and develop concept knowledge, choose the Concept Literacy Leveled Readers.

Grade 3 Alignment with DRA2

Many educators use the Developmental Reading Assessment, or DRA2, to assess students' reading achievement. This chart shows how *Reading Street* aligns with DRA2.

GRADE THREE Instructional Strand	Focus for Instruction	DRA2 Benchmark	*Reading Street* Unit/ Week Lesson Plan	Materials
Phonics				
	Short vowels	28–38	1/1	DI pages: U1v1 DI1–DI15 Decodable Readers: 1A, 1C Leveled Readers*
	Plurals	28–38	1/2	DI pages: U1v1 DI126–DI140 Decodable Readers: 2A, 2C Leveled Readers*
	Endings	28–38	1/3	DI pages: U1v1 DI151–DI165 Decodable Readers: 3A, 3C Leveled Readers*
	Vowel Digraphs	28–38	1/4	DI pages: U1v1 DI76–DI90 Decodable Readers: 4A, 4C Leveled Readers*
	Vowel Diphthongs	28–38	1/5	DI pages: U1v1 DI101–DI115 Decodable Readers: 5A, 5C Leveled Readers*
	Syllables VC/CV, V/CV, VC/V, VCCCV	28–38	1/1, 2/1, 2/2, 4/5, 5/1, 6/3	DI pages: U1v1 DI1–DI15, U2v1 DI1–DI15, DI26–DI40, U4v2 DI101–DI115, U5v1 DI1–DI15, U6v1 DI51–DI65 Decodable Readers: 1A, 1C, 6A, 6C, 7A, 7C, 20A, 20C, 21A, 21C, 28A, 28C Leveled Readers*
	Compound words	28–38	2/3	DI pages: U2v1 DI51–DI65 Decodable Readers: 8A, 8C Leveled Readers*
	Consonant blends	28–38	2/4	DI pages: U2v2 DI76–DI90 Decodable Readers: 9A, 9C Leveled Readers*
	Consonant digraphs	28–38	2/5	DI pages: U2v2 DI101–DI115 Decodable Readers: 10A, 10C Leveled Readers*

* See following pages for a list of Leveled Readers.

GRADE THREE Instructional Strand	Focus for Instruction	DRA2 Benchmark	*Reading Street* Unit/ Week Lesson Plan	Materials
	Contractions	28–38	3/1	DI pages: U3v1 DI1–DI15 Decodable Readers: 11A, 11C Leveled Readers*
	Prefixes and/or suffixes	28–38	3/2, 3/4, 4/3, 4/4, 5/5, 6/4	DI pages: U3v1 DI26–DI40, U3v2 DI76–DI90, U4v1 DI51–DI65, U4v2 DI76–DI90, U5v2 DI101–DI115, U6v2 DI76–DI90 Decodable Readers: 12A, 12C, 14A, 14C, 18A, 18C, 19A, 19C, 25A, 25C, 29A, 29C Leveled Readers*
	Consonant patterns	28–38	3/5	DI pages: U3v2 DI101–DI115 Decodable Readers: 15A, 15C Leveled Readers*
	r-controlled vowels	28–38	4/2	DI pages: U4v1 DI26–DI40 Decodable Readers: 17A, 17C Leveled Readers*
	Vowel patterns	28–38	5/3, 5/4	DI pages: U5v1 DI51–DI65, U5v2 DI76–DI90 Decodable Readers: 23A, 23C, 24A, 24C Leveled Readers*
	Vowel Sounds *oo, ow, ue, ui, oo, u*	28–38	6/1	DI pages: U6v1 DI1–DI15 Decodable Readers: 26A, 26C Leveled Readers*
Comprehension				
Questioning	Teach students to generate questions before and during reading	28–38	2/3, 4/4, 6/1	DI pages: U2v1 DI51–DI65, U4v2 DI76–DI90, U6v1 DI1–DI15 Leveled Readers*
Prediction	Guide how to focus on title, and opening paragraphs	28–38	2/4, 3/5	DI pages: U2v2 DI76–DI90, U3v2 DI101–DI115 Leveled Readers*
Story Structure	Teach students how to use information from fiction text features (e.g., title, illustrations, text)	28–38	1/5, 3/4, 6/4	DI pages: U1v2 DI101–DI115, U3v2 DI76–DI90, U6v2 DI76–DI90 Leveled Readers*
Monitor and Clarify	Model how to monitor meaning across pages /short chapters	28–38	2/1, 4/5, 5/3	DI pages: U2v1 DI1–DI15, U4v2 DI101–DI115, U5v1 DI51–DI65 Leveled Readers*

* See following pages for a list of Leveled Readers.

GRADE THREE Instructional Strand	Focus for Instruction	DRA2 Benchmark	*Reading Street* Unit/ Week Lesson Plan	Materials
Background Knowledge	Model and support using background knowledge to make meaning connections	28–38	1/1, 1/4, 5/5	DI pages: U1v1 DI1–DI15, U1v2 DI76–DI90, U5v2 DI101–DI115 Leveled Readers*
Summarize	Share and identify character-istics of good summaries	28–38	1/2, 4/1, 5/4	DI pages: U1v1 DI126–DI140, U4v1 DI1–DI15, U5v2 DI76–DI90 Leveled Readers*
Visualize	Use sensory images to deter-mine word meaning	28–38	1/3, 2/2, 5/1	DI pages: U1v1 DI51–DI65, U2v1 DI26–DI40, U5v1 DI1–DI15 Leveled Readers*
Important Ideas	Teach how to use a graphic organizer to create a sum-mary. Identify more and less important ideas and details.	28–38	3/1, 4/2, 6/3	DI pages: U3v1 DI1–DI15, U4v1 DI26–DI40, U6v1 DI51–DI65 Leveled Readers*
Text Structure	Gain information from fiction and nonfiction text features	28–38	2/5, 3/3	DI pages: U2v2 DI101–DI115, U3v1 DI51–DI65 Leveled Readers*
Inferring	Model and teach how to support inferences with examples from text.	28–38	3/2, 4/3, 5/2, 6/2, 6/5	DI pages: U3v1 DI26–DI40, U4v1 DI51–DI65, U5v1 DI26–DI40, U6v1 DI26–DI40, U6v2 DI101–DI115 Leveled Readers*

* See following pages for a list of Leveled Readers.

Leveled Reader Skills Chart

How do I find the right reader for every student?

The books in this list were leveled using the criteria suggested in Matching Books to Readers *and* Leveled Books for Readers, Grades 3–6 *by Irene C. Fountas and Gay Su Pinnell. For more on leveling, see the* Reading Street Leveled Readers Leveling Guide. *Complete books may also be found on* the Leveled Readers Database.

Grade 3 — Title	Level*	DRA Level*	Genre	Target Comprehension Skill	
The Opposite Cousins	F	10	Realistic Fiction	Character, Setting, and Theme	
It's a Fair Swap!	F	10	Expository Nonfiction	Sequence	
Life in the Arctic	F	10	Nonfiction	Sequence	
Let's Surprise Mom	F	10	Realistic Fiction	Compare and Contrast	
E-mail Friends	F	10	Realistic Fiction	Author's Purpose	
The Frozen Continent: Antarctica	F	10	Expository Nonfiction	Main Idea and Details	
Buddy Goes to School	G	12	Realistic Fiction	Compare and Contrast	
The Metal Detective	G	12	Realistic Fiction	Draw Conclusions	
Growing Vegetables	G	12	Narrative Nonfiction	Author's Purpose	
All About Birds	G	12	Nonfiction	Main Idea and Details	
Raisins	G	12	Nonfiction	Draw Conclusions	
The Hunters and the Elk	G	12	Fiction	Character, Setting, and Plot	
Pictures in the Sky	H	14	Expository Nonfiction	Graphic Sources	
Rescuing Whales	H	14	Expository Nonfiction	Generalize	
The Field Trip	H	14	Expository Nonfiction	Cause and Effect	
The Winning Point	H	14	Realistic Fiction	Generalize	
How to Measure the Weather	H	14	Expository Nonfiction	Graphic Sources	
Grandpa's Rock Kit	H	14	Narrative Nonfiction	Fact and Opinion	
Across the English Channel	H	14	Expository Nonfiction	Fact and Opinion	
Swimming Like Buck	I	16	Animal Fantasy	Cause and Effect	
A Tea Party with Obâchan	I	16	Realistic Fiction	Compare and Contrast	
Celebrate Independence Day/ Celebra el Día de la Independencia	I	16	Nonfiction	Main Idea and Details	
A Child's Life in Korea	I	16	Expository Nonfiction	Sequence	
The World of Bread!	I	16	Expository Nonfiction	Draw Conclusions	
A Walk Around the City	I	16	Expository Nonfiction	Author's Purpose	
The Statue of Liberty: A Gift From France	I	16	Expository Nonfiction	Fact and Opinion	
Camping with Aunt Julie	J	18	Realistic Fiction	Character and Setting	
Let's Make a Trade!	J	18	Expository Nonfiction	Sequence	
Ice Fishing in the Arctic	J	18	Nonfiction	Sequence	
The Shopping Trip	J	18	Fiction	Compare and Contrast	

* Suggested Guided Reading level. Use your knowledge of children's abilities to adjust levels as needed.

Additional Comprehension Instruction	Comprehension Strategy	Vocabulary	Content Connection
Draw Conclusions	Background Knowledge	Context Clues/Homonyms	Social Studies
Fact and Opinion	Summarize	Word Structure/Compound Words	Economics/Geography
Generalize	Visualize	Dictionary/Glossary/Unfamiliar Words	Life Science
Main Idea	Background Knowledge	Context Clues/Multiple Meanings	Social Studies
Compare and Contrast	Story Structure	Word Structure/Prefixes and Suffixes	Culture
Generalize	Monitor and Clarify	Context Clues/Synonyms	Earth Science
Sequence	Visualize	Context Clues/Unfamiliar Words	Social Studies
Realism and Fantasy	Questioning	Compound Words/Word Structure	Economics
Generalize	Predict and Set Purpose	Context Clues/Antonyms	Life Science
Compare and Contrast	Text Structure	Context Clues/Unfamiliar Words	Life Science
Generalize	Important Ideas	Homophones/Context Clues	Life Science
Theme	Inferring	Unknown Words/Dictionary/Glossary	Life Science
Author's Purpose	Text Structure	Unknown Words/Dictionary/Glossary	Earth Science
Sequence	Story Structure	Context Clues/Unfamiliar Words	Life Science
Draw Conclusions	Predict and Set Purpose	Prefixes/Suffixes/Word Structure	Life Science
Plot	Summarize	Unfamiliar Words/Context Clues	Social Studies
Main Idea	Important Ideas	Unknown Words/Dictionary/Glossary	Earth Science
Fact and Opinion	Inferring	Context Clues/Multiple Meanings	Earth Science
Generalize	Questioning	Context Clues/Multiple Meanings	History
Character	Monitor and Clarify	Unknown Words/Dictionary/Glossary	Life Science
Generalize	Visualize	Context Clues/Synonyms	Culture
Draw Conclusions	Inferring	Context Clues/Antonyms	History
Author's Purpose	Monitor and Clarify	Word Structure/Compound Words	Culture
Main Idea	Summarize	Context Clues/Unfamiliar Words	Culture
Generalize	Background Knowledge	Context Clues/Homonyms	Culture
Fact and Opinion	Questioning	Word Structure/Prefixes	History
Theme	Background Knowledge	Context Clues/Homonyms	Social Studies
Draw Conclusions	Summarize	Word Structure/Compound Words	Economics/Geography
Author's Purpose	Visualize	Dictionary/Glossary/Unfamiliar Words	Life Science/Economics
Character	Background Knowledge	Context Clues/Multiple Meanings	Economics

Leveled Reader Skills Chart (*continued*)

Grade 3 — Title	Level*	DRA Level*	Genre	Target Comprehension Skill	
New York's Chinatown	J	18	Expository Nonfiction	Cause and Effect	
One Forest, Different Trees	J	18	Realistic Fiction	Graphic Sources	
Swimming in a School	J	18	Animal Fantasy	Plot and Theme	
Greek Myths	J	18	Nonfiction	Generalize	
The Market Adventure	K	20	Realistic Fiction	Author's Purpose	
These Birds Can't Fly!	K	20	Expository Nonfiction	Main Idea and Details	
Iguana Takes a Ride	K	20	Animal Fantasy	Compare and Contrast	
The Last Minute	K	20	Realistic Fiction	Draw Conclusions	
Our Garden	K	20	Realistic Fiction	Author's Purpose	
Bills and Beaks	L	24	Historical Fiction	Main Idea and Details	
In the Fields	L	24	Historical Fiction	Draw Conclusions	
The Thunder and Lightning Men	L	24	Folktale	Character, Setting, and Plot	
Meet the Stars	L	24	Realistic Fiction	Graphic Sources	
What a Day!	L	24	Realistic Fiction	Generalize	
Desert Life	L	24	Expository Nonfiction	Cause and Effect	
A Trip	M	28	Realistic Fiction	Generalize	
Measuring the Earth	M	28	Expository Nonfiction	Graphic Sources	
Fun with Hobbies and Science!	M	28	Expository Nonfiction	Fact and Opinion	
Great Women in U.S. History	M	28	Biography	Fact and Opinion	
Buddy Ran Away	M	28	Realistic Fiction	Cause and Effect	
Cowboy Slim's Dude Ranch	M	28	Realistic Fiction	Compare and Contrast	
Celebrate Around the World	N	30	Nonfiction	Main Idea and Details	
Joanie's House Becomes a Home	N	30	Realistic Fiction	Sequence of Events	
Kapuapua's Magic Shell	N	30	Folktale	Draw Conclusions	
Bobby's New Apartment	N	30	Realistic Fiction	Author's Purpose	
Symbols, Signs, and Songs of America	N	30	Narrative Nonfiction	Main Idea	
A Pet Bird	O	34	Expository Nonfiction	Cause and Effect	
Lily's Adventure Around the World	O	34	Realistic Fiction	Graphic Sources	
The Three Bears and Goldilocks	O	34	Animal Fantasy	Plot and Theme	
Sweet Freedom!	O	34	Nonfiction	Generalize	

* Suggested Guided Reading level. Use your knowledge of children's abilities to adjust levels as needed.

Additional Comprehension Instruction	Comprehension Strategy	Vocabulary	Content Connection
Generalize	Inferring	Context Clues/Antonyms	Culture
Generalize	Important Ideas	Dictionary/Glossary/Unknown Words	Culture
Realism and Fantasy	Story Structure	Word Structure/Prefixes and Suffixes	Life Science
Compare and Contrast	Inferring	Homographs/Context Clues	History/Culture
Generalize	Story Structure	Word Structure/Prefixes and Suffixes	Economics/Geography
Compare and Contrast	Monitor and Clarify	Context Clues/Synonyms	Life Science
Draw Conclusions	Visualize	Context Clues/Unfamiliar Words	Culture
Sequence	Questioning	Compound Words/Word Structure	Culture
Plot	Predict and Set Purpose	Context Clues/Antonyms	Citizenship
Setting	Text Structure	Context Clues/Unfamiliar Words	Life Science
Author's Purpose	Important Ideas	Homophones/Context Clues	Life Science
Main Idea	Inferring	Unknown Words/Dictionary/Glossary	Culture
Plot	Text Structure	Unknown Words/Dictionary/Glossary	Science and Technology
Character	Story Structure	Context Clues/Unfamiliar Words	Earth Science
Generalize	Predict and Set Purpose	Dictionary/Glossary/Unfamiliar Words	Life Science
Author's Purpose	Summarize	Unfamiliar Words/Context Clues	History
Fact and Opinion	Important Ideas	Unknown Words/Dictionary/Glossary	Earth Science
Draw Conclusions	Inferring	Context Clues/Multiple Meanings	Earth Science
Main Idea and Details	Questioning	Context Clues/Multiple Meanings	History
Sequence	Monitor and Clarify	Unknown Words/Dictionary/Glossary	Life Science
Main Idea	Visualize	Context Clues/Synonyms	Culture
Compare and Contrast	Inferring	Homophones/Context Clues	Culture
Draw Conclusions	Monitor and Clarify	Word Structure/Compound Words	Economics/Geography
Theme	Summarize	Context Clues/Unfamiliar Words	Culture
Realism and Fantasy	Background Knowledge	Context Clues/Homonyms	Culture
Fact and Opinion	Text Structure	Word Structure/Prefixes	Citizenship/Culture
Main Idea	Inferring	Context Clues/Antonyms	Life Science
Compare and Contrast	Important Ideas	Unknown Words/Dictionary/Glossary	Culture/Geography
Character	Story Structure	Word Structure/Prefixes and Suffixes	Culture
Author's Purpose	Inferring	Homographs/Context Clues	Citizenship

Leveled Reader Skills Chart (*continued*)

grade 3 Title	Level*	DRA Level*	Genre	Target Comprehension Skill	
Mr. Post's Project	P	38	Realistic Fiction	Character and Setting	
What's Money All About?	P	38	Expository Nonfiction	Sequence	
Journey Across the Arctic	P	38	Fiction	Sequence	
The Road to New York	P	38	Realistic Fiction	Compare and Contrast	
With a Twist	P	38	Fantasy	Author's Purpose	
All About Penguins	P	38	Expository Nonfiction	Main Idea and Details	
Puppy Problems	Q	40	Realistic Fiction	Compare and Contrast	
A Family of Collectors	Q	40	Realistic Fiction	Graphic Sources	
The Magic of Coyote	Q	40	Realistic Fiction	Author's Purpose	
Animals of the Concrete Jungle	Q	40	Expository Nonfiction	Main Idea and Details	
Grape Season	Q	40	Realistic Fiction	Draw Conclusions	
Grandmother Spider Steals the Sun	Q	40	Folktale	Character, Setting, and Plot	
Animal Tracking: Learn More About Animals	Q	40	Expository Nonfiction	Graphic Sources	
Whales and Other Amazing Animals	R	40	Expository Nonfiction	Generalize	
Coral Reefs	R	40	Expository Nonfiction	Cause and Effect	
Extraordinary Athletes	R	40	Biography	Generalize	
Largest, Fastest, Lightest, Longest	R	40	Expository Nonfiction	Compare and Contrast	
Gemstones Around the World	R	40	Expository Nonfiction	Fact and Opinion	
Changing Times: Women in the Early Twentieth Century	R	40	Expository Nonfiction	Fact and Opinion	
Toby the Smart Dog	R	40	Humorous Fiction	Cause and Effect	
His Favorite Sweatshirt	S	40	Realistic Nonfiction	Compare and Contrast	
Life Overseas	S	40	Expository Nonfiction	Main Idea and Details	
It's a World of Time Zones	S	40	Expository Nonfiction	Sequence	
Mixing, Kneading, and Baking: The Baker's Art	S	40	Narrative Nonfiction	Draw Conclusions	
Let's Go Have Fun!	S	40	Expository Nonfiction	Author's Purpose	
The French Connection	S	40	Narrative Nonfiction	Fact and Opinion	
China's Special Gifts to the World	T	50	Expository Nonfiction	Cause and Effect	
Thomas Hart Benton: Painter of Murals	T	50	Biography	Graphic Sources	
The Best Field Trip Ever!	T	50	Expository Fiction	Plot and Theme	
Free in the Sea	T	50	Expository Nonfiction	Generalize	

* Suggested Guided Reading level. Use your knowledge of children's abilities to adjust levels as needed.

Additional Comprehension Instruction	Comprehension Strategy	Vocabulary	Content Connection
Theme	Background Knowledge	Context Clues/Homonyms	Economics
Draw Conclusions	Summarize	Word Structure/Compound Words	Economics/Geography
Setting	Visualize	Dictionary/Glossary/Unfamiliar Words	Earth Science
Character	Background Knowledge	Context Clues/Multiple Meanings	Culture
Sequence	Story Structure	Word Structure/Prefixes and Suffixes	History
Compare and Contrast	Monitor and Clarify	Context Clues/Synonyms	Social Studies
Cause and Effect	Visualize	Context Clues/Unfamiliar Words	Social Studies
Realism and Fantasy	Important Ideas	Compound Words/Word Structure	Economics
Sequence	Predict	Context Clues/Antonyms	Culture/History
Fact and Opinion	Text Structure	Context Clues/Unfamiliar Words	Life Science
Main Idea	Important Ideas	Homophones/Context Clues	Life Science
Fact and Opinion	Inferring	Dictionary/Glossary/Unfamiliar Words	Culture
Compare and Contrast	Text Structure	Unknown Words/Dictionary/Glossary	Life Science
Author's Purpose	Story Structure	Context Clues/Unfamiliar Words	Life Science
Draw Conclusions	Predict and Set Purpose	Prefixes and Suffixes/Word Structure	Life Science
Draw Conclusions	Summarize	Unfamiliar Words/Context Clues	History
Author's Purpose	Ask Questions	Word Structure/Compound Words	Life Science
Cause and Effect	Inferring	Context Clues/Multiple Meanings	Earth Science
Generalize	Questioning	Context Clues/Multiple Meanings	History
Character and Setting	Monitor and Clarify	Unknown Words/Dictionary/Glossary	Life Science
Draw Conclusions	Visualize	Context Clues/Synonyms	Culture
Cause and Effect	Inferring	Homophones/Context Clues	Culture/Geography
Draw Conclusions	Monitor and Clarify	Word Structure/Compound Words	Economics/Geograpy
Main Idea	Summarize	Context Clues/Unfamiliar Words	Culture
Compare and Contrast	Background Knowledge	Context Clues/Homonyms	Culture
Generalize	Questioning	Word Structure/Prefixes	Culture/Geography
Generalize	Graphic Organizers	Context Clues/Antonyms	Culture/Geography
Author's Purpose	Important Ideas	Unknown Words/Dictionary/Glossary	History
Realism and Fantasy	Story Structure	Word Structure/Prefixes and Suffixes	Life Science
Compare and Contrast	Predict	Context Clues/Synonyms	Life Science

Leveled Reader Skills Chart (*continued*)

Need more choices? Look back to Grade 2.

Grade 2 Title	Level*	DRA Level*	Genre	Target Comprehension Skill	
The Rescue Dogs	C	3	Narrative Nonfiction	Cause and Effect	
Country Mouse and City Mouse	D	4	Traditional Tales	Character and Setting	
All About Astronauts	D	4	Expository Nonfiction	Main Idea	
Camping with Pup	D	4	Animal Fantasy	Character and Setting	
Deserts	D	4	Expository Nonfiction	Main Idea	
Too Many Rabbit Holes	D	4	Fantasy/Play	Facts and Details	
A Class Play	D	4	Realistic Fiction	Author's Purpose	
The Barn Raising	D	4	Nonfiction	Facts and Details	
Working Dogs	D	4	Expository Nonfiction	Cause and Effect	
Where is Fish?	D	4	Fantasy	Compare and Contrast	
Our School Science Fair	D	4	Realistic Fiction	Author's Purpose	
Let's Send a Letter!	D	4	Narrative Nonfiction	Draw Conclusions	
Using a Net	D	4	Expository Nonfiction	Compare and Contrast	
Ana Is Shy	E	6–8	Realistic Fiction	Sequence	
Sink or Float?	E	6–8	Narrative Nonfiction	Fact and Opinion	
The Camping Trip	E	6–8	Realistic Fiction	Draw Conclusions	
How to Grow Tomatoes	E	6–8	How-to	Sequence	
How a Seed Grows	E	6–8	Expository Nonfiction	Fact and Opinion	
Snakeskin Canyon	E	6–8	Realistic Fiction	Plot and Theme	
Blizzard!	E	6–8	Realistic Fiction	Plot and Theme	
The New Kid in Bali	F	10	Realistic Fiction	Character and Setting	
An Astronaut Space Walk	F	10	Expository Nonfiction	Character and Setting	
Desert Animals	F	10	Expository Nonfiction	Main Idea	
Camping at Crescent Lake	F	10	Realistic Fiction	Character and Setting	
Service Workers	F	10	Expository Nonfiction	Fact and Opinion	
What Can You Do?	F	10	Narrative Nonfiction	Cause and Effect	
Sally and the Wild Puppy	F	10	Humorous Fiction	Plot and Theme	
Join an Adventure Club!	F	10	Narrative Nonfiction	Character and Setting	
Andrew's Mistake	F	10	Realistic Fiction	Main Idea	
Glooskap and the First Summer: An Algonquin Tale	G	12	Folk Tale	Facts and Details	

* Suggested Guided Reading level. Use your knowledge of children's abilities to adjust levels as needed.

Additional Comprehension Instruction	Comprehension Strategy	Vocabulary	Content Connection
Fact and Opinion	Summarize	High-Frequency Words	Citizenship
Fact and Opinion	Monitor and Clarify	High-Frequency Words	Economics/Geography
Author's Purpose	Text Structure	High-Frequency Words	Space and Technology/ Life Science
Main Idea	Story Structure	High-Frequency Words	Citizenship/Culture
Compare and Contrast	Important Ideas	High-Frequency Words	Earth Science
Character and Setting	Predict and Set Purpose	High-Frequency Words	Life Science
Fact and Detail	Text Structure	High-Frequency Words	History
Cause and Effect	Background Knowledge	High-Frequency Words	Citizenship
Compare and Contrast	Story Structure	High-Frequency Words	Citizenship
Author's Purpose	Inferring	High-Frequency Words	Life Science
Plot and Theme	Questioning	High-Frequency Words	Physical Science/ Earth Science
Sequence	Visualize	High-Frequency Words	Government
Draw Conclusions/ Make Inferences	Summarize	High-Frequency Words	Citizenship
Cause and Effect	Predict and Set Purpose	High-Frequency Words	Culture
Sequence	Inferring	High-Frequency Words	Physical Science
Character and Setting	Background Knowledge	Word Structure/Prefixes	Culture
Fact and Opinion	Important Ideas	Context Clues/Antonyms	Life Science
Facts and Details	Questioning	Context Clues/Unfamiliar Words	Life Science
Draw Conclusions/ Make Inferences	Visualize	Context Clues/Multiple Meanings	Economics/Geography
Main Idea	Monitor and Clarify	Picture Clues/Multiple Meanings	Earth Science
Plot and Theme	Monitor and Clarify	High-Frequency Words	Culture
Sequence	Story Structure	High-Frequency Words	Science and Technology
Compare and Contrast	Important Ideas	High-Frequency Words	Space and Technology/ Earth Science
Main Idea	Story Structure	High-Frequency Words	Life Science
Author's Purpose	Important Ideas	Word Structure/Suffixes	Citizenship
Facts and Details	Visualize	Dictionary Skills/Unfamiliar Words	Citizenship
Sequence	Background Knowledge	Dictionary Skills/Unfamiliar Words	Citizenship
Plot and Theme	Story Structure	Dictionary Skills/Unfamiliar Words	Citizenship
Character and Setting	Inferring	Word Structure/Compound Words	Citizenship
Character and Setting	Predict and Set Purpose	High-Frequency Words	Culture

Leveled Reader Skills Chart (continued)

Grade 2 Title	Level*	DRA Level*	Genre	Target Comprehension Skill	
Be Ready for an Emergency	G	12	Narrative Nonfiction	Cause and Effect	
Let's Work Together!	G	12	Realistic Fiction	Author's Purpose	
Farming Families	G	12	Expository Nonfiction	Facts and Details	
Growing Up	G	12	Realistic Fiction	Cause and Effect	
Three Great Ballplayers	G	12	Autobiography/Biography	Compare and Contrast	
America's Birthday	G	12	Expository Nonfiction	Author's Purpose	
Special Chinese Birthdays	G	12	Narrative Nonfiction	Draw Conclusions	
Down on the Ranch	G	12	Historical Fiction	Sequence	
Just Like Grandpa	G	12	Realistic Fiction	Facts and Details	
Showing Good Manners	H	14	Nonfiction	Compare and Contrast	
Dotty's Art	H	14	Realistic Fiction	Author's Purpose	
Living in Seoul	H	14	Narrative Nonfiction	Draw Conclusions	
Arachnid or Insect?	H	14	Expository Nonfiction	Compare and Contrast	
The International Food Fair	H	14	Realistic Fiction	Sequence	
Thomas Adams: Chewing Gum Inventor	I	16	Biography	Fact and Opinion	
Making Travel Fun	I	16	Expository Nonfiction	Draw Conclusions	
How Do Plants Grow?	I	16	Expository Nonfiction	Sequence	
A Slice of Mud Pie	I	16	Realistic Fiction	Fact and Opinion	
Too Many Frogs!	I	16	Humorous Fiction	Plot and Theme	
Rainbow Crow Brings Fire to Earth	J	18	Narrative Nonfiction	Plot and Theme	
Keeping Our Community Safe	J	18	Expository Nonfiction	Fact and Opinion	
Annie Makes a Big Change	J	18	Realistic Fiction	Cause and Effect	
Hubert and Frankie	J	18	Animal Fantasy	Plot and Theme	
Everyone Can Make a Difference!	K	20	Narrative Nonfiction	Character and Setting	
Freda the Signmaker	K	20	Humorous Fiction	Main Idea	
Women Play Baseball	K	20	Narrative Nonfiction	Compare and Contrast	
American Revolution Heroes	K	20	Biography	Author's Purpose	
Country Friends, City Friends	L	24	Realistic Fiction	Character and Setting	
Look at Our Galaxy	L	24	Expository Nonfiction	Main Idea	
At Home in the Wilderness	L	24	Historical Fiction	Character and Setting	

* Suggested Guided Reading level. Use your knowledge of children's abilities to adjust levels as needed.

Additional Comprehension Instruction	Comprehension Strategy	Vocabulary	Content Connection
Fact and Opinion	Summarize	High-Frequency Words	Citizenship
Facts and Details	Text Structure	High-Frequency Words	Citizenship
Cause and Effect	Background Knowledge	High-Frequency Words	Life Science
Compare and Contrast	Story Structure	High-Frequency Words	Life Science
Draw Conclusions/Make Inferences	Monitor and Clarify	Context Clues/Homophones	History
Fact and Opinion	Summarize	Context Clues/Unfamiliar Words	Citizenship
Cause and Effect	Questioning	Context Clues/Synonyms	Culture
Main Idea	Story Structure	Word Structure/Suffixes	History
Compare and Contrast	Predict and Set Purpose	Word Structure/Compound Words	Culture
Author's Purpose	Inferring	High-Frequency Words	Culture
Plot and Theme	Questioning	High-Frequency Words	Culture
Sequence	Visualize	High-Frequency Words	Culture
Draw Conclusions/Make Inferences	Summarize	High-Frequency Words	Life Science
Cause and Effect	Predict and Set Purpose	High-Frequency Words	Culture
Sequence	Inferring	High-Frequency Words	History
Character and Setting	Background Knowledge	Word Structure/Prefixes	History
Fact and Opinion	Important Ideas	Context Clues/Antonyms	Life Science
Fact and Details	Questioning	Context Clues/Unfamiliar Words	Earth Science
Draw Conclusions/Make Inferences	Visualize	Context Clues/Multiple Meanings	Citizenship
Main Idea	Monitor and Clarify	Context Clues/Multiple Meanings	Earth Science
Author's Purpose	Important Ideas	Word Structure/Suffixes	Citizenship
Facts and Details	Visualize	Dictionary Skills/Unfamiliar Words	Life Science/Citizenship
Sequence	Background Knowledge	Dictionary Skills/Unfamiliar Words	Citizenship
Plot and Theme	Story Structure	Dictionary Skills/Unfamiliar Words	Citizenship
Character and Setting	Inferring	Word Structure/Compound Words	Citizenship
Draw Conclusions/Make Inferences	Monitor and Clarify	Context Clues/Homophones	History
Fact and Opinion	Summarize	Context Clues/Unfamiliar Words	History
Plot and Theme	Monitor and Clarify	Amazing Words	Culture
Author's Purpose	Text Structure	Amazing Words	Space and Technology
Main Idea	Story Structure	Amazing Words	History

Leveled Reader Skills Chart (*continued*)

Grade 2 Title	Level*	DRA Level*	Genre	Target Comprehension Skill	
The First People to Fly	L	24	Realistic Fiction	Facts and Details	
A World of Birthdays	L	24	Narrative Nonfiction	Draw Conclusions	
A Cowboy's Life	L	24	Historical Fiction	Sequence	
Voting Day	L	24	Realistic Fiction	Facts and Details	
The Hummingbird	M	28	Expository Nonfiction	Main Idea	
Special Animal Helpers	M	28	Narrative Nonfiction	Cause and Effect	
The Hoover Dam	M	28	Expository Nonfiction	Author's Purpose	
Many Types of Energy	M	28	Expository Nonfiction	Facts and Details	
Stripes and Silver	M	28	Play	Cause and Effect	
Saint Bernards and Other Working Dogs	N	30	Nonfiction	Compare and Contrast	
Maggie's New Sidekick	N	30	Fantasy	Author's Purpose	
Communicating Then and Now	N	30	Expository Nonfiction	Draw Conclusions	
How Can Animals Help?	N	30	Narrative Nonfiction	Compare and Contrast	
Hank's Tortilla Factory	N	30	Realistic Fiction	Sequence	
A Few Nifty Inventions	N	30	Expository Nonfiction	Fact and Opinion	
Starting a New Life	N	30	Expository Nonfiction	Draw Conclusions	
Plants Grow Everywhere	O	34	Expository Nonfiction	Sequence	
Compost: Recycled Waste	O	34	Narrative Nonfiction	Fact and Opinion	
A Quiet Place	O	34	Realistic Fiction	Plot and Theme	
Hurricane!	O	34	Expository Nonfiction	Plot and Theme	
Services and Goods	O	34	Narrative Nonfiction	Fact and Opinion	
A Vet for All Animals	O	34	Narrative Nonfiction	Cause and Effect	
Training Peanut	O	34	Realistic Fiction	Plot and Theme	
Protect the Earth	P	38	Narrative Nonfiction	Character and Setting	
Marty's Summer Job	P	38	Realistic Fiction	Main Idea	
Baseball Heroes Make History	P	38	Autobiography/Biography	Compare and Contrast	
Living in a Democracy	P	38	Expository Nonfiction	Author's Purpose	
Celebrations and Family Traditions	P	38	Narrative Nonfiction	Draw Conclusions	
Living on a Ranch	P	38	Realistic Fiction	Sequence	
Happy New Year!	P	38	Realistic Fiction	Facts and Details	

* Suggested Guided Reading level. Use your knowledge of children's abilities to adjust levels as needed.

Additional Comprehension Instruction	Comprehension Strategy	Vocabulary	Content Connection
Character and Setting	Predict and Set Purpose	Amazing Words	Culture
Cause and Effect	Questioning	Context Clues/Synonyms	Culture
Main Idea	Text Structure	Word Structure/Suffixes	History
Compare and Contrast	Predict and Set Purpose	Word Structure/Compound Words	Culture
Compare and Contrast	Important Ideas	Amazing Words	Physical Science
Cause and Effect	Summarize	Amazing Words	Citizenship
Fact and Detail	Text Structure	Amazing Words	History
Cause and Effect	Background Knowledge	Amazing Words	Physical Science
Compare and Contrast	Story Structure	Amazing Words	Citizenship/Life Science
Author's Purpose	Inferring	Amazing Words	History
Plot and Theme	Questioning	Amazing Words	Space and Technology
Sequence	Visualize	Amazing Words	Government
Draw Conclusions/ Make Inferences	Summarize	Amazing Words	Life Science
Cause and Effect	Predict and Set Purpose	Amazing Words	History
Sequence	Inferring	Amazing Words	History
Character and Setting	Background Knowledge	Word Structure/Prefixes	History
Fact and Opinion	Important Ideas	Context Clues/Antonyms	Life Science
Fact and Details	Questioning	Context Clues/Unfamiliar Words	Life Science
Draw Conclusions/ Make Inferences	Visualize	Context Clues/Multiple Meanings	Economics/Geography
Main Idea	Monitor and Clarify	Context Clues/Multiple Meanings	Earth Science
Author's Purpose	Important Ideas	Word Structure/Suffixes	Economics/Geography
Facts and Details	Visualize	Dictionary Skills/Unfamiliar Words	Life Science
Sequence	Background Knowledge	Dictionary Skills/Unfamiliar Words	Citizenship
Plot and Theme	Story Structure	Dictionary Skills/Unfamiliar Words	Citizenship
Character and Setting	Inferring	Word Structure/Compound Words	Citizenship
Draw Conclusions/ Make Inferences	Monitor and Clarify	Context Clues/Homophones	History
Fact and Opinion	Summarize	Context Clues/Unfamiliar Words	History
Cause and Effect	Questioning	Context Clues/Synonyms	Culture
Main Idea	Text Structure	Word Structure/Suffixes	Culture
Compare and Contrast	Predict and Set Purpose	Word Structure/Compound Words	Culture

Leveled Reader Skills Chart *(continued)*

Need more choices? Look ahead to Grade 4.

Grade 4 Title	Level*	DRA Level*	Genre	Target Comprehension Skill	
Florida Everglades: Its Plants and Animals	K	20	Expository Nonfiction	Sequence	
The Long Journey West	K	20	Expository Nonfiction	Author's Purpose	
From Sea to Shining Sea	K	20	Realistic Fiction	Setting and Plot	
Flash Flood	K	20	Realistic Fiction	Author's Purpose	
America's National Parks	K	20	Expository Nonfiction	Main Idea and Details	
Cheers for the Cheetahs	K	20	Realistic Fiction	Cause and Effect	
Ranches in the Southwest	L	24	Expository Nonfiction	Draw Conclusions	
What It Takes to Stage a Play	L	24	Expository Nonfiction	Draw Conclusions	
Animal Helpers	L	24	Nonfiction	Fact and Opinion	
A Trip to Capitol Hill	L	24	Expository Nonfiction	Main Idea and Details	
Looking For Changes	L	24	Expository Nonfiction	Graphic Features	
The Gray Whale	L	24	Expository Nonfiction	Fact and Opinion	
Day For Night	M	28	Narrative Nonfiction	Generalize	
Surviving Hurricane Andrew	M	28	Realistic Fiction	Graphic Sources	
Saving Trees Using Science	M	28	Nonfiction	Generalize	
Mini Microbes	M	28	Expository Nonfiction	Compare and Contrast	
Dolphins: Mammals of the Sea	M	28	Expository Nonfiction	Compare and Contrast	
Speaking in Code	M	28	Expository Nonfiction	Sequence	
The Rosetta Stone: The Key to Ancient Writings	M	28	Expository Nonfiction	Graphic Features	
Something to Do	N	30	Realistic Fiction	Sequence	
Lewis, Clark, and the Corps of Discovery	N	30	Biography	Author's Purpose	
Protecting Wild Animals	N	30	Realistic Fiction	Setting and Plot	
From Spain to America	N	30	Expository Nonfiction	Author's Purpose	
Top Hat Tompkins, The Detective	N	30	Mystery Fiction	Character and Plot	
Putting a Stop to Wildfires	N	30	Expository Nonfiction	Author's Purpose	
Let's Get to Know the Incas	N	30	Expository Nonfiction	Compare and Contrast	
Mountain Rescue	N	30	Fiction	Character, Plot, Theme	
Plants and Animals in Antarctica	N	30	Expository Nonfiction	Main Idea and Details	
Stuart's Moon Suit	N	30	Realistic Fiction	Draw Conclusions	
The Wonders of Western Geography	O	34	Expository Nonfiction	Main Idea and Details	

* Suggested Guided Reading level. Use your knowledge of children's abilities to adjust levels as needed.

Additional Comprehension Instruction	Comprehension Strategy	Vocabulary	Content Connection
Draw Conclusions	Summarize	Word Structure/Suffixes	Life Science
Main Idea and Details	Questioning	Word Structure/Endings	History
Sequence of Events	Background Knowledge	Dictionary/Glossary/Multiple Meanings	Social Studies
Main Idea and Details	Story Structure	Context Clues/Synonyms/Antonyms	Earth Science
Generalize	Text Structure	Word Structure/Suffixes	Geography
Plot	Background Knowledge	Word Structure/Prefixes/Suffixes	Culture
Graphic Sources	Prior Knowledge	Unknown Words/Dictionary/Glossary	Economics/Geography
Generalize	Questioning	Word Structure/Prefixes/Suffixes	Culture
Draw Conclusions	Monitor and Clarify	Unknown Words/Dictionary/Glossary	Social Studies
Generalize	Inferring	Unknown Words/Dictionary/Glossary	Geography/Citizenship
Compare and Contrast	Important Ideas	Context Clues/Multiple Meanings	Earth Science
Main Idea and Details	Text Structure	Context Clues/Multiple Meanings	Life Science
Cause and Effect	Visualize	Context Clues/Unfamiliar Words	Space and Technology
Plot and Character	Predict	Root Words/Word Structure	Earth Science
Main Idea and Details	Inferring	Word Structure/Suffixes	Life Science
Fact and Opinion	Visualize	Context Clues/Synonyms and Antonyms	Life Science
Generalize	Summarize	Context Clues/Multiple Meanings	Life Science
Author's Purpose	Important Ideas	Unknown Words/Dictionary/Glossary	History
Draw Conclusions	Predict and Set Purpose	Word Structure/Greek and Latin Roots	History
Draw Conclusions	Summarize	Word Structure/Suffixes	Culture
Compare and Contrast	Questioning	Word Structure/Endings	History
Sequence of Events	Background Knowledge	Dictionary/Glossary/Multiple Meanings	Life Science
Compare and Contrast	Story Structure	Context Clues/Synonyms/Antonyms	Culture/Economics/Geography
Fact and Opinion	Monitor and Clarify	Context Clues/Synonyms/Antonyms	Physical Science
Fact and Opinion	Important Ideas	Homographs/Dictionary/Glossary	Earth Science
Main Idea and Details	Visualize	Word Structure/Greek and Latin Roots	History
Cause and Effect	Story Structure	Context Clues/Unfamiliar Words	Citizenship
Graphic Sources	Text Structure	Word Structure/Greek and Latin Roots	Life Science
Main Idea and Details	Monitor and Clarify	Synonyms/Context Clues	Space and Technology
Graphic Sources	Text Structure	Word Structure/Suffixes	Geography

Leveled Reader Skills Chart (continued)

grade 4 Title	Level*	DRA Level*	Genre	Target Comprehension Skill	
Amazing Female Athletes	O	34	Biography	Cause and Effect	
Ranching in the Great American Desert	O	34	Expository Nonfiction	Draw Conclusions	
The Black Ensemble Theater	O	34	Nonfiction	Draw Conclusions	
Animal Helpers	O	34	Nonfiction	Fact and Opinion	
We Shall Overcome	O	34	Expository Nonfiction	Cause and Effect	
The Sauk and Fox Native Americans	O	34	Expository Nonfiction	Fact and Opinion	
Living with Grandpa Joseph	O	34	Realistic Fiction	Sequence	
To Be a Star	O	34	Realistic Fiction	Generalize	
Earth's Closest Neighbor	O	34	Expository Nonfiction	Graphic Features	
The United States Government	P	38	Expository Nonfiction	Main Idea and Details	
Storm Chasers	P	38	Nonfiction	Graphic Features	
Migration Relocation	P	38	Expository Nonfiction	Fact and Opinion	
Darkness into Light	P	38	Expository Nonfiction	Generalize	
Severe Weather: Storms	P	38	Expository Nonfiction	Cause and Effect	
Maine Now and Then	P	38	Expository Nonfiction	Generalize	
Mysterious Monsters	Q	40	Expository Nonfiction	Compare and Contrast	
Come Learn About Dolphins	Q	40	Expository Nonfiction	Compare and Contrast	
The Super Secret Surprise Society	Q	40	Realistic Fiction	Sequence	
Code Breaking: Uncovering German Messages	Q	40	Expository Nonfiction	Graphic Features	
The Missing Iguana Mystery	Q	40	Mystery	Character and Plot	
The Grizzly Bear Hotshots	Q	40	Fiction	Author's Purpose	
Pompeii, the Lost City	R	40	Expository Nonfiction	Compare and Contrast	
Bessie Coleman: Queen of the Skies	R	40	Historical Fiction	Character, Plot, Theme	
Let's Explore Antarctica!	R	40	Expository Nonfiction	Main Idea and Details	
To the Moon!	R	40	Science Fiction	Draw Conclusions	
The Civil Rights Movement	R	40	Expository Nonfiction	Cause and Effect	
The Story of Libraries	S	40	Expository Nonfiction	Sequence	
Two Powerful Rivers	S	40	Expository Nonfiction	Author's Purpose	
Exploring the Moon	S	40	Realistic Fiction	Setting and Plot	
The Diné	S	40	Expository Nonfiction	Author's Purpose	

* Suggested Guided Reading level. Use your knowledge of children's abilities to adjust levels as needed.

Additional Comprehension Instruction	Comprehension Strategy	Vocabulary	Content Connection
Author's Purpose	Background Knowledge	Dictionary/Prefixes/Suffixes	Culture
Main Idea and Details	Story Structure	Unknown Words/Dictionary/Glossary	Economics/Geography
Fact and Opinion	Questioning	Word Structure/Prefixes	Culture
Compare and Contrast	Monitor and Clarify	Unknown Words/Dictionary/Glossary	Citizenship
Sequence	Questioning	Root Words/Word Structure	History
Plot and Theme	Summarize	Multiple Meanings/Dictionary/Glossary	History
Character	Inferring	Context Clues/Unfamiliar Words	Culture
Cause and Effect	Predict and Set Purpose	Context Clues/Unfamiliar Words	Culture
Main Idea and Details	Background Knowledge	Multiple Meanings/Context Clues	Space and Technology
Generalize	Inferring	Unknown Words/Dictionary/Glossary	Government/History
Sequence	Important Ideas	Context Clues/Multiple Meanings	Earth Science
Draw Conclusions	Text Structure	Context Clues/Multiple Meanings	Life Science
Compare and Contrast	Visualize	Context Clues/Unfamiliar Words	Space and Technology
Graphic Sources	Predict and Set Purpose	Root Words/Word Structure	Earth Science
Fact and Opinion	Inferring	Word Structure/Suffixes	Geography
Main Idea and Details	Visualize	Context Clues/Synonyms and Antonyms	Life Science
Fact and Opinion	Summarize	Context Clues/Multiple Meanings	Life Science
Cause and Effect	Important Ideas	Unknown Words/Dictionary/Glossary	Social Studies
Main Idea and Details	Predict and Set Purpose	Word Structure/Greek and Latin Roots	History
Cause and Effect	Monitor and Clarify	Context Clues/Synonyms and Antonyms	Culture/Life Science
Sequence	Important Ideas	Homographs/Dictionary/Glossary	Culture
Generalize	Visualize	Word Structure/Greek and Latin Roots	History
Generalize	Story Structure	Context Clues/Unfamiliar Words	History
Generalize	Text Structure	Word Structure/Greek and Latin Affixes	Earth Science
Compare and Contrast	Monitor and Clarify	Context Clues/Synonyms	Space and Technology
Sequence	Questioning	Root Words/Word Structure	History
Main Idea and Details	Summarize	Word Structure/Suffixes	History
Compare and Contrast	Questioning	Word Structure/Endings	Economics/Geography/History
Sequence of Events	Background Knowledge	Dictionary/Glossary/Multiple Meanings	Space and Technology
Compare and Contrast	Story Structure	Context Clues/Synonyms	Culture/History

Leveled Reader Skills Chart (*continued*)

Grade 4 Title	Level*	DRA Level*	Genre	Target Comprehension Skill	
Becoming a Melting Pot	S	40	Expository Nonfiction	Fact and Opinion	
The Seahaven Squids Host a Pet Wash	S	40	Realistic Fiction	Sequence	
Birthday Surprise	S	40	Realistic Fiction	Generalize	
One Giant Leap	S	40	Narrative Nonfiction	Graphic Features	
John Muir: Protector of the Wilderness	T	50	Biography	Main Idea and Details	
Equality in American Schools	T	50	Expository Nonfiction	Cause and Effect	
The Legacy of César Chávez	T	50	Biography	Draw Conclusions	
Journey to Hong Kong	T	50	Nonfiction	Draw Conclusions	
Danger! Children at Work	T	50	Expository Nonfiction	Fact and Opinion	
The Power of the People	T	50	Expository Nonfiction	Main Idea and Details	
Sharing Our Planet	U	50	Expository Nonfiction	Graphic Features	
Birds Take Flight	U	50	Expository Nonfiction	Fact and Opinion	
Orbiting the Sun	U	50	Expository Nonfiction	Generalize	
Wondrously Wild Weather	U	50	Narrative Nonfiction	Cause and Effect	
The Alaskan Pipeline	U	50	Expository Nonfiction	Generalize	
What in the World Is That?	U	50	Expository Nonfiction	Compare and Contrast	
How Does Echolocation Work?	U	50	Expository Nonfiction	Compare and Contrast	
The Incredible Alexander Graham Bell	U	50	Historical Fiction	Sequence	
The Navajo Code Talkers	V	50	Expository Nonfiction	Graphic Features	
The Salamander Stumper	V	50	Realistic Fiction	Character and Plot	
Thor Heyerdahl's Incredible Raft	V	50	Narrative Nonfiction	Author's Purpose	
Meet the Maya	V	50	Expository Nonfiction	Compare and Contrast	
A Book of Their Own	V	50	Realistic Fiction	Character, Plot, Theme	
Danger: The World Is Getting Hot!	V	50	Expository Nonfiction	Main Idea and Details	
Life on Mars: The Real Story	V	50	Realistic Fiction	Draw Conclusions	
The Women's Movement	V	50	Expository Nonfiction	Cause and Effect	
Jim Thorpe: The World's Greatest Athlete	W	60	Biography	Fact and Opinion	
A New Home	W	60	Realistic Fiction	Sequence	
The Show Must Go On!	W	60	Realistic Fiction	Generalize	
The Mysteries of Space	W	60	Expository Nonfiction	Graphic Features	

* Suggested Guided Reading level. Use your knowledge of children's abilities to adjust levels as needed.

Additional Comprehension Instruction	Comprehension Strategy	Vocabulary	Content Connection
Sequence	Summarize	Multiple Meanings/Dictionary/Glossary	History
Author's Purpose	Inferring	Context Clues/Unfamiliar Words	Economics
Fact and Opinion	Predict and Set Purpose	Context Clues/Unfamiliar Words	Social Studies
Cause and Effect	Background Knowledge	Context Clues/Homonyms	Space and Technology
Generalize	Text Structure	Word Structure/Suffixes	Economics/Geography
Sequence	Background Knowledge	Word Structure/Prefixes/Suffixes	Citizenship
Sequence	Story Structure	Unknown Words/Dictionary/Glossary	Culture/Government/History
Graphic Sources	Questioning	Word Structure/Prefixes	Culture/Geography
Draw Conclusions	Monitor and Clarify	Unknown Words/Dictionary/Glossary	Citizenship
Draw Conclusions	Inferring	Unknown Words/Dictionary/Glossary	Government/History
Theme	Important Ideas	Context Clues/Multiple Meanings	Life Science
Author's Purpose	Text Structure	Context Clues/Multiple Meanings	Life Science
Main Idea and Details	Visualize	Context Clues/Unfamiliar Words	Space and Technology
Compare and Contrast	Predict and Set Purpose	Root Words/Word Structure	Earth Science
Sequence	Inferring	Word Structure/Suffixes	Economics/Geography
Author's Purpose	Visualize	Context Clues/Synonyms and Antonyms	Life Science
Cause and Effect	Summarize	Context Clues/Multiple Meanings	Life Science
Character and Setting	Important Ideas	Unknown Words/Dictionary/Glossary	History
Author's Purpose	Predict and Set Purpose	Word Structure/Greek and Latin Roots	History
Fact and Opinion	Monitor and Clarify	Context Clues/Synonyms and Antonyms	Life Science
Fact and Opinion	Important Ideas	Homographs/Dictionary/Glossary	History
Draw Conclusions	Visualize	Word Structure/Greek and Latin Roots	History
Generalize	Story Structure	Context Clues/Unfamiliar Words	Culture
Fact and Opinion	Text Structure	Word Structure/Greek and Latin Roots	Earth Science
Graphic Sources	Monitor and Clarify	Synonyms/Context Clues	Space and Technology
Draw Conclusions	Questioning	Word Structure/Root Words	History
Author's Purpose	Summarize	Multiple Meanings/Dictionary/Glossary	History
Plot	Inferring	Context Clues/Unfamiliar Words	Culture
Main Idea and Details	Predict and Set Purpose	Context Clues/Unfamiliar Words	Social Studies
Fact and Opinion	Background Knowledge	Multiple Meanings/Context Clues	Space and Technology

Concept Literacy Leveled Reader Chart

Concept Literacy Leveled Readers align with the weekly concepts in each unit. Each book is written at a lower level than the Below-Level Reader for the week to provide struggling readers with a way to practice independent reading as they build understanding and develop concept knowledge. Concept Literacy Readers play a role in the instruction for the Strategic Intervention group, but they can be used for independent reading practice for any struggling readers.

Grade 3 — Title	Level*	DRA Level*	Concept	Content Connection
Learning New Things!	B	2	Living and Learning	Social Studies
Trading This for That	B	2	Living and Learning	Economics
We Want Soup!	B	2	Living and Learning	Social Studies
The Supermarket	B	2	Living and Learning	Economics
I Have a Dollar	B	2	Living and Learning	Economics
Keeping Warm	B	2	Smart Solutions	Life Science
Which Way Is Better?	B	2	Smart Solutions	Social Studies
You Can Solve It!	B	2	Smart Solutions	Citizenship
Let's Be Fair!	B	2	Smart Solutions	Citizenship
Birds' Nests	B	2	Smart Solutions	Life Science
Grapes into Raisins	C	3	People and Nature	Life Science
Explaining Nature	C	3	People and Nature	Culture
Take a Look!	C	3	People and Nature	Space and Technology
Helping Whales	C	3	People and Nature	Life Science
The Hot Desert	C	3	People and Nature	Life Science
What Can Athletes Do?	C	3	One of a Kind	Social Studies
Extremes	C	3	One of a Kind	Earth Science
I Collect Rocks	C	3	One of a Kind	Earth Science
Women Who Were First!	C	3	One of a Kind	History
What Can Animals Do?	C	3	One of a Kind	Life Science
Kiko's Kimono	D	4	Cultures	Culture
Happy New Year!	D	4	Cultures	Culture
Our New Home	D	4	Cultures	Culture
Bread!	D	4	Cultures	Culture
From Country to City	D	4	Cultures	Culture
The Statue of Liberty	D	4	Freedom	History/Citizenship
The Eagle Is Free	D	4	Freedom	Citizenship/Life Science
Many Voices	D	4	Freedom	Social Studies
We Have Rules	D	4	Freedom	Citizenship
Freedom for All!	D	4	Freedom	Citizenship

* Suggested Guided Reading level. Use your knowledge of children's abilities to adjust levels as needed.

Concept Literacy Leveled Reader Chart *(continued)*

Need more choices? Look back to Grade 2.

Grade 2 Title	Level*	DRA Level*	Concept	Content Connection
The Country and the City	A	1	Exploration	Culture
How Do We Explore Space?	A	1	Exploration	Space and Technology
Our Camping Trip	A	1	Exploration	Life Science
In the Dry Desert	A	1	Exploration	Life Science
How Can You Find Animals?	A	1	Exploration	Life Science
Who Helps?	A	1	Working Together	Citizenship
Working Together	A	1	Working Together	Citizenship
What a School Needs	A	1	Working Together	Economics
Let's Clean Up the Park!	A	1	Working Together	Citizenship
We Make Soup!	A	1	Working Together	Social Studies
Help from a Friend	B	2	Creative Ideas	Citizenship
How I Feel	B	2	Creative Ideas	Social Studies
What Should We Do?	B	2	Creative Ideas	Social Studies
Good Ideas!	B	2	Creative Ideas	Culture
What Can You Make?	B	2	Creative Ideas	Science
When Things Change	B	2	Our Changing World	Social Studies
Harvest Time	B	2	Our Changing World	Life Science
Who Needs Soil?	B	2	Our Changing World	Life Science
New Faces and Places	B	2	Our Changing World	Social Studies
All Kinds of Weather	B	2	Our Changing World	Physical Science
Who Helps on Your Street?	C	3	Responsibility	Citizenship
Helping Our World	C	3	Responsibility	Citizenship
Our Dog Buster	C	3	Responsibility	Citizenship
Neighbors Help Neighbors	C	3	Responsibility	Citizenship
I Follow the Rules	C	3	Responsibility	Citizenship
At the Ballpark	C	3	Traditions	Social Studies
Flag Day	C	3	Traditions	History
Happy Birthday!	C	3	Traditions	Social Studies
Cowboys	C	3	Traditions	Culture/History
Election Day	C	3	Traditions	History

* Suggested Guided Reading level. Use your knowledge of children's abilities to adjust levels as needed.

Concept Literacy Leveled Reader Chart (continued)

Need more choices? Look ahead to Grade 4.

Grade 4 Title	Level*	DRA Level*	Concept	Content Connection
Coming Together	D	4	Turning Points	Culture
The Dog That Discovered the West	D	4	Turning Points	History
Laura Ingalls Wilder: Pioneer Girl	D	4	Turning Points	History
The Horned Toad	D	4	Turning Points	Life Science
Yosemite National Park	D	4	Turning Points	Earth Science
We All Have Talent	E	6–8	Teamwork	Social Studies
At the Rodeo	E	6–8	Teamwork	Culture
Be a Historian	E	6–8	Teamwork	History
Teamwork!	E	6–8	Teamwork	Citizenship
The President's Promise	E	6–8	Teamwork	Citizenship
Looking for Patterns	E	6–8	Patterns in Nature	Earth Science/Life Science
Gray Whales on the Go	E	6–8	Patterns in Nature	Life Science
Day and Night	E	6–8	Patterns in Nature	Earth Science
Hurricane!	E	6–8	Patterns in Nature	Earth Science
Rocks, Wind, and Water	E	6–8	Patterns in Nature	Earth Science
Is Yeast a Beast?	F	10	Puzzles and Mysteries	Life Science
The Mysterious Amazon River Dolphin	F	10	Puzzles and Mysteries	Life Science
Sending Secrets	F	10	Puzzles and Mysteries	Social Studies
Crack the Code!	F	10	Puzzles and Mysteries	Social Studies
Tiger Salamander's Amazing Tail	F	10	Puzzles and Mysteries	Life Science
Fire!	F	10	Land, Air, and Water	Earth Science
Discovering Machu Picchu	F	10	Land, Air, and Water	History
Dogs to the Rescue!	F	10	Land, Air, and Water	Life Science
Exploring Antarctica	F	10	Land, Air, and Water	Earth Science/Life Science
Moonscape: The Surface of the Moon	F	10	Land, Air, and Water	Space and Technology
A Boy Named Martin	G	12	Reaching for Goals	History
Dreamers and Doers	G	12	Reaching for Goals	History
Roberto Clemente	G	12	Reaching for Goals	History
Quanah Parker: Last Chief of the Comanche	G	12	Reaching for Goals	History
Apollo 11	G	12	Reaching for Goals	History/Space and Technology

* Suggested Guided Reading level. Use your knowledge of children's abilities to adjust levels as needed.

21st Century Skills
on Reading Street

Your third grade students are "digital natives." So when you tell them to *Get Online!* they jump at the chance. The world of information and communication technology (ICT) is a natural part of their everyday lives.

In **Section 8**, you'll discover the visually engaging and entertaining Digital Path locations on *Scott Foresman Reading Street*. These exciting, research-based tools motivate your students to explore the new literacies of the 21st Century and their own ideas through technology.

The next step is easy. To begin exploring content and features, just visit www.ReadingStreet.com!

21st Century Skills

The world today is one of rapid technological advancement and change. The third grade students in your classroom now will quickly become part of tomorrow's workforce. As a teacher of literacy, you are providing them valuable literacy skills as they grow up in this information, media, and information-rich context.

Technology on *Scott Foresman Reading Street* can be used both for enhancing student experiences and preparing them for the future. Throughout the year, you can choose from research-based technology options that enrich your instruction and assist you in the management of classroom learning.

What Are New Literacies?

Right before our eyes, the nature of reading and learning is changing. The Internet and other technologies create new opportunities, new solutions, and new literacies—new ways to make meaning out of what we see and read onscreen. Each new technology for reading, writing, and communicating requires new literacies to take full advantage of its potential. The future calls for new comprehension skills too. Students must adapt and use new reading comprehension skills when they are online. These literacies are increasingly important to our students and our society.

Research has shown that technology is a powerful motivational tool as well as a critical literacy area for the future. It has the power to engage and hold students' attention, maximize time on task, and help you scaffold students' learning. Student engagement leads to willingness to practice and practice leads to real learning. To be effective, technology and digital media for literacy learning must be carefully designed to include instructionally effective visuals, audio, and interactivity.

"Locating information on the Internet requires very different reading skills from locating information in a book."
Donald J. Leu, Jr., 2008

How Can I Help Students Adjust to Changing Technology?

Technology is part of our lives, so what we are used to now changes rapidly. New uses for technology are constantly being envisioned, and teachers respond by changing their instruction. They see the benefits of student-centered learning that technology makes possible. In the future, technology will foster even more learner-based instruction. Your third grade students don't have to wait for opportunities to control how they will achieve certain learning goals. *Scott Foresman Reading Street* has multiple destinations on its Digital Path that help make the transition to student-centered instruction effective. With these research-based multimedia tools, you can guide students to See It!, Hear It!, and Do It!

Big Question Videos introduce the unit level Big Question that students explore throughout the unit. Students use the Journal activity to capture their questions and ideas in a graphic organizer.

Concept Talk Videos support you in providing critical background building information. Students learn background about text topics before they begin to read. Seeing and hearing concept vocabulary prepares students to talk about the topic with others in the class.

Envision It! Animations make cause and effect, compare and contrast, and other comprehension skills come to life in an animated context. After students watch, they can talk about and understand the skill. The next stop, learning the academic vocabulary for each comprehension skill, comes more easily. Students can click on to retellings, which include concept vocabulary, and access definitions. The picture prompts help students retell. Envision It! also includes a paired selection, with audio, that expands on the theme or topic in a new way.

What Skills Do Students Need for New Literacies?

Five comprehension skill areas are important for students to develop as they read online. These skills build on the decoding, vocabulary, and text comprehension skills that are also necessary for reading on the Internet.

1. **Ask, identify, and generate important questions.**
   What motivates students to read on the Internet? Most begin with a question or another need to find information. Students need to know how to ask important questions. They also need to use the Internet to generate questions.

2. **Use multiple comprehension skills to locate information.**
   Students encounter separate search engines to find information. Then they read search results and make inferences to select the best links for their needs.

3. **Critically evaluate information on the Internet.**
   Students read information that anyone may have published on the Internet, so they must pay attention to accuracy. Students need to determine who created the information and consider why and when it was published. They need to detect bias in the information. They must also know how to use other sources to check if information is accurate for their own purposes.

4. **Synthesize information to create unique answers.**
   Readers on the Internet are putting together a new, or external, text as they find information in different places. A critical new comprehension skill is learning to make wise choices as they select links and add information. Each student's synthesis may be different because different links may be chosen. Students also must learn to create the external text that answers their question, or answers additional questions that arose as they searched.

5. **Communicate the answers to others.**
   Reading and writing are integrated when using the Internet. Students must learn to compose texts through the links that they select during reading. They use blogs, e-mail, text messaging, and other communication technologies to send the new information.

   When students follow the Digital Path in *Scott Foresman Reading Street*, they are learning 21st Century literacy skills. As students read Paired eSelections, which extend concepts, vocabulary, and the topic of the main selection, they can select the Read Online feature. This interactive lesson is like a private tutor that teaches students information and communication technology (ICT) comprehension skills and strategies for e-mail, Web sites, and media awareness.

How Does Technology Help Students Acquire Vocabulary?

Have you observed that students who use academic vocabulary in classroom conversations—even before they can read the words—are at an advantage? Later, when students see the words in print, you notice that they comprehend more quickly. Your observations align with what research is pointing to. Students who view images, video, and animation while listening to audio gain important information. But they won't use those sources alone. In the 21st century, students will use multimedia information sources and read traditional text often. The reason is obvious: we can read text far faster than we can listen to or view it. The need for speed and information management will require all readers to depend on a balance of technological and traditional text sources—as well as their expanded knowledge of literacy skills.

eReaders Leveled books are available as audio books. Teachers can assign the book matched to each student based on his or her reading profile, or choose another book based on a different instructional purpose.

Vocabulary Activities on the Digital Path show students that words are fun. Activities include Vocabulary Flashcards, Crossword Puzzle, Memory Match, Trivia, and Poetry.

Journal Word Bank is a rich source of vocabulary practice. Students respond to prompts and use weekly tested vocabulary as they write in complete sentences.

Grammar Jammer has songs and rhymes that help students remember the weekly conventions skills.

Interactive Sound-Spelling Cards are engaging activities for phonemic awareness and phonics skills. Students select images and hear words with target spelling patterns. They see, hear and do as they select and see images—and hear and read words.

What Makes Technology Powerful?

Watch students as they engage in technology. They have a "Do It!" attitude and seem to be aware that they're actively learning. Your third grade students are eager to make choices in response to reading prompts. They become motivated when they receive immediate feedback and are receptive to thought-provoking questions about their use of strategies. Technology is also a powerful tool for the student writer. Research shows that technology for writing instruction helps students think as they write, especially when the technology has prompts to support reflection on writing, spelling, and grammar. When you use carefully designed technology, your instruction has more power because it's more student-centered.

While these literacy and learning outcomes are important, new literacies can also lead to important new realizations for students. When you use the Internet, students have the potential to travel across information bridges and interact with authors, experts, communities, and students from around the globe. Meaningful interactions with other students from diverse communities spark new questions in your students about the larger world around them. As they search for answers, their insights and understanding broaden too.

How Does Technology Support Teachers?

As a teacher in the 21st century, you want to be skilled in the effective use of information and communication technology (ICT) for teaching and learning. You expect a literacy curriculum that integrates the new literacies of ICT into your instructional programs. You need assessment practices in literacy that include reading on the Internet and writing using word-processing. When you go to the Student and Teacher Resources and Download Center in the *Scott Foresman Reading Street* Digital Path, you can choose digital supports for all your needs. The Teacher's Edition, Student Edition, and practice books are available online. You'll also find a variety of online assessment tools that help you adjust your instruction and make grouping decisions. You can search by standards or skill key word to find additional resources that target student needs. Your students will get the specific extra practice they need before reassessment. You'll also find many other teacher and student materials in CD and CD-ROM formats.

Online Assessment has weekly tests, Fresh Reads Tests, Unit Tests, and more for data-driven decision-making. When you need to customize a test, use the Teacher Build-a-Test.

Story Sort allows students to drag and drop retelling cards and place them in correct order. This interactive sequencing is a visual way to practice retelling stories, a critical comprehension skill. Students build comprehension as they write an Image Essay about one picture.

Decodable eReaders show students word-by-word highlighting as they hear the decodable text read aloud. You can use underlining and highlighting tools for group or one-on-one instruction.

Letter Tile Drag and Drop is a word building game designed that teachers can use whenever students are ready to extend vocabulary and explore words. They manipulate the familiar yellow tiles that appear in Teacher Edition lessons for word work.

New Literacies on *Reading Street*

Did you know that many nations are preparing their students for the reading demands of the Internet? Students need to be prepared for a global information economy. The ability to read information online to learn, solve problems, and communicate solutions is central to success.

As our reliance on technology and the Internet increases, it is essential that students learn digital skills. Starting in First Grade, *Reading Street* weaves these basic digital skills—e-mail, Web sites, parts of a computer— with the core knowledge that schools and teachers have instilled in students for generations. More than ever, America's students require an emphasis on 21st century skills and basic digital know-how to grow into successful and effective adults. Writing e-mail weekly or daily, students practice the comprehension and writing skills taught in *Reading Street*. School projects call students to search engines, online directories, and reference sources that support the research skills taught in *Reading Street* Teacher Editions.

As students progress in school, *Reading Street* teaches increasingly important ways to write e-mail, browse Web sites, research with online directories and search engines, and evaluate online sources. By teaching these important digital skills using easily understood and fun-to-read selections, *Reading Street* prepares our youth for the success that they deserve as they move through school.

You change the world when you teach a child to read. And now, with the new literacies of the Internet, this can happen in profoundly powerful ways. The Internet opens your classroom windows to the world.

E-mail The preferred method of written communication is no longer the hand- or typewritten letter sent through the post office; it's e-mail. Americans send e-mails every day, to friends and family, to potential employers, to work colleagues. Students use e-mail to discuss school projects with classmates or simply to make new friends. By writing and mastering e-mail, students practice their comprehension and vocabulary skills, exchange ideas, engage in dialogue with peers, and articulate their thoughts, while gaining the electronic skills vital to their future.

Web Sites With almost every click of a mouse button, students encounter information on Web sites. Students browse Web sites for fun, for researching school projects, and for learning about other nations and cultures. Browsing the Internet is one of the easiest ways for students to improve comprehension and develop a thirst for learning. All the information imaginable is at their fingertips. Encourage students to keep on clicking!

Online Directories Students browse online directories when they want to find information about specific topics. Using the same set of skills they hone while browsing Web sites, students punch key words into directories to discover organized information and articles that assist them in research and broaden their view of the environment around them.

Evaluating Online Sources Two questions to listen for from Web-browsing students: *Who wrote that? Can I trust them?* As students learn to research information on the Internet, they also must learn to evaluate online sources. Information on the Internet can be inaccurate or even false. Today's successful students evaluate online information for accuracy and reliability, and understand how media shapes and influences their views. Evaluating online sources is a crucial step in students' development into independent individuals.

Search Engines When students use the Internet for research, they are amateur sleuths, clicking on links and typing in key words to hunt down the information they need. One of the best tools for information-hunting on the Internet is the search engine. Learning to use a search engine helps students identify questions and frame information in a way that helps them solve their problems. As they use search engines, students train themselves to evaluate sources and brainstorm ideas.

Online Reference Sources Dictionaries, almanacs, encyclopedias: These are the essential tools at our fingertips to complete projects and learn about our world. Students must learn to access online reference sources and analyze the information they find to answer questions or define words in a vocabulary list. By learning to navigate these sources, students gain research skills and learn how to construct better solutions to problems.

Teacher Resources
for Grade 3

Oral Vocabulary/Amazing Words

UNIT 1

WEEK 1

appetizing
cringed
grit
physical
plentiful
reaction
reject
suitable

WEEK 2

barter   wilt
expensive   worthless
lovely
mania
obvious
peddler
permanent

WEEK 3

adequate   funds
admirably   rehearsal
amusement
announcement
brainstorm
collaborate
design
enthusiasm

WEEK 4

bargain   product
browse   resource
budget
compromise
exchange
export
hastily
import

WEEK 5

amount   tempted
consumer   thrift shop
denomination
income
investor
resist
retail
savings

UNIT 2

WEEK 1

absorb   saliva
brace   vibration
earthen
flourish
inhospitable
predatory
refuge
reinforce

WEEK 2

budge   stubborn
disagree   unite
implement
obstinate
prevent
quarrel
rally
supervise

WEEK 3

bulky   portable
decade   rubble
device
drastic
exception
impress
inflatable
petrify

WEEK 4

claim   satisfaction
convince   vain
distribute
divvy
humiliate
jealous
official
reasonable

WEEK 5

burrow   spine
concoction   vital
disguise
dormant
evaporate
extreme
moisture
nutrient

UNIT 3

WEEK 1

admire   trek
backpack   wildlife
elevation
jumble
nature
stumble
tame
teem

WEEK 2

abundant   shrivel
elder   torrent
existence
fertile
irritable
pierce
scarce
scorch

WEEK 3

active   species
detect   twilight
downwind
dusk
intimate
microscopic
reflect
sensitive

WEEK 4

biologists   salt marsh
catastrophe   starvation
conservation
hover
inhumane
illegally
overpopulation
prohibit

WEEK 5

appreciate   preserve
behold   relationship
birch
border
cedar
centipede
dew
origin

WEEK 1

audition	succeed
ecstatic	thrill
idle	verge
mock	
necessary	
potential	
result	
rise	

WEEK 2

acrobat	valuable
champ	weaken
competitors	
evergreens	
lumber	
plunged	
ranger	
sprinter	

WEEK 3

ancestor	ornament
compartment	project
descendant	
forge	
hobby	
leftover	
murmur	

WEEK 4

accompany	spectacle
assemble	suspend
erect	
imagination	
magnificent	
ordinary	
organize	
provision	

WEEK 5

agile	snout
armor	unfurl
coil	
extraordinary	
intersection	
pesky	
protrude	
scenery	

WEEK 1

acceptable	stylish
drape	traditional
elegant	
fabric	
fret	
inspire	
robe	
scarves	

WEEK 2

barbecue	settler
belief	shield
chant	
clan	
concentrate	
dwelling	
headdress	
procession	

WEEK 3

advantage	native
aspect	sponsor
conscious	
habit	
homeland	
impolite	
insult	
manner	

WEEK 4

agent	spice
allergic	wholesome
calorie	
flavor	
grate	
grumble	
nutmeg	
nutrition	

WEEK 5

bitter	taxicab
gutter	vendor
hurl	
meager	
ramble	
scamper	
scurry	
skyscraper	

WEEK 1

competition	staggering
contribution	tribute
dedication	
disgrace	
enlighten	
fund	
impressive	
recognizable	

WEEK 2

affectionate	territory
companion	wandering
deserve	
loyal	
manage	
nag	
release	
retrieve	

WEEK 3

artistic	significant
creative	view
emotion	
expressive	
exquisite	
lecture	
lyrics	
pause	

WEEK 4

citizen	permission
consequence	responsibility
eerie	
encounter	
fascinate	
forbid	
guilt	
obey	

WEEK 5

blight	wept
demonstrate	witty
equality	
justice	
mourn	
perish	
violence	

You've learned 295 **Amazing Words** this year!

Word Lists for Unit 1

When Charlie McButton Lost Power

Selection Vocabulary

bat
battery
blew
fuel

plug
term
vision

Spelling Words
Short vowels VC/CV

basket	lettuce	sister	supper
collar	monster	spelling	traffic
happen	napkin	subject	winter
lesson	puppet	suggest	

What About Me?

Selection Vocabulary

carpenter
carpetmaker
knowledge
marketplace

merchant
plenty
straying
thread

Spelling Words
Plurals -s, -es

bodies	families	parties	pockets
bunches	glasses	pencils	supplies
copies	inches	pennies	wishes
crashes	lists	plants	

Kumak's Fish

Selection Vocabulary

gear
parka
splendid

twitch
willow
yanked

Spelling Words
Adding -ed, -ing, -er, and -est

angrier	funniest	leaving	swimming
easiest	getting	pleased	using
emptied	greatest	shopped	worried
freezing	heavier	strangest	

Supermarket

Selection Vocabulary

laundry
section
shelves
spoiled

store
thousands
traded
variety

Spelling Words
Long vowel digraphs

agree	coach	grain	teeth
braid	display	peach	thrown
cheese	dream	shadow	window
clean	float	Sunday	

My Rows and Piles of Coins

Selection Vocabulary

arranged
bundles
dangerously
errands

excitedly
steady
unwrapped
wobbled

Spelling Words
Vowel sounds in *out* and *toy*

amount	bounce	hour	shower
annoy	broil	poison	thousand
appoint	choice	proud	voyage
avoid	employ	prowl	

Word Lists for Unit 2

Penguin Chick

Selection Vocabulary

cuddles
flippers
frozen
hatch

pecks
preen
snuggles

Spelling Words
Syllable pattern V/CV, VC/V

camel	focus	pupil	silent
even	lemon	rapid	tulip
female	music	robot	wagon
finish	pilot	salad	

I Wanna Iguana

Selection Vocabulary

adorable
compassionate
exactly
iguana

mature
mention
trophies

Spelling Words
Words ending in *-le*

gentle	middle	poodle	table
handle	noodle	riddle	trouble
juggle	people	saddle	uncle
little	pickle	simple	

Prudy's Problem

Selection Vocabulary

butterflies
collection
enormous

scattered
shoelaces
strain

Spelling Words
Compound words

blueberry	football	popcorn	snowstorm
butterflies	haircut	railroad	sunglasses
campground	homework	sandbox	toothbrush
earring	lawnmower	scarecrow	

Tops & Bottoms

Selection Vocabulary

bottom
cheated
clever
crops

lazy
partners
wealth

Spelling Words
Words with *spl, thr, squ, str*

scratch	splurge	street	thrill
scream	square	strength	throne
splash	squeak	strike	throw
split	squeeze	three	

Amazing Bird Nests

Selection Vocabulary

bill
goo
hunters
material

platform
tons
twigs

Spelling Words
Digraphs *sh, th, ph, ch, tch*

alphabet	English	nephew	trophy
athlete	fashion	other	watch
catch	father	pitcher	weather
chapter	flash	shrink	

Word Lists for Unit 3

How do you Raise a Raisin

Selection Vocabulary

area   proof
artificial   raise
grapevine   raisin
preservative

Spelling Words
Contractions

can't	he'd	should've	when's
didn't	I'd	they'll	won't
hasn't	let's	wasn't	you'll
haven't	she'd	we'd	

Pushing Up the Sky

Selection Vocabulary

antlers   narrator
imagined   overhead
languages poked

Spelling Words
Prefixes *un-, re-, mis-, dis-, non-*

disagree	mislead	recall	unknown
disappear	misspell	replace	unload
dishonest	mistake	rewrite	unroll
dislike	react	unhappy	

Seeing Stars

Selection Vocabulary

dim   patterns
gas   shine
gigantic   temperature
ladle

Spelling Words
Consonant Sounds /j/ and /k/

brake	crack	kitten	page
budge	edge	large	pocket
change	jacket	mark	ridge
clock	judge	orange	

A Symphony of Whales

Selection Vocabulary

anxiously   melody
bay   supplies
blizzards   surrounded
channel   symphony
chipped

Spelling Words
Suffixes *-ly, -ful, -ness, -less*

beautiful	finally	painful	suddenly
cheerful	helpful	quietly	wireless
daily	illness	safely	worthless
fairness	kindness	spotless	

Around One Cactus: Owls, Bats and Leaping Rats

Selection Vocabulary

lofty   survivors
incredible topic
noble   unseen
search   waterless
stinging

Spelling Words
Words with *wr, kn, mb, gn*

assign	gnaw	know	wrinkle
climb	knit	lamb	wrist
crumb	knob	thumb	written
design	knot	wrench	

Word Lists for Unit 4

The Man who Invented Basketball: James Naismith and His Amazing Game

Selection Vocabulary

disease	study
guard	popular
freeze	sports
terrible	basketball

Spelling Words
Plurals

banjos	feet	knives	sheep
children	geese	men	wolves
cuffs	halves	mice	women
elves	heroes	scarves	

Hottest, Coldest, Highest, Deepest

Selection Vocabulary

average	outrun
depth	peak
deserts	tides
erupted	waterfalls

Spelling Words
Vowels with _r_

certain	earth	third	workout
dirty	herself	thirsty	world
early	nerve	verb	worm
earn	perfect	word	

Rocks in His Head

Selection Vocabulary

attic	labeled
board	spare
chores	stamps
customer	

Spelling Words
Prefixes _pre-, mid-, over-, out-_

midnight	outfield	overdue	prefix
midpoint	outgoing	overflow	prepaid
Midwest	outline	overgrown	pretest
outdoors	outside	overtime	

Gertrude Ederle

Selection Vocabulary

celebrate	medals
continued	stirred
current	strokes
drowned	

Spelling Words
Suffixes _-er, -or, -ess, -ist_

actress	dentist	lioness	swimmer
artist	editor	organist	tourist
chemist	hostess	seller	tutor
conductor	investor	shipper	

Fly, Eagle, Fly!

Selection Vocabulary

clutched	scrambled
echoed	thatch
gully	valley
reeds	

Spelling Words
Syllable pattern VCCCV

address	control	inspect	sample
children	district	instant	substance
complete	explode	monster	surprise
contrast	hundred	pilgrim	

Word Lists for Unit 5

Suki's Kimono

Selection Vocabulary

cotton
festival
graceful
handkerchief

paces
pale
rhythm
snug

Spelling Words
Syllable Pattern CV/VC

audio	medium	radio	trio
create	patio	rodeo	video
duo	piano	stadium	violin
idea	pioneer	studio	

I Love Saturdays y domingos

Selection Vocabulary

bouquet
circus
difficult
nibbling

pier
soars
swallow

Spelling Words
Homophones

bare	right	stare	weak
bear	road	to	week
knew	rode	too	write
new	stair	two	

Good-Bye, 382 Shin Dang Dong

Selection Vocabulary

airport
cellar
curious
delicious
described

farewell
homesick
memories
raindrops

Spelling Words
Vowel Sound in *ball*

author	could	fought	through
because	daughter	sausage	touch
bought	enough	should	would
brought	faucet	taught	

Jalapeño Bagels

Selection Vocabulary

bakery
batch
boils
braided

dough
ingredients
mixture

Spelling Words
More Vowel Sound in *ball*

ceiling	either	neighbor	sleigh
conceited	freight	neither	weigh
deceive	height	protein	weight
eighteen	leisure	receive	

Me and Uncle Romie

Selection Vocabulary

cardboard
feast
fierce
flights

pitcher
ruined
stoops
treasure

Spelling Words
Suffixes *-y, -ish, -hood, -ment*

bumpy	foolish	payment	shipment
childhood	movement	rainy	sleepy
childish	neighborhood	rocky	treatment
crunchy	parenthood	selfish	

Word Lists for Unit 6

The Story of the Statue of Liberty

Selection Vocabulary

crown | tablet
liberty | torch
models | unforgettable
symbol | unveiled

Spelling Words
Vowel sounds in *tooth* and *cook*

balloon	cookie	glue	suit
bookmark	cushion	goose	Tuesday
bushel	few	noodle	true
chew	fruit	school	

Happy Birthday Mr. Kang

Selection Vocabulary

bows | narrow
chilly | perches
foolish | recipe
foreign |

Spelling Words
Schwa

above	circus	melon	sugar
afraid	family	nickel	travel
animal	gallon	open	upon
another	item	paper	

Talking Walls

Selection Vocabulary

encourages | settled
expression | social
local | support
native |

Spelling Words
Words with *-tion, -sion, -ture*

action	culture	fiction	sculpture
celebration	direction	furniture	vacation
collision	division	mansion	vision
creature	feature	question	

Two Bad Ants

Selection Vocabulary

crystal | journey
disappeared | joyful
discovery | scoop
goal | unaware

Spelling Words
Multisyllabic words

carefully	misbehaving	reappeared	unbearably
gracefully	oncoming	refreshment	uncomfortable
impossibly	overdoing	remarkable	unprepared
leadership	ownership	unacceptable	

Atlantis

Selection Vocabulary

aqueducts | honor
content | pillar
crouched | thermal
guidance |

Spelling Words
Related words

ability	deal	natural	sign
able	dealt	nature	signal
cloth	mean	pleasant	signature
clothes	meant	please	

Looking Back
Grade 2 Vocabulary

Use this list of second grade tested vocabulary words for review and leveled activities.

A
above
adventure
afternoon
ago
agriculture
alone
animals
annoy
answer
armadillo
around
astronaut
awaken

B
balance
bear
beautiful
become
been
behind
believe
blame
bought
brave
break
brought
build
building
bumpy
burning
buy

C
cactus
canyons
caught
certainly
chased
chewing
chiles
clearing
cliffs
climate
climbed
clothes
clubhouse
collar
college
company
complain
coral
couldn't

country
cousins
coyote
crashed
creature

D
dangerous
daughters
delicious
desert
door
dripping
drooled

E
early
either
electricity
enough
envelope
everybody
everywhere
excitement
experiment
exploring
eyes

F
family
faraway
father
fault
finally
friend
front
fruit
full

G
gnaws
gone
goodbye
grabbed
grains
grateful
gravity
great
greatest
greenhouse
groaned
guess

H
half
harsh
harvest

heard
honest
hours
hurricanes

I
idea
important

J
justice

L
laboratory
lanterns
laugh
lawyer
lazy
learn
listen
live
love
luckiest

M
machines
many
masks
materials
meadow
mill
minute
money
monsters
mother
mountain
move
mumbles
musician

N
narrator
neighbor
nothing
noticed

O
often
once
only

P
P.M.
parents
particles
people
perfect
persimmons

photograph
picture
pieces
pleasant
pond
practice
pretty
prize
probably
promise
pull

Q
question
quickly

R
rainbow
rattle
relatives
resources
roar
robbers
robot
root

S
scarce
scarcity
scared
school
science
second
seeps
shall
shivered
shoe
shrugs
shuttle
sign
signature
signmaker
slipped
slivers
smooth
smudged
snorted
snuggled
soil
someone
somewhere
spilling
splashing
station
stories

straight
substances
suffer
sway

T
taught
telescope
texture
their
thought
tightly
today
together
tomorrow
took
tortillas
toward
townspeople
trade-off
trash
traveled
treat
truest

V
very
village
vine
volcano

W
wad
wagged
warm
wash
watch
water
weave
whatever
whisper
whole
woman
won
wondered
word
work
world
worst

Y
youngest
you're

Looking Ahead
Grade 4 Vocabulary
Use this list of fourth grade tested vocabulary words for review and leveled activities.

A
abundance
advance
advice
affords
ambition
amphibians
analysis
ancestors
ancient
announcement
anticipation
apprentice
aquarium
argument
arrangements
astronauts
atmosphere
avoided

B
backdrop
badger
bank
bargain
bawling
beakers
biologist
bluff
boarding
brilliant
bristled

C
capsule
ceremonial
chemical
chorus
club
coil
colonel
concentrating
Constitution
continent
convergence
coward
coyote
crime
curiosity

D
dedication
depart
descendents
descent
destruction
developed
dishonest
docks
dolphins
dormitory
drought
dudes

E
enchanted
endurance
essay
essential
exhausting
exhibit
expected

F
favor
feature
flexible
forbidding
forecasts
foresaw
fouled

G
generations
glacier
gleamed
glimpses
glint
glorious
grand
granite
graze

H
harness
hatch
headquarters
heaves
hollow
hoop
horizon

howling
humble

I
icebergs
identify
impossible
impressive
infested
inland
intense

J
jersey
jointed

L
lagoon
landslide
lassoed
lecture
link
lizards
loomed
lumberjacks
lunar
lurking

M
manual
manufacturing
marveled
massive
memorial
messages
method
microscope
migrating
minister
module

N
naturalist
numerous

O
offended

P
palettes
parachute
patched
peculiar
politics

positive
prairie
precise
preserve
pressure
prideful
pulpit
pulses

Q
quaint
quarantine
quicksand

R
rappel
recalls
reference
relentless
reptiles
requirements
resemblance
reservation
resistance
responsibility
reveal
rickety
ridge
rile
rim
riverbed
roamed
roundup
ruffled
ruins
rumbling
runt
rushes

S
salamanders
scales
scan
scent
scholars
school
script
seeker
selecting
shaft
shatter

shielding
shimmering
shock
shrieked
slopes
snag
society
solemnly
species
speechless
spurs
staggered
steer
stumped
summoning
surface
surge
swatted

T
taunted
temple
terraced
thaw
thickets
torrent
translate
trekked
trench
triumph
tropical
trudged

U
unbelievable
uncover
underbrush
unnatural
untamed

V
vain
vast
void

W
wharf
wilderness
wind

Y
yearned

Glossary of Reading Terms

This glossary includes academic language terms used with students as well as reading terms provided for your information and professional use.

abbreviation a shortened form of a word. *Dr.* is an abbreviation for *doctor.*

accuracy reading words in text without errors, an element of fluency

action verb a word that shows action

adjective a word that describes a person, place, or thing. An adjective tells how many, what kind, or which one.

adverb a word that tells how, when, or where something happens. Adverbs also tell how much or how little is meant. Adverbs often end in *-ly.*

affix a prefix, suffix, or inflected ending that is added to a base word to form a new word

alliteration the repetition of a consonant sound in a group of words, especially in poetry

allusion a word or phrase that refers to something else the reader already knows from history, experience, or reading

alphabetical order the arrangement of words according to the letters of the alphabet

animal fantasy a story about animals that talk and act like people

answer questions a reading strategy in which readers use the text and prior knowledge to answer questions about what they are reading

antecedent the noun or nouns to which a pronoun refers

antonym a word that means the opposite of another word

apostrophe punctuation (') that shows where letters have been left out in a contraction or that is used with *s* at the end of a noun to show possession

appositive a word or phrase that explains the word it follows

ask questions a reading strategy in which readers ask themselves questions about the text to help make sense of what they read

author a person who writes books, stories, poems, or plays

author's point of view the author's opinion on the subject he or she is writing about

author's purpose the reason the author wrote the text

autobiography tells about a real person's life written by the person who lived it

automaticity the ability to read words or connected text automatically, with little or no attention to decoding

background knowledge the information and experience that a reader brings to a text

base word a word that can stand alone or take endings, prefixes, and suffixes

biography tells about a real person's life. It is written by another person

blend combine a series of sounds in sequence without pausing between them

cause why something happens

character a person, animal, or personalized object in a story

choral reading reading aloud in unison as a group

chronological order events in a selection, presented in the order in which they occurred

chunking a decoding strategy for breaking words into manageable parts to read them

classify and categorize put things, such as pictures or words, into groups

clause a group of words having a subject and predicate and used as part of a compound or complex sentence

climax the point in a story at which conflict is confronted

collective noun a noun that names a group of persons or things, such as *audience* or *herd*

colon punctuation (:) that may introduce a list or separate hours from minutes to show time

comma punctuation (,) that can be used, for example, to indicate a pause in a sentence or to separate items in a series

comparative adjective an adjective used to compare two people, places, or things. Add *-er* to most adjectives to make them comparative.

compare tell how things are the same

complete predicate all the words in the predicate

complete subject all the words in the subject

complex sentence a sentence made up of one independent clause and one or more dependent clauses

composition a short piece of written work

compound sentence a sentence that contains two or more independent clauses. The clauses are joined either by a comma and a conjunction or by a semicolon.

compound word a word made up of two or more short words

comprehension understanding of text being read—the ultimate goal of reading

comprehension strategy a conscious plan used by a reader to gain understanding of text. Comprehension strategies may be used before, during, or after reading.

conclusion a decision or opinion arrived at after thinking about facts and details and using prior knowledge

conflict the problem or struggle in a story

conjunction a word, such as *and, but,* and *or,* that connects words, phrases, clauses, or sentences

consonant any letter of the alphabet that is not a vowel

consonant blend two or more consecutive consonants, each of which is pronounced and blended with the other, such as *cl* in *clock*

consonant digraph two consecutive consonants, that stand for a single sound, such as *ch, sh, th.* Its pronunciation usually differs from the sound of either individual consonant.

context clue the words, phrases, or sentences near an unknown word that give the reader clues to the word's meaning

continuous sound a sound that can be sustained without distortion, such as /m/, /f/, and /s/

contraction a shorter word formed by combining two words. The omitted letters are replaced with an apostrophe.

contrast tell how things are different

cursive handwriting handwriting in which the letters are joined

declarative sentence a sentence that tells something and ends with a period

decode apply knowledge of sound-spellings and word parts to read a new word

definition the meaning of a word

dependent clause a clause that cannot stand alone as a sentence

details small pieces of information

dialect form of a language spoken in a certain region or by a certain group of people that differs from the standard form of that language

dialogue written conversation

diary a day-to-day record of one's activities and thoughts

digraph two letters that stand for a single sound

diphthong two consecutive vowels whose sounds are pronounced in immediate sequence within a syllable, such as *oi* in *noise*

direct object a noun or pronoun that follows an action verb and tells who or what receives the action of the verb

discussion talking something over with other people

draft the first attempt at a composition. A draft is a rough copy that usually requires revision and editing before publication.

drama a story written to be acted out for others

draw conclusions arrive at decisions or opinions after thinking about facts and details and using prior knowledge

edit the stage in the writing process when a draft is corrected for facts and such mechanical errors as grammar, punctuation, usage, and spelling

Glossary of Reading Terms

effect what happens as the result of a cause

elaborate add more detail to what has already been said or written

entry word the word being defined in a dictionary or glossary. It is printed in boldface type.

etymology an explanation of the origin and history of a word and its meaning

exaggeration a statement that makes something seem larger or greater than it actually is

exclamation mark punctuation (!) following a word, phrase, or sentence that was exclaimed, or spoken with strong feeling

exclamatory sentence a sentence that expresses strong feeling or surprise and ends with an exclamation mark

expository text tells facts about a topic

expression emotion put into words while reading or speaking

fable a story that teaches a lesson

fact piece of information that can be proved to be true

fairy tale a folk story with magical characters and events

fantasy a make-believe story that could never happen in the real world

fiction writing that tells about imaginary people, things, and events

figurative language the use of language that gives words a meaning beyond their usual definitions in order to add beauty or force

flashback an interruption in the sequence of events of a narrative to include an event that happened earlier

fluency the ability to read quickly, accurately, and with expression. Fluent readers can focus their attention on the meaning of the text.

folk tale a story that has been handed down over many years

foreshadowing the use of hints or clues about what will happen later in a story

generalize make a broad statement or rule after examining particular facts

gesture a meaningful movement of the hands, arms, or other part of the body. Gestures may be used instead of words or with words to help express an idea or feeling.

glossary an alphabetical list of words and their definitions, usually found at the back of a book

graphic organizer a drawing, chart, or web that illustrates concepts or shows how ideas relate to each other. Readers use graphic organizers to help them keep track of and understand important information and ideas as they read. Story maps, word webs, Venn diagrams, and K-W-L charts are graphic organizers.

graphic source a chart, diagram, or map within a text that adds to readers' understanding of the text

guide words the words at the top of a dictionary or glossary page that show the first and last entry words on that page

high-frequency words the words that appear most commonly in print. The one hundred most frequent words account for about 50 percent of printed words. They are often called *sight words* since automatic recognition of these words is necessary for fluent reading.

historical fiction realistic fiction that takes place in the past

homograph a word that is spelled the same as another word, but has a different meaning and history. The words may or may not be pronounced the same. *Bass,* meaning a low singing voice, and *bass,* meaning a fish, are homographs.

homophone a word that sounds the same as another word, but has a different spelling, meaning, and history. *Ate* and *eight* are homophones.

humor writing or speech that has a funny or amusing quality

humorous fiction a funny story about imaginary people and events

hyperbole an exaggerated statement not meant to be taken literally, such as *I'm so hungry I could eat a horse.*

idiom a phrase whose meaning differs from the ordinary meaning of the words. *A stone's throw* is an idiom meaning "a short distance."

illustrative phrase or sentence an example showing how an entry word in a dictionary may be used in a sentence or phrase. It is printed in italic type.

illustrator a person who draws the pictures to go with a selection

imagery the use of language to create beautiful or forceful pictures in the reader's mind

imperative sentence a sentence that gives a command or makes a request. It usually ends with a period.

indent to begin the first line of a paragraph farther in from the left margin than the other lines

independent clause a clause that can stand by itself as a sentence

index an alphabetical list of people, places, and things that are mentioned in a book. An index gives the page numbers where each of these can be found. It appears at the end of a book.

indirect object a noun or pronoun that shows to whom or for whom the action of the verb is done

inference conclusion reached on the basis of evidence and reasoning

inflected ending a letter or group of letters added to the end of a base word that does not change the part of speech of the base word. Inflected endings are *-s, -es, -ed, -ing, -er,* and *-est.*

inflection a grammatical change in the form of a word, usually by adding an ending

inform give knowledge, facts, or news to someone

informational text often gives facts about real people, places and events that reflect history or the traditions of communities

interjection a word that is used to express strong feeling, such as *Oh!*

interrogative sentence a sentence that asks a question and ends with a question mark

interview a face-to-face conversation in which someone responds to questions

intonation the rise and fall of a reader's or speaker's voice

introductory paragraph the first paragraph of a composition or piece of writing. It sets up what is to come in the composition.

introductory sentence the first sentence of the first paragraph in a composition or a piece of writing. It sets up what is to come in the paragraph.

irony a way of speaking or writing in which the ordinary meaning of the words is the opposite of what the speaker or writer is thinking; a contrast between what is expected and what actually happens

irregular verb a verb that does not add *-ed* to form the past tense

jargon the language of a special group or profession

legend an old story that tells about the great deeds of a hero

legible clear and easy to read

linking verb a verb that does not show action, such as *is, seem,* and *become*

literary elements the characters, setting, plot, and theme of a narrative text

literary nonfiction tells about a true event or a series of events like a story

long vowel sound a vowel sound that is the same as the name of a vowel letter—*a, e, i, o,* and *u*

main idea the big idea that tells what a paragraph or a selection is mainly about; the most important idea of a text

media often, **the media** print and electronic sources such as newspapers, magazines, TV, radio, the Internet, and other such means of communication

Glossary of Reading Terms

metacognition an awareness of one's own thinking processes and the ability to monitor and direct them to a desired goal. Good readers use metacognition to monitor their reading and adjust their reading strategies.

metaphor a comparison that does not use *like* or *as*, such as *a heart of stone*

meter the pattern of beats or accents in poetry

modulation the variance of the volume, tone, or pitch of one's voice

monitor and clarify a comprehension strategy by which readers actively think about understanding their reading and know when they understand and when they do not. Readers use appropriate strategies to make sense of difficult words, ideas, or passages.

mood the atmosphere or feeling of a written work

moral the lesson or teaching of a fable or story

morpheme the smallest meaningful unit of language, including base words and affixes. There are three morphemes in the word *unfriendly—un, friend*, and *ly.*

motive the reason a character in a narrative does or says something

multiple-meaning word a word that has more than one meaning. Its meaning can be understood from the context in which it is used.

mystery a story about mysterious events that are not explained until the end, so as to keep the reader in suspense

myth an old story that often explains something about nature

narrative a story, made up or true, that someone tells or writes

narrator the character in a selection who tells the story

negative a word that means "no" or "not"

nonfiction writing that tells about real things, real people, and real events

noun a word that names a person, place, animal, or thing

onomatopoeia the use of words that sound like their meanings, such as *buzz* and *hum*

onset the part of a word or syllable that comes before the vowel. In the word *black, bl* is the onset. Also see *rime.*

opinion someone's judgment, belief, or way of thinking

oral rereading repeated reading of text until it can be read fluently

oral vocabulary the words needed for speaking and listening

outcome the resolution of the conflict in a story

pace (in fluency) the speed at which someone reads

paired reading reading aloud with a partner who provides help identifying words and other feedback. Also called *partner reading.*

paragraph a group of sentences about one main idea. Each paragraph begins on a new line and is indented.

paraphrase retell the meaning of a passage in one's own words

parentheses two curved lines ( ) used to set off words or phrases in text

participle a word formed from a verb and often used as an adjective or a noun

period the dot (.) that signifies the end of most sentences or shows an abbreviation, as in *Dec.*

personification a figure of speech in which human traits are given to animals or inanimate objects, as in *The sunbeam danced on the waves.*

persuade convince someone to do or to believe something

phoneme the smallest part of spoken language that makes a difference in the meaning of words. The word *sat* has three phonemes—/s/, /a/, and /t/.

phoneme blending orally combining a series of phonemes in sequence to form a word

phoneme isolation the ability to identify and pronounce an individual phoneme in a word

phoneme manipulation adding, deleting, or substituting phonemes in spoken words, for example, Say *fox* without the /f/: *ox*.

phonemic awareness one kind of phonological awareness. It includes the ability to hear individual sounds in words and to identify and manipulate them.

phonics the study of the relationship between sounds and their spellings

phonogram the part of a one-syllable word comprised of a vowel and all the letters that follow it, as *ack* in *back, crack, track, shack.* Words that share a phonogram are called a *word family.*

phonological awareness an awareness of the sounds that make up spoken language

photo essay a collection of photographs on one theme, accompanied by text

phrasing breaking text into natural thought units when reading

pitch degree of highness or lowness of a sound or of a speaker's voice

play a story that is written to be acted out for an audience

plot a series of related events at the beginning, middle, and end of a story; the action of a story

plural noun a noun that names more than one person, place, or thing

plural possessive noun a noun that shows there are two or more owners of something. Add an apostrophe to a plural noun ending in *-s* to make it a plural possessive noun.

poem an expressive, imaginative piece of writing often arranged in lines having rhythm and rhyme. In a poem, the patterns made by the sounds of the words have special importance.

possessive noun a noun that shows ownership or possession

possessive pronoun a pronoun that shows who or what owns or has something

pourquoi tale a type of folk story that explains why things in nature came to be. *Pourquoi* is a French word meaning "why."

predicate a word or group of words that tells what the subject is or does

predict tell what a selection might be about or what might happen in a text. Readers use text features and information to predict. They confirm or revise their predictions as they read.

prefix a word part added at the beginning of a base word to change its meaning or make another word, such as *un* in *unbutton*

preposition a word that shows the relationship of a noun or pronoun to another word. It is the first word in a prepositional phrase.

prepositional phrase a group of words that begins with a preposition and ends with a noun or pronoun

presentation something that is presented to an audience

preview look over a text before reading it

prewrite an initial stage in the writing process when topics may be brainstormed, ideas may be considered, and planning may occur

prior knowledge the information and experience that a reader brings to a text. Readers use prior knowledge to help them understand what they read.

procedural text a set of directions and graphic features telling how to do something

pronoun a word that can take the place of a noun or nouns

pronunciation key the explanation of the symbols used in a dictionary or glossary

pronunciation the letters and diacritical marks appearing in parentheses after an entry word in a dictionary that show how the word is pronounced

prop an item, such as an object, picture, or chart, used in a performance or presentation

proper noun a word that names a particular person, place, or thing. A proper noun begins with a capital letter.

Glossary of Reading Terms

punctuation the marks used in writing to separate sentences and their elements and to make meaning clear. Periods, commas, question marks, semicolons, and colons are punctuation marks.

question mark a punctuation mark (?) used at the end of a sentence to indicate a question

quotation marks the punctuation marks (" ") used to indicate the beginning and end of a speaker's exact words

reading vocabulary the words we recognize or use in print

realistic fiction a story of imaginary people and events that could happen in real life

r-controlled vowel sound the sound of a vowel immediately followed by *r* in the same syllable. Its sound is neither long nor short.

regular verb a verb that adds *-ed* to form the past tense

repetition the repeated use of some aspect of language

resolution the point in a story where the conflict is resolved

revise the stage in the writing process when a draft may be changed to improve such things as focus, ideas, organization, word choice, or voice

rhyme to end in the same sound(s)

rhythm a pattern of strong beats in speech or writing, especially in poetry

rime the part of a word or syllable that includes the vowel and any following consonants. In the word *black, ack* is the rime. Also see *onset.*

rising action the buildup of conflicts and complications in a story

root a word part, usually of Greek or Latin origin, that cannot stand alone, but is used to form a family of words. *Trans* in *transfer* and *transportation* is a root.

rubric a set of guidelines used to evaluate a product such as writing

run-on sentence two sentences written together without correct punctuation

salutation the words of greeting in a letter that address the person to whom the letter is being written

schwa the vowel sound in an unaccented syllable, such as the sound of *a* in *above*

science fiction a story based on science that tells what life in the future might be like

segment break a spoken word into its individual sounds

semantic map a graphic organizer, often a web, used to display words or concepts that are meaningfully related

semicolon punctuation (;) that indicates a pause between two clauses in a sentence

sensory language the use of words that help the reader understand how things look, sound, smell, taste, or feel

sentence a group of words that tells or asks something; asks a question; or makes a request, a command, or an exclamation

sequence the order of events in a selection or the order of the steps in which something is done

sequence words clue words such as *first, next, then,* and *finally* that signal the order of events in a selection

setting where and when a story takes place

short vowel sound the sound of *a, e, i, o,* and *u* as heard in *bat, bet, bit, box,* and *but*

simile a comparison that uses *like* or *as,* as in as *busy as a bee*

simple predicate the verb in the complete predicate

simple subject the main noun or pronoun in the complete subject

singular noun a noun that names one person, place, or thing

singular possessive noun a noun that shows there is one owner of something. Add an apostrophe and *-s* to a singular noun to make it a singular possessive noun.

sound boxes a graphic consisting of a row of boxes in which each box represents a single phoneme. A marker is placed in a box for each sound heard in a given word. Also called *Elkonin boxes.*

speech a public talk to a group of people made for a specific purpose

stanza a group of lines in a poem

statement a sentence that tells something. A statement ends with a period.

steps in a process the order of the steps in which something is done

stop sound a phoneme that can be said without distortion for only an instant. /b/, /k/, and /g/ are all stop sounds.

story map a graphic organizer used to record the literary elements and the sequence of events in a narrative text

story structure how the characters, setting, and events of a story are organized into a plot

subject a word or group of words that tells whom or what a sentence is about

subject-verb agreement when the subject and verb in a sentence work together, or agree. A sentence with a singular subject must have a verb that works, or agrees, with a singular subject.

suffix a word part added at the end of a word to change its meaning and part of speech, such as -ly in *friendly*

summarize give the most important ideas of what was read. Readers summarize important information in the selection to keep track of what they are reading.

superlative adjective an adjective used to compare three or more people, places, or things. Add -est to most adjectives to make them superlative.

supporting detail piece of information that tells about the main idea

syllable a word part that contains a single vowel sound

symbolism the use of one thing to suggest something else; often the use of something concrete to stand for an abstract idea

synonym a word with the same or nearly the same meaning as another word

table of contents list of chapters, articles, or stories in a book. It appears at the beginning of the book.

tall tale a story that uses exaggeration

tempo (in speaking) the speed at which someone speaks

text structure the organization of a piece of writing. Text structures of informational text include cause/effect, chronological, compare/contrast, description, problem/solution, proposition/support, and ask/answer questions.

theme the big idea or author's message in a story

think aloud an instructional strategy in which a teacher verbalizes his or her thinking to model the process of comprehension or the application of a skill

timed reading a method of measuring fluency by determining words correct per minute (WCPM)

title the name of a written work; a word or abbreviation that can come before the name of a person, such as *Dr.* or *Mrs.*

tone author's attitude toward the subject or toward the reader

topic the subject of a discussion, conversation, or piece of text

topic sentence the sentence that tells the main idea of a paragraph

verb a word that tells what something or someone does or is

visualize picture in one's mind what is happening in the text. Visualizing helps readers imagine the things they read about.

volume (in speaking) degree of loudness of a speaker's voice

vowel digraph two vowels together that stand for a single sound, such as *oa* in *boat* or *ea* in *leaf*

vowel the letters *a, e, i, o, u,* and sometimes *y*

WCPM words correct per minute; the number of words read correctly in one minute

word analysis decoding a word by using its parts, such as suffixes, prefixes, and syllables

word family a group of words that rhyme and share the same phonogram, such as *fill, still, will*

D'Nealian™ Cursive

a b c d e f g
h i j k l m n
o p q r s t u
v w x y z

A B C D E F G
H I J K L M N
O P Q R S T U
V W X Y Z . , ' ?

1 2 3 4 5 6
7 8 9 10

D'Nealian™ Alphabet

a b c d e f g h i

j k l m n o p q r s t

u v w x y z

A B C D E F G

H I J K L M N O

P Q R S T U V

W X Y Z . , ' ?

1 2 3 4 5 6

7 8 9 10

Manuscript Alphabet

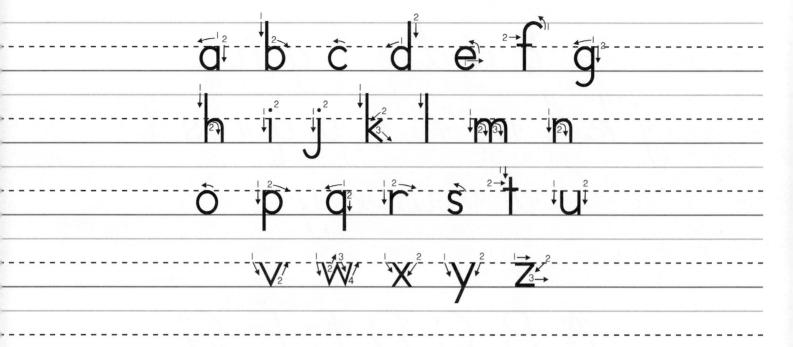

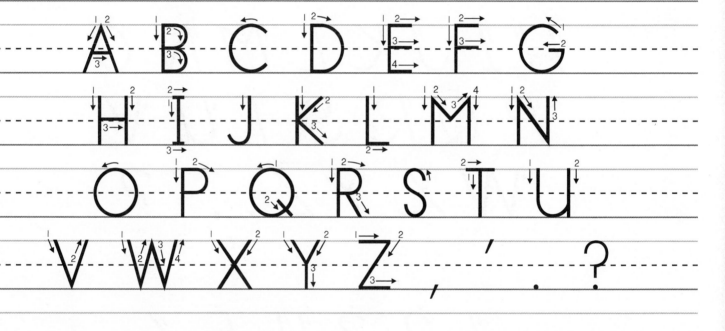

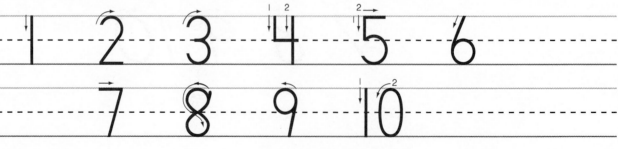

Reteach Lessons: Grade 3

Reteach Phonics

Reteach Comprehension

Reteach Phonics
Short Vowels

1 Teach

Remind students that knowing short vowel patterns can help them decode words. A single vowel in a short word or syllable usually makes a short vowel sound. These short vowel sounds usually occur at the beginning of the word or between two consonants.

Write *hat, bed, bib, mom, sun,* and *bread* on the board. Read the word *hat* aloud with students, stretching out the short *a* sound. Explain that the letter for the short *a* sound in *hat* is *a*. Continue the activity with the short vowel sound-spellings in the other words.

Write the following phrases on the board:

too late for <u>supper</u>   time for <u>breakfast</u>

<u>hot ham</u> for <u>lunch</u>   <u>fish</u> for <u>dinner</u>

Tell students that words with a VC/CV pattern are often divided into syllables, or parts, between the two consonants. Ask students to point to the letter or letters for the short vowel sound in each underlined word.

2 Practice

Write the following words on the board. Have students read each word. If the word has a short vowel sound, tell students to use the word in a sentence.

camp   dime   bend   hunt   spray

head   mitt   cube   shop   feet

Write the word *pan* on the board and have students write *pan* on a sheet of paper. Ask them to listen to your instructions and write the new words.

Change the *a* to *e*. Write the new word. (*pen*)
Change the *e* to *i*. Write the new word. (*pin*)
Change the *n* to *t*. Write the new word. (*pit*)
Change the *i* to *e*. Write the new word. (*pet*)
Change the *e* to *a*. Write the new word. (*pat*)
Change the *p* to *c*. Write the new word. (*cat*)

Reteach Phonics
Plural *-s, -es, -ies*

1 Teach

Write the following sentences on the board and read them aloud with students.

We picked cherries from the trees.
Grandma made pies.
Grandpa put them in boxes.

Tell students that when we talk or write about more than one person, animal, place, or thing, we use a plural noun. Remind students that while *-s* is added to the end of most words to make plurals, *-es* is added to words that end with *s, ss, x, ch,* or *sh,* and words that end with a consonant and *y* change the *y* to *i* and then add *-es.*

Underline the words *cherries, trees, pies,* and *boxes.* Have students read the word, identify the base word, tell what ending was added, *-s, -es,* or *-ies,* and explain why.

2 Practice

Draw a two-column chart on the board and label the columns *Singular Nouns* and *Plural Nouns.* Read the following words and have students write them in the appropriate column: *matches, dress, lion, benches, pencil, hammer, city, inches, wagons, brush, babies, apples.* Tell students to leave a space in the column next to each word so that they can fill in the missing singular or plural form for each word.

Singular Nouns	Plural Nouns
(match)	matches
dress	*(dresses)*
lion	*(lions)*
(bench)	benches
pencil	*(pencils)*
hammer	*(hammers)*

Reteach Phonics
Base Words and Endings
-ed, -ing, -er, -est

① Teach

Write these sentences on the board:

> *Peg cooks dinner for her family.*
> *Pete cooked eggs for breakfast.*
> *Paul is cooking hamburgers for lunch.*

Underline *cook* and tell students that *cook* is a base word. Adding *-ed* or *-ing* to the base word makes new words: *cooked, cooking.* Explain the four rules to remember when adding the endings *-ed, -ing, -er,* and *-est* to base words.

- Some base words do not change: *jump, jumped, jumping.*
- If a one-syllable base word ends with a consonant-vowel-consonant (CVC) pattern, double the final consonant: *skip, skipped, skipping.*
- If the base word ends with *e*, drop the *e*: *cute, cuter, cutest.*
- If the base word ends with *y*, change the *y* to *i* before adding *-ed, -er,* or *-est: easy, easier, easiest; try, tried.* Keep the *y* when adding *-ing: try, trying.*

② Practice

Draw a four-column chart as shown below:

No Change	Double Final Consonant	Drop *e*	Change *y* to *i*

Write the following words on self-stick notes: *started, singing, played, clapped, stopped, planned, saddest, shopping, waved, finest, smiling, tiniest, cried, frying, studied.* Have students take turns selecting a word, reading it aloud, and identifying the base word. Then have them stick their word on the chart in the appropriate column. When the chart is complete, have students choose a word to use in an oral sentence.

Reteach Phonics
Long Vowel Digraphs
ee, ea; ai, ay; oa, ow

① Teach

Remind students that understanding long vowel sounds can help them decode unfamiliar words. A long vowel sound says the name of the vowel.

Write the words *team, dear, feet,* and *cheer* on the board. Ask students what vowel sound they hear in these words. Frame *ea* or *ee* in each word and explain that *ea* and *ee* make the long *e* sound in these words.

Write the words *boat* and *grow* on the board. Ask students what vowel sound they hear in *boat* and *grow*. Frame *oa* or *ow* in each word and explain that *oa* and *ow* make the long *o* sound in *boat* and *grow*.

Write the words *pail, chair,* and *say* on the board. Say the words and ask students what vowel sound they hear in these words. Frame *ai* or *ay* in each word and explain that *ai* and *ay* make the long *a* sound in these words.

② Practice

Write the following words on the board:

   deep   east   fail   stay   moan   snow

Provide students with a set of the following word cards: *goat, clear, clay, steer, pair, peas, day, know, jail, screen, show, road, seem, tease, grown, chain, play, fair.* Read the words aloud with students. Tell them to sort the cards by vowel sounds. Have volunteers choose a word, identify the long vowel sound, and tell the letters for the sound. Then tell them to write the word on the board under the word that has the same vowel sound-spelling.

Reteach Phonics
Vowel Diphthongs
/ou/ *ou, ow;* /oi/ *oi, oy*

1 Teach

Remind students that sometimes when vowels are side by side, they make one sound, and this sound is called a vowel diphthong.

Write the words *out* and *now* on the board. Tell students that the vowel diphthong /ou/ can be spelled *ou* or *ow*. Underline the letters for /ou/.

Write the words *boy* and *coin* on the board. Explain to students that the vowel diphthong /oi/ can be spelled *oi* or *oy*. Underline the letters for /oi/.

Write *toy, noise, cloud,* and *clown* on the board. Ask students what vowel sound they hear in each word. Have them identify the letters that spell /ou/ and /oi/.

2 Practice

Write these sentences on the board:

> *The clown found a cow roaming around town.*
> *How did that mouse get in our house?*
> *We enjoyed the corn that Roy boiled.*
> *The sly boy buried gold coins in the soil.*

Ask students to read the sentences and underline the letters for the /ou/ and /oi/ sounds.

Prepare cards with the following words: *broil, spoil, point, moist, joy, toy, royal, employ, loud, ground, flour, blouse, shout, towel, down, scowl, gown, frown.*

Have students work with a partner to read and sort the words first by the vowel sounds /ou/ and /oi/ and then by the letters for the vowel sounds.

Reteach Phonics
Syllable Patterns
V/CV, VC/V

1 Teach

Write the words *bacon* and *lemon* on the board. Remind students that a word is made up of parts called syllables, and each syllable in a word has one vowel sound. The words *bacon* and *lemon* have two vowel sounds, so they have two syllables.

Point out the VCV pattern in bacon and show students how to divide the word into syllables by drawing a line between the first vowel and the consonant (V/CV). Tell students that when a word has a vowel-consonant-vowel pattern, the middle consonant usually goes with the second syllable, and the vowel sound in the first syllable is usually long—/bā/ /kən/.

Point out the VCV pattern in *lemon* and show students how to divide the word into syllables after the consonant (VC/V). Tell students that if they divide the word after the *e*, the vowel will have the long sound—/lē/ /mən/. But that doesn't sound like a word. Then they should put the middle consonant with the first syllable and the vowel sound in the first syllable will be short—/lem/ /ən/. That sounds like a word.

2 Practice

Write the following words on the board:

token	*seven*	*baker*
pupil	*robin*	*music*
future	*radar*	*limit*
tiger	*profit*	*river*
palace	*siren*	*cabin*

Draw a two-column chart with the headings *V/CV* and *VC/V*. Have students sort the words according to their syllable patterns by writing them in the appropriate columns. After the chart is completed, have students read each word and identify the vowel sound in the first syllable. Remind them that they may need to try different vowel sounds in the first syllable to figure out the word.

Reteach Phonics
Syllable Pattern C + *le*

1 Teach

Remind students that each syllable has one vowel sound. Write the word *table* on the board and underline the letters *ble*. Explain that when a consonant + *le* appears at the end of a word, the consonant + *le* forms the final syllable. Write the following sentence on the board. Read the sentence, emphasizing the consonant + *le* words.

> *Anna put a candle in the middle of the table.*

Repeat the words *candle, middle,* and *table* as you underline each word. Show students how to divide each word before the consonant + *le*: *mid/dle, can/dle, ta/ble*. Point out that if the first syllable ends in a consonant, the vowel sound is short, as in *middle* and *candle*. If the first syllable ends in a vowel, the vowel sound is long, as in *table*.

2 Practice

Display the following word cards on the chalk ledge: *jungle, ladle, bugle, pebble, maple, title, circle*. Read the following clues. As students guess each answer, have them write the word on a sheet of paper, divide the word into syllables, and read the word aloud.

> I'm a round shape. What am I? *(circle)*
> I'm a small rock. What am I? *(pebble)*
> I'm a place where lions and tigers live. What am I? *(jungle)*
> I'm a kind of tree. What am I? *(maple)*
> I'm a musical instrument. What am I? *(bugle)*
> I'm the name of a book. What am I? *(title)*
> I'm a kitchen tool. What am I? *(ladle)*

Reteach Phonics
Compound Words

1 ## Teach

Make cards for the words *fire, place, house, wood*, and *fighter*. Display the word cards on the chalk ledge. Tell students that a compound word is made from two smaller words that are put together. Point to the word cards *fire* and *fighter* and read each card separately. Slide the cards together and read the word *firefighter*. Explain that a *firefighter* is "a person who fights fires."

Repeat the routine using the word cards to make the compound words *fireplace, firehouse*, and *firewood*.

Tell students that if they know the meanings of the two smaller words in a compound word, they can often figure out the meaning of the compound word.

2 ## Practice

Write these sentences on the board:

> *I can't find my raincoat.*
> *I looked all around the classroom.*
> *Nobody has seen it.*
> *Is it in my backpack on the playground?*

Read the sentences aloud and point out that the underlined words are compound words. Ask students to identify the two smaller words that make up each compound word.

Make cards for the words *book, shelf, store, air, port, plane, sun, light, shine, set, rise, earth, worm, quake, home, town, work, made*, and *sick*. Have students make compound words using the word cards. List students' compound words on the board. Tell students to choose a compound word from the list and write a sentence using the compound word.

Reteach Phonics
Consonant Blends

1 Teach

Remind students that recognizing consonant blends will help them decode unfamiliar words. Write *squ, spl, scr, spr, str,* and *thr* on the board. Remind students that blends are two or more consonants grouped together, but each consonant or consonant digraph maintains its own sound. You can hear each sound.

Write the word *stripe* on the board and underline the consonant blend *str.* Tell students that when you say *stripe,* you hear /s/ /t/ /r/ at the beginning of the word.

Write these words on the board. Tell students to read the words and underline the consonant blend.

thread	*spray*	*scribble*	*brush*
squirt	*string*	*splash*	*plant*

2 Practice

Show students how to fold a sheet of paper into thirds horizontally and vertically to make a nine-square tic-tac-toe game board. Read the following words slowly and have students write each word in any square on their game board: *scrape, squint, scream, splash, sprinkle, strong, throat, thrill, straw.* Point out to students that each word on their game board begins with a consonant blend.

Tell students to listen to each word you say and to circle the words on their game board that begin with the same consonant blend. When a student has circled three words in a vertical, horizontal, or diagonal row, the student should raise his or her hand, read the words, and identify the consonant blend. Say these words one at a time: *stranger, throne, spring, scratch, split, squeeze.*

Reteach
Consonant Digraphs
sh, th, wh, ph, ch, tch,
/sh/ch, ng

1 Teach

Remind students that sometimes two consonants together make one sound. Point out, for example, that the consonants *c* and *h* together make the /ch/ sound in words such as *chicken* and *coach*. Write the following words on the board:

telephone	father	kitchen	singer
machine	teacher	fashion	whittle

Read each word, emphasizing the consonant digraph. Ask students to underline the consonants in each word that make one sound.

2 Practice

Have students suggest other words that begin or end with the consonant digraphs *sh, th, wh, ph, ch, tch,* /sh/*ch,* and *ng*. Have students list the words on a sheet of paper and underline the consonants in each word that stand for one sound.

Write the following words on index cards: *shed, bath, when, graph, chain, fetch, chef, ring*. Have students sit in a circle. Read the first word card aloud, pass it to the student on your left, and ask him or her to say another word with the same consonant digraph. If the student's response is correct, have him or her pass the card to the next student to continue the routine. When a student cannot respond with an appropriate word, start the routine over with another word card.

Reteach Phonics
Contractions

1 Teach

Remind students that a contraction is a shortened form of two words in which the words are joined together and an apostrophe replaces one or more letters. Write *you're* on the board and explain that *you're* is made from the two words *you are*. The apostrophe takes the place of the missing letter *a*.

Write these sentences on the board. Have students identify the contraction in each sentence and tell what two words are used to make the contraction.

They're identical twins.
Most people couldn't tell them apart.
I'm not sure which is which.
Isn't that twin Tom?

2 Practice

Write the following contractions on the board:

I'm	*you'll*	*we've*	*didn't*
it's	*there's*	*haven't*	*you're*
won't	*aren't*	*shouldn't*	*we'll*
she'll	*don't*	*hasn't*	*weren't*

Prepare cards for the following words: *I, you, we, she, did, it, there, have, are, should, do, has, were, am, will, not, is.* (Make more than one card for *will* and *not*.) Distribute the cards to students.

Read a contraction from the board and ask the two students who are holding the words that make this contraction to stand up. Have them identify the letter(s) replaced by the apostrophe and use the contraction in an oral sentence.

Reteach Phonics
Prefixes *un-, re-, mis-, dis-, non-*

1 Teach

Write these sentences on the board and underline the prefix *un-* in the second sentence.

> Jan wrapped her gift in colorful paper.
> Ted <u>un</u>wrapped the gift quickly.

Remind students that a prefix is a group of letters added at the beginning of a base word. Adding a prefix changes the meaning of the base word.

Tell students that the prefixes *un-, dis-,* and *non-* mean "not" or "the opposite of." Write the words *unhappy, disobey,* and *nonfiction* on the board and underline the prefixes. Explain that *unhappy* means "not happy," *disobey* means "the opposite of obey," and *nonfiction* means "the opposite of fiction" or "not fiction."

Write the words *misbehave* and *rewrite* on the board and underline the prefixes. Explain that the prefix *mis-* means "badly or wrongly," so *misbehave* means "behave badly." The prefix *re-* means "again," so *rewrite* means "write again."

2 Practice

Write the following on the board:

> *un-, dis-, non-* = not, the opposite of
> *re-* = again
> *mis-* = badly, wrongly

Ask students to write words that mean

- "the opposite of _____" by adding a prefix to *tidy, respect, agree, stop, common,* and *profit.*
- "_____ again" by adding a prefix to *copy* and *pack.*
- "_____ wrongly" by adding a prefix to *use* and *understand.*

Have students use a word from above to complete each sentence:

> A room that is not neat is _____. *(untidy)*
> A person who talks during a play shows _____ to the actors and the audience. *(disrespect)*
> If a plane flies straight from Chicago to Houston, it is a _____ flight. *(nonstop)*
> If you can't close your suitcase, you will have to _____ it. *(repack)*
> If you don't speak clearly, others may _____ you. *(misunderstand)*

Reteach Phonics
Consonants /j/g, j, dge; /s/s, c; /k/c, k, ck, ch

1 Teach

Write these sentences on the board and read them aloud with students:

> *Ginger gave the message to the judge.*
> *Officer Sam saw the notice at the city center.*
> *Kate came over to pick up the chameleon.*

Reread the first sentence and have students raise their hand when they hear /j/. Point out that /j/ can be spelled *g, j,* or *dge.* Underline the letters that spell /j/ in *Ginger, messa~~g~~e,* and *jud~~ge~~.*

Reread the second sentence and have students clap their hands when they hear /s/. Point out that /s/ can be spelled *s* or *c.* Underline the letters that spell /s/ in *Officer, Sam, saw, notice, city,* and *center.*

Reread the third sentence and have students tap their feet when they hear /k/. Point out that /k/ can be spelled *c, k, ck,* or *ch.* Underline the letters that spell /k/ in *Kate, came, pick,* and *chameleon.*

Ask students to silently brainstorm words with /j/, /s/, and /k/. Call on different students to offer words. As they say their words, write them on the board and circle the words that spell the target sound-spellings.

2 Practice

Write the following words on self-stick notes: *advice, badge, cane, celery, cement, chemistry, choir, curve, dance, dodge, gentle, giant, gym, jumper, jeep, job, kettle, kind, kitten, locket, manager, minus, orange, picnic, prince, register, ridge, snack, south, voice.*

Draw a three-column chart with the headings /j/, /s/, and /k/. Have students choose a self-stick note, read the word aloud, and place it in the appropriate column of the chart. When all the words have been sorted, have students sort the words again, this time according to their spellings for /j/, /s/, and /k/. Have students pick one word from each of the three groups and write a sentence using all three words.

Reteach Phonics
Suffixes *-ly, -ful, -ness, -less, -able, -ible*

1 Teach

Write these suffixes and their meanings on the board:

-ly   in a _____ way   *-ness* state of being _____
-less without _____   *-able* able to be _____
-ful full of _____   *-ible* able to be _____

Tell students that a suffix is a group of letters added to the end of a base word. The suffix adds a syllable to the base word and changes its meaning. For example, adding *-ly* to the base word quick makes the word *quickly*, which means "in a quick way."

Explain how adding *-ful, -less, -ness, -able,* and *-ible* to the words *peace, air, sick, pack,* and *flex* makes new words with new meanings.

Ask students to identify the base word and suffix in the following words:

healthful   *slowly*   *acceptable*
darkness   *spotless*   *reversible*

2 Practice

Have students choose a base word and suffix from the chart to make a word to complete each sentence below. Read the sentences slowly and have students write the new words on a sheet of paper.

Base Words	Suffixes
notice	-able
use	-ly
cheer	-ful
brave	-less
access	-ness
harm	-ible

A snow shovel is _____ in Hawaii. *(useless)*
The knight _____ defended the castle. *(bravely)*
Although my dog has a loud bark, he is _____. *(harmless)*
Ramps and board paths make the new park _____. *(accessible)*
The clown's pink and purple hair was _____. *(noticeable)*
The _____ crossing guard smiled at the children. *(cheerful)*

Ask students to use the new words in their own oral sentences.

Reteach Phonics
Silent Consonants
wr, kn, st, mb, gn

1 Teach

Write this sentence on the board:

Dad hung the wreath on the knob.

Blend the word wreath as you run your fingers under the letters. Point out that the beginning sound in *wreath* is /r/ and underline the letters *wr*. Explain to students that sometimes a letter does not make a sound in a word; it is silent, like the *w* in *wreath*. Ask students to list other words that begin with *wr* on the board.

Have students repeat the word *knob* and listen for the beginning sound. Point out that although /n/ in *knob* is spelled *kn*, the *k* is silent. Ask students to think of other *kn* words.

Use the words *gnarl*, *climb*, and *listen* to review the silent consonants in *gn*, *mb*, and *st*.

2 Practice

Write the following questions on the board and read them aloud with students. Have them tell what sound the underlined letters make.

Can a <u>kn</u>ight <u>kn</u>it a sweater?
Will you fa<u>st</u>en the <u>wh</u>istle around your neck?
Does a <u>gn</u>ome wear colo<u>gn</u>e?
Why did that lam<u>b</u> eat cookie cru<u>mb</u>s?
Can you <u>wr</u>ite with a broken <u>wr</u>ist?

Write these words on the board:

gnat   comb   listen   wrong   knock

Have students write a word with a silent letter to complete each of these sentences:

A _____ answer is incorrect. *(wrong)*
If you want to look neat, be sure to _____ your hair. *(comb)*
I like to _____ to music. *(listen)*
Always _____ before opening the door. *(knock)*
A _____ is a small insect. *(gnat)*

Reteach Phonics
Plurals *-f, -fe* to *-ves;*
Irregular Plurals

① Teach

Remind students that we use the plural form of a noun when we mean more than one. The plurals of most nouns are made by adding an *-s* to the singular form, but some plurals are made in other ways. Write these phrases on the board:

one wolf	*one knife*
a pack of wol<u>ves</u>	*a set of kni<u>ves</u>*

Underline the *ves* in *wolves*. Explain that *wolves* is the plural form of *wolf*. To make the plural, change the final *f* to *v* and add *-es*. Ask students how the plural of *knife* is formed.

Remind students that some nouns have completely different spellings for their plurals. These are called irregular plurals. Use the nouns *mouse/mice, child/children, woman/women, tooth/teeth,* and *man/men* in sentences.

② Practice

Have students draw a chart as shown below without the words. Read each of the following sentences aloud. Have students identify two or more plural nouns in each sentence and write the plurals in the appropriate columns in the chart.

Plurals with *-s*	Other Plurals
pots	women
spoons	elves
forks	teeth
students	men
books	knives
bags	shelves
coins	thieves
piles	leaves

The women stirred the pots of soup.
The elves brushed their teeth twice a day.
The men washed the spoons, knives, and forks.
The students put their books on the shelves.
The sneaky thieves stole bags of coins.
We raked the leaves into big piles.

Reteach Phonics
R-controlled /er/
er, ir, ur, ear, or

① Teach

Write these sentences on the board and read them aloud, emphasizing the words with /er/. Ask students what vowel sound they hear several times in each sentence.

> *The early birds perched on the birch's branches.*
> *That girl purchased the biggest purse in the world.*

Remind students that vowels followed by *r* sound different than the same vowels alone. Underline the words with /er/. Point out that /er/ can be spelled *er, ir, ur, ear,* or *or.*

② Practice

Write the following letter on chart paper and underline each word that is spelled incorrectly. Ask students to rewrite the letter on a sheet of paper and to correct each misspelled word.

Dear Aunt Sue,

   Last Thirsday my class took a field trip. We went to a supirb farm. Furst I saw many terkeys. Then I saw beautiful furns. I also saw pigs with cirly tails. We watched the farmer's wife chirn butter. I thought we left too urly. In one wurd—our trip was fantastic!!

Annie

Reteach Phonics
Prefixes *pre-, mid-, over-, out-, bi-*

① Teach

Write the prefixes *pre-, mid-, over-, out-,* and *bi-* on the board. Remind students that these are prefixes. A prefix is a group of letters added to the beginning of a base word. The prefix changes the meaning of the base word. Review the meanings of these prefixes:

pre-	before
mid-	in the middle
over-	too much
out-	go beyond; too great
bi-	two, twice

Write the word *prewash* on the board. Explain the different meanings of the words *wash* and *prewash.* Point out that adding the prefix *pre-* to the base word *wash* changes the meaning of wash. *Prewash* means "wash before." Ask students to explain how adding prefixes changes the meanings of the following words: *preview, midstream, bicycle, overtime, outgrow.*

② Practice

Write the following words on the board. Ask students to first identify the base word and prefix and then choose a word to complete each sentence.

bimonthly	*outrun*	*oversleep*
midnight	*preheat*	

I set my alarm clock for 8 a.m. so that I wouldn't _____.
(oversleep)

Our class magazine comes out _____ during the school year.
(bimonthly)

At _____ the hall clock chimed twelve times. *(midnight)*

My dog is so fast that he can _____ me every time. *(outrun)*

I _____ the oven, and then I put the meat loaf in. *(preheat)*

Reteach Phonics
Suffixes
-er, -or, -ess, -ist

1 Teach

Remind students that a suffix is a group of letters that is added to the end of the base word. The suffix changes the meaning of the base word. The suffixes *-er, -or,* and *-ist* are added to base words to make new words that mean "one who _____." Write *speak* and *speaker* on the board. Explain that adding the suffix *-er* to the base word *speak* makes the word *speaker*, which means "one who speaks."

Write the words *act, actor,* and *actress* on the board. Underline the suffixes *-or* and *-ess*. Tell students that the suffix *-or* added to the base word *act* makes the word *actor*, which means "one who acts." The suffix *-ess* added to the base word act makes the word *actress*, which means "a female actor." Other words with the *-ess* suffix are *princess, lioness, hostess,* and *heiress.*

2 Practice

Write the following base words on the board:

art	*tour*	*invent*	*host*
edit	*farm*	*read*	*govern*
violin	*paint*	*teach*	*guitar*

Have students form new words by adding *-er, -or, -ess,* or *-ist* to the base words. Then ask students to use the new words to complete these sentences.

A person who farms is a _____. *(farmer)*
A person who reads is a _____. *(reader)*
A person who edits books is an _____. *(editor)*
A woman who hosts a party is a _____. *(hostess)*
A person who plays the violin is a _____. *(violinist)*
A person who invents things is an _____. *(inventor)*
A person who plays the guitar is a _____. *(guitarist)*
A person who paints pictures is a _____. *(painter)*
A person who tours the world is a _____. *(tourist)*
A person who governs a state is a _____. *(governor)*
A person who teaches is a _____. *(teacher)*
A person who creates art is an _____. *(artist)*

Reteach Phonics
Syllable Patterns
VC/CCV, VCC/CV

1 Teach

Write the words *control, explode,* and *westward* on the board. Remind students that each syllable in a word has one vowel sound. The words *control, explode,* and *westward* each have two vowel sounds; therefore, the words each have two syllables.

Tell students that words with three or more consonants in the middle almost always contain a blend or a digraph. Underline the *tr, pl,* and *st* blends in *control, explode,* and *westward.* Point out the VCCCV pattern in the words and show students how to divide each word between the consonant and the consonant blend (VC/CCV or VCC/CV). Remind them that the letters in a blend or digraph always stay together. Tell students that recognizing the VCCCV pattern in two-syllable words can help them decode words: when the syllable ends in a consonant, like the syllable *con* in *control,* sometimes the vowel sound is short.

Write this sentence on the board:

The partners made a hundred sandwiches.

Read the sentence aloud and have volunteers underline the words with the VCCCV pattern. Have them draw a line between the syllables in each word: *part/ners, hun/dred, sand/wich/es.*

2 Practice

Have students write the following words on index cards: *complete, purchase, pilgrim, monster, merchant, inspect, constant, explain, handsome, orphan.* Ask them to take turns reading words aloud and folding cards to show the syllables.

Write these words on the board:

   dolphin   orchard   improve   panther

Give these clues. Have students write the word that answers the clue on a sheet of paper. Orally review the clues and answers as students draw a line between the syllables in each word.

This mammal lives in the ocean. *(dolphin)*
If you get better at something, you do this. *(improve)*
This is a place where apples grow. *(orchard)*
This is a wild black cat. *(panther)*

Reteach Phonics
Syllable Pattern
CV/VC

1 Teach

Write this sentence on the board and underline the words *duet* and *piano*.

Jim and Jan played a duet on the piano.

Read the sentence aloud and repeat the word *duet*, stressing the syllables. Remind students that each syllable has one vowel sound. Ask them to identify the vowel sounds in *duet*. Draw a line between *u* and *e*. Explain to students that only a few words divide between the vowels. The vowel in the first syllable is usually long, like the *u* in *duet*, because the syllable ends in a vowel. Repeat the routine with *piano*.

Write the words *create* and *idea* on the board. Read the words aloud and ask students how many syllables they hear. Draw a line between the syllables in each word as you point out the CV/VC pattern.

2 Practice

Write the following words on the board and have students copy them on a sheet of paper. Read the words aloud and tell students to cross out any words that do not have the CV/VC pattern.

science	*stereo*	*radio*	*rabbit*
cameo	*boat*	*lion*	*canoe*
does	*poet*	*jail*	*triumph*

On the board, draw a two-column chart with the headings *Two-Syllable Words* and *Three-Syllable Words*. Have students take turns coming to the board and writing a CV/VC word from their paper in the correct column on the chart.

Reteach Phonics
Homophones

① ## Teach

Write these sentences on the board:

Ken <u>ate</u> a piece of pie.
Trina read <u>eight</u> books.

Remind students that *ate* and *eight* are called homophones. Homophones are words that sound alike but have different spellings and meanings. Tell students that they can use context clues to help determine the meaning of a homophone.

Write the following homophone pairs on the board and ask students to choose a homophone to complete each of the following sentences.

pear	*our*	*blew*
pair	*hour*	*blue*

I picked a juicy _____ off the tree. *(pear)*
I bought a new _____ of shoes. *(pair)*
_____ house is one block from the school. *(Our)*
I try to read for one _____ every day. *(hour)*
The wind _____ the leaves off the tree. *(blew)*
The color of my favorite sweater is _____. *(blue)*

② ## Practice

Write the following homophone pairs on the board. Have students write a sentence for each homophone in the pair, leaving a blank for the homophone. Have students exchange papers and write the correct homophone to complete each sentence.

dear	*hear*	*I*	*seen*	*fare*
deer	*here*	*eye*	*scene*	*fair*

Reteach Phonics
Vowel Sound in *ball*:
a, au, aw, al

1 Teach

Write the words *wall*, *squawk*, *paw*, and *walk* on the board. Ask students what vowel sound they hear in all four words. Underline *a* in *wall*, *au* in *squawk*, *aw* in *paw*, and *al* in *walk*. Point out that the /ȯ/ vowel sound can be spelled *a*, *au*, *aw*, or *al*.

Write the following words on the board and ask students to identify the word in each row that does not have the same vowel sound as the other two words.

mall	*mail*	*thaw*
hawk	*launch*	*heart*
start	*pause*	*lawyer*
August	*laundry*	*April*
yawn	*marsh*	*sausage*

2 Practice

Write the following words on the board:

talk	*autumn*	*small*
always	*awful*	*launch*

Ask students to write the word from the board that means the opposite of each of these words:

1. land   *(launch)*
2. large   *(small)*
3. wonderful   *(awful)*
4. never   *(always)*
5. spring   *(autumn)*
6. listen   *(talk)*

Have students unscramble the sets of letters below to make words that have the vowel sound in *ball*.

wstar (straw)	*fulat (fault)*	*thoaru (author)*
lmta (malt)	*lcla (call)*	*csaeu (sauce)*
luah (haul)	*ndwa (dawn)*	*wlac (claw)*

Have students sort and rewrite the words according to the spelling patterns for /ȯ/.

Reteach Phonics
Vowel Sound in *ball*: *augh, ough*

1 Teach

Write this sentence on the board:

I bought my daughter new shoes.

Read the sentence aloud. Then repeat the words *bought* and *daughter*, emphasizing the /ȯ/ vowel sound. Point out that the words have the same vowel sound but different spellings for that vowel sound. Frame the letters *ough* in *bought* and the letters *augh* in *daughter* and point out that /ȯ/ can be spelled *ough* or *augh*.

Write the following words on the board and have students identify and repeat the words that have the vowel sound in *ball*.

country	*tooth*	*ought*	*salute*
naughty	*caught*	*would*	*fought*

2 Practice

Write the following sentences on the board and have students copy them on a sheet of paper. Tell students to circle the spelling patterns for the /ȯ/ vowel sound in the underlined words. Have students read the sentences aloud.

We <u>bought</u> fresh corn at the farmers' market.
Uncle Ted <u>taught</u> me to play the piano.
The <u>naughty</u> puppy chewed a hole in the shoe.
The outfielder <u>caught</u> the ball.
I <u>thought</u> the party started at 5:00 p.m.
My dad <u>brought</u> a pizza home for dinner.

Reteach Phonics
Vowel Patterns
ei, eigh

1 Teach

Write the following sentence on the board:

The reindeer pulled the sleigh through the snow.

Read the sentence aloud. Repeat the words *reindeer* and *sleigh*, placing emphasis on the vowel pattern *ei* in reindeer and *eigh* in *sleigh*. Underline *ei* in r<u>ei</u>ndeer and *eigh* in sl<u>eigh</u>. Explain that these are long vowels that make the same long *a* sound, even though they are spelled differently.

Write the following words on the board, and ask students to identify the word in each row that has a long vowel pattern spelled with *ei* or *eigh*.

cat	rein	find
park	wide	weigh
vein	window	freight

2 Practice

Write the following sentences on the board:

The king reigns over his subjects.
Our neighbor mows his lawn every week.
There are eight people standing in line for ice cream.

Read the sentences aloud. Have students write each sentence on a sheet of paper. Ask students to underline the word with the vowel patterns *ei* or *eigh* in each sentence, and circle the vowel pattern in each underlined word. Have students read the sentences aloud.

Reteach Phonics
Suffixes
-y, -ish, -hood, -ment

1 Teach

List these suffixes and their meanings on the board.

-y   having _____
-ish   like a _____
-hood   state or quality of _____
-ment   act or process of _____

Remind students that a suffix is a group of letters that is added to the end of a base word. The suffix changes the meaning of the base word.

Write the words *dirty*, *foolish*, *brotherhood*, and *enjoyment* in a second list on the board. Point out that suffixes have been added to base words to make these words. Ask students to identify the base word and suffix in each word and tell the word's meaning.

2 Practice

Write these base words and suffixes on the board.

child   neighbor   agree   cloudy
-y   -ish   -hood   -ment

Read the following sentences. Have students add a suffix to a base word and write the new word to complete one of the sentences.

A day with a sky full of clouds is a _____ day. *(cloudy)*
A contract between two people is an _____. *(agreement)*
Another name for a community is a _____. *(neighborhood)*
A person who acts silly and immature is _____. *(childish)*

Reteach Phonics
Vowel Sounds in *moon* and *foot:* *oo, ew, ue, ui, u*

1 Teach

Write *moon, grew, clue,* and *juice* on the board. Have students read the words aloud and identify the vowel sound in the words. Frame *oo* in *moon* and explain that these are letters for /ü/ in *moon.* Frame *ew* in *grew* and explain that these are letters for /ü/ in *grew.* Frame *ue* in *clue* and explain that these are the letters for /ü/ in *clue.* Frame *ui* in *juice* and explain that these are the letters for /ü/ in *juice.* Point out that the four words have the same vowel sound, but different letters spell the vowel sound in each word.

Write *foot* and *put* on the board. Underline *oo* and *u.* Repeat the words several times, emphasizing the vowel sound. Point out to students that the letters *oo* and *u* spell the /ù/ vowel sound they hear in *foot* and *put.*

2 Practice

Write the following story on the board.

> *Marty Moose had a loose tooth.*
> *Marty felt blue because he could not chew.*
> *Then Marty had a good idea.*
> *He hooked a loop of string around his tooth.*
> *He pushed and pulled and soon it flew out.*
> *Marty said, "This is cool! Now I can eat fruit!"*

Tell students to divide a sheet of paper into four squares and write one of these spelling patterns in each square: *oo, ew, ue, ui.* Tell students to sort the /ü/ words from the story according to their spellings by writing them in the appropriate squares. Tell students to circle the /ü/ words and underline the sound-spelling in each word.

194

Reteach Phonics
Unaccented Syllables (Schwa)

① Teach

Write the following words on the board:

about   *upon*   *pilot*   *circus*

As you say each word, emphasize the unaccented syllable that contains the schwa sound. Explain to students that the schwa sound is the vowel sound they hear in the first syllable of *about* and *upon* and in the second syllable of *pilot* and *circus*. The schwa sound, which sounds like "uh," can be spelled by the vowels *a, e, i, o,* and *u.*

Tell students that in English most words that have two or more syllables have at least one schwa sound. Remind them that a syllable with the schwa sound is always unstressed and said very quickly. Write /ə/ on the board and tell students that this is the symbol for the schwa sound.

Write the following words on the board, read them aloud, and have students circle the vowel for the schwa sound in each word:

extra   *happen*   *paper*
focus   *family*   *atom*

② Practice

Display word cards for the following words, one at a time. Have students identify the letter for the schwa sound in each word and read the word.

future	*celebrate*	*afraid*	*astronaut*
cabinet	*mammal*	*pencil*	*sailor*
removal	*enemy*	*correct*	*sentence*
volunteer	*product*	*dragon*	*easily*

Have students sort the cards according to the letters that spell the schwa sound in the words. Tell them to use a dictionary to confirm their word sorts. Remind students to look for /ə/ in the respelling in each word's dictionary entry.

Reteach Phonics
Final Syllables
-tion, -sion, -ion, -ture, -ive, -ize

1 Teach

Write these words on the board:

infection	*solution*	*culture*
centralize	*expansion*	*effective*

Say the word *infection* and clap out the syllables. Point out that you clapped three times because *infection* has three word parts, or syllables.

Repeat the routine with the words *solution, culture, centralize, expansion,* and *sensitive.* Ask students to tell how many syllables each word has. Tell them that dividing a word into syllables can make reading the word easier.

Underline *-ion* in *infection, -tion* in *solution,* and *-sion* in *expansion* and point out that *-ion, -tion,* and *-sion* are all pronounced /shən/.

Underline *-ture* in *culture, -ize* in *centralize,* and *-ive* in *effective.* Explain that, as with *-ion/-tion/-sion, -ture, -ive,* and *-ize* add a syllable to a word.

2 Practice

Write the following word equations on the board:

mix + ture	*legal + ize*	*act + ive*
expand + sion	*televise + ion*	*mass + ive*
convene + tion	*modern + ize*	*react + ion*
general + ize	*attend + tion*	*decide + sion*

Have students fold a sheet of papers into thirds vertically and label the columns *2 syllables, 3 syllables,* and *4 syllables.* Ask students to solve the word equations by combining the base words and suffixes to make new words. Remind them that they may need to modify some words by dropping a letter or two before adding the suffix. Then have them count the syllables in the new words and write the words in the appropriate columns on their paper.

Reteach Phonics
Prefixes *im-*, *in-*

1 Teach

Write the following words on the board:

correct   incorrect
polite   impolite

Underline the prefixes *in-* and *im-*. Remind students that a prefix is a group of letters that is added to the beginning of a base word. A prefix changes the base word's meaning. Explain that the prefixes *in-* and *im-* mean "not." Read the words aloud and ask students to tell how the prefixes *in-* and *im-* change the meanings of the base words *correct* and *polite*.

Write these sentences on the board.

The facts in the magazine article were accurate.
The people standing in line were patient.

Read the sentences aloud. Ask students how adding the prefix *in-* to *accurate* and the prefix *im-* to *patient* changes the meanings of the base words. Write the words *inaccurate* and *impatient* in the sentences and discuss these words change the meanings of the sentences.

2 Practice

Write these base words on the board:

formal   possible   active   visible
movable   expensive   perfect   passable

Read the following sentences. Have students add the prefix *in-* or *im-* to one of the base words to make a new word that completes each sentence. As students figure out each answer, tell them to write the word on a sheet of paper. Have students draw a line between the syllables in each word they write.

The scratched table is _____. *(imperfect)*
A person who doesn't exercise is _____. *(inactive)*
Something that can't be seen is _____. *(invisible)*
We use _____ language when we talk to our friends. *(informal)*
The snowstorm made the road _____. *(impassable)*
Something that can't be done is _____. *(impossible)*
The boulder was so big that it was _____. *(immovable)*
Something that is not costly is _____. *(inexpensive)*

Reteach Phonics
Related Words

1 ## Teach

Write the following sentences on the board and ask students to look for two words that are similar.

Kate is able to do a back flip.
A good gymnast has that ability.

Underline *able* and *ability*. Tell students that *able* and *ability* are related words. Explain that related words have parts that are similar but pronounced differently. Often the emphasized syllable changes.

Write the following related words on the board. Have students read them aloud and underline the similar word parts.

sign   signal
heal   health
crumb   crumble

2 ## Practice

Arrange word cards for *anger, nature, unity, major, meter,* and *compose* on the chalk ledge. Display word cards for the following words, one at a time and have students match the related words.

angry   natural   unite
majority   metric   composition

Have students write a word that is related to the underlined word in each sentence to complete the sentence:

The famous <u>poet</u> Joyce Kilmer wrote the _____ "Trees."
(poem)
Solve the <u>equation</u> to find out how to divide an orange into
_____ parts. *(equal)*
The teacher decided to _____, so she handed in her
<u>resignation</u>. *(resign)*
The <u>humans</u> cared for the animals in a _____ way. *(humane)*
The _____ weightlifter has strong, well-developed <u>muscles</u>.
(muscular)

Reteach Comprehension
Character

Understanding character helps readers comprehend a story and make good predictions about what will happen next. Use this routine to help students understand character.

① Review Character

Remind students that characters are the people or animals in a story. Readers learn about characters by thinking about what they do, say, and think and how they interact with other characters. Readers make inferences about characters by thinking about these clues and their own experiences.

② Teach Character Development

Explain that events in a story often cause a character to change in an important way. Such a change might be in a character's attitudes or beliefs. Students should read to see if this happens to the main character.

③ Model Inferring Traits

Provide an example from a story you have read. Model making inferences about a character from the character's words and actions. Point out how and why the character changes. Compare characters with each other and with real people.

④ Apply To a Selection

Read with students a story in which there are well-developed characters. Have students draw conclusions about characters from clues in the story and their own experiences.

⑤ Use a Graphic Organizer

Have students record clues about a character in a web. They can record details about what the character says and does and how characters interact. Remind students that they can extend the web by adding as many ovals and connecting lines as they need.

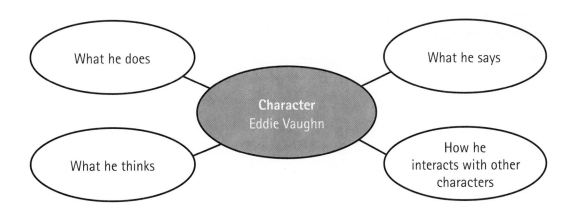

Reteach Comprehension
Setting

When students can describe the setting of a story—both place and time—they better understand the story. Use this routine to teach setting.

1 Define Setting

Explain that setting is the time and place in which a story takes place. It may be general (large forest) or it may be specific (Sutter's Mill, California, 1849).

2 Teach Setting

Explain that sometimes an author tells what the setting is, but sometimes a reader has to figure it out from details in the story. Tell students to look for details that help them visualize the setting.

3 Model Analyzing Setting

Choose a passage that describes a setting from a story students have not read. Model analyzing the setting from descriptions and details. Ask questions like these:

- Does the author or narrator tell you directly where and when the story takes place?

- What are some descriptions and details that help you figure out the setting?

- Do any character's actions help you figure out the setting? (for example, waiting for a bus, looking in the refrigerator)

4 Use a Graphic Organizer

Have students fill in a web with details that help them visualize the setting of a story. Tell them to look for details that describe the sights, sounds, feelings, tastes, and smells. Remind students that they can add as many ovals and connecting lines as they need.

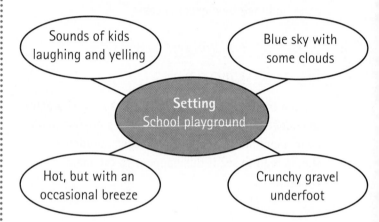

Reteach Comprehension
Theme

Students who determine the theme of a story understand the "why" of the story, the point the author is trying to make. Use this routine to teach theme.

1 Define Theme

Explain that the theme is a big idea about life that is the basic meaning of a story. A theme can be stated in a generalization, such as "Family is important." Sometimes the theme is stated, but more often it is implied.

2 Model Finding the Theme

Discuss with students a story they all know, such as a folk tale or fairy tale. Review the characters and events of the story. Then model finding their theme by thinking about story events and characters. Often, theme is the result of what a character wants and the outcome of his or her trying to get it.

Explain that students should give details from the story to support a theme.

3 Practice Choosing a Theme

Before students state a theme on their own, have them choose themes from options. Offer three possible theme statements for a story. Have students choose the one they think is best and explain why.

4 Use a Graphic Organizer

Rework a main idea chart. Change the Main Idea box to read *Theme*. Have students write a theme statement and supporting details.

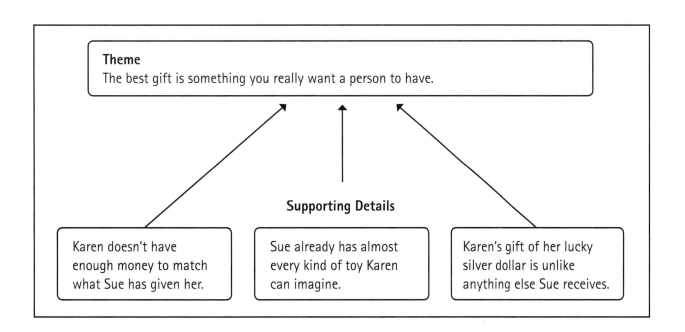

Theme
The best gift is something you really want a person to have.

Supporting Details

Karen doesn't have enough money to match what Sue has given her.

Sue already has almost every kind of toy Karen can imagine.

Karen's gift of her lucky silver dollar is unlike anything else Sue receives.

Reteach Comprehension
Sequence

Keeping track of the sequence of events helps students understand what they read. Use this routine to help students develop sequence skills.

① Discuss Sequence

Tell students it is important to keep track of the sequence, or order, of events to understand some stories and articles. Discuss a story recently read in which the sequence of events was important to a correct understanding of the story.

② Teach Clue Words

Write clue words on the board that can signal sequence, such as *first*, *next*, *then*, and *finally*. Explain that these words show the order in which things happen. Also teach that dates and times of the day signal sequence.

③ Sequence Sentence Strips

Write a clear sequence of events on sentence strips. Partners can work together to place the strips in the correct order. They can retell the events, inserting clue words to show the sequence.

④ Record a Sequence On a Chart

- After reading a story, students can work in pairs to create story sequence charts to show the order of events.

- For a nonfiction selection, partners can create time lines to show the chronological (time order) sequence of events.

Beginning
Meg can't figure out what she can get for her mother's birthday that will be special.

Middle
She asks Grandma Pearl, who suggests that she paint a family portrait and add faces copied from photos in Grandma's album.

End
Meg's mother is surprised and thrilled by Meg's thoughtful gift.

Reteach Comprehension
Compare and Contrast

Noticing, understanding, and making comparisons and contrasts can clarify for students what they read. Use this routine to teach comparing and contrasting.

1 Define the Terms

Explain that when you compare and contrast, you tell how two things are alike and different. Point out that, in some contexts, questions asking students to compare may be asking students to describe both similarities and differences.

2 Give an Example

Provide a simple example, such as comparing an apple and a banana.

- Alike: Both are fruits; both grow on trees; both are good for you.

- Different: One is red; the other is yellow. One is round; the other is long and thin. With one you can eat the skin; with the other you throw away the peel.

3 Discuss Clue Words

Students should look for clue words that signal comparisons and contrasts as they read. List some examples on the board:

Compare	Contrast
like	unlike
alike	on the other hand
similarly	however

4 Use a Venn Diagram

Students can use a Venn diagram to record comparisons and contrasts.

5 Provide Practice

- Ask students to compare and contrast two characters in a story or two characters in different stories.

- Ask students to compare and contrast information in a nonfiction article.

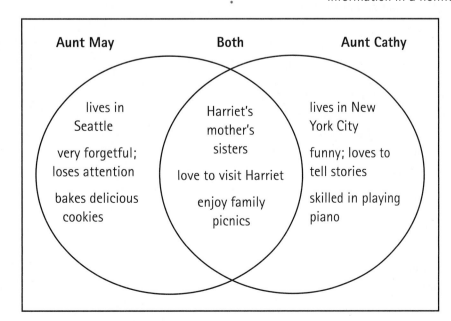

Aunt May — Both — Aunt Cathy

Aunt May: lives in Seattle; very forgetful; loses attention; bakes delicious cookies

Both: Harriet's mother's sisters; love to visit Harriet; enjoy family picnics

Aunt Cathy: lives in New York City; funny; loves to tell stories; skilled in playing piano

Reteach Comprehension
Author's Purpose and Viewpoint

Evaluating the author's purpose for writing helps students decide how quickly or slowly and carefully to read. Inferring the author's viewpoint helps students evaluate the information given. Use this routine to teach author's purpose and viewpoint.

① Discuss Author's Purpose

Explain that the author's purpose is the author's reason or reasons for writing. Four common reasons for writing are to persuade, to inform, to entertain, or to express ideas or feelings.

② Explain Its Use

Tell students that one reason they need to consider the author's purpose is to adjust their reading rate. If a story is meant to be fun, they may decide to read quickly. If the author wants to explain how something works, they may need to read slowly and carefully.

③ Explain Author's Viewpoint

Explain that the author's viewpoint is the way he or she looks at the subject—his or her opinion of the subject. To learn the author's viewpoint, look at what the author says and leaves out and at the opinions the author expresses.

④ Ask Questions

Authors don't usually state their purposes for writing, and they often have more than one purpose. Before, during, and after reading a selection, students should ask questions to help them draw conclusions about the author's purposes and viewpoint:

- *Why did the author write this selection?*

- *What is the author trying to tell readers?*

- *How does the author seem to feel about that?*

⑤ Ask Questions

Have students predict the author's purpose before reading by previewing the title, illustrations, and graphics. During and after reading, students should check and confirm their predictions. Have them record ideas and evidence in a three-column chart. Do the same for the author's viewpoint.

	Author's Purpose	Why Do You Think So?
Before you read: What do you think it will be?	to entertain	The characters are animals, but they act like people.
After you read: What was it?	to entertain and to teach a lesson	The story was fun to read, and the animals learned a lesson at the end.

Reteach Comprehension
Main Idea/Details

Determining the main idea in a text helps readers distinguish between important and less important information. When students can correctly identify the main idea, they understand the gist of what they read. Use this routine to teach main idea.

1 ## Explain Its Use

Explain that finding the main idea is an important tool in helping students understand and remember what they read.

2 ## Define the Terms

Explain that the topic is the subject, what the selection is all about. The main idea is the most important idea about the topic. The main idea can be stated in a sentence.

3 ## Model Finding the Main Idea

Read a nonfiction paragraph with a stated main idea. Have students identify the topic by asking: *What is this paragraph about?* Then model how you determine the main idea.

4 ## Finding Supporting Details

Explain that supporting details are small pieces of information that tell more about the main idea. Model how to identify supporting details.

5 ## Use a Graphic Organizer

Have students find the main idea and supporting details in a nonfiction selection. Use a main idea chart to help students organize their thoughts.

Choose passages carefully to practice this succession of skills:

- Stated main idea in a paragraph
- Implied main idea in a paragraph
- Stated main idea in an article

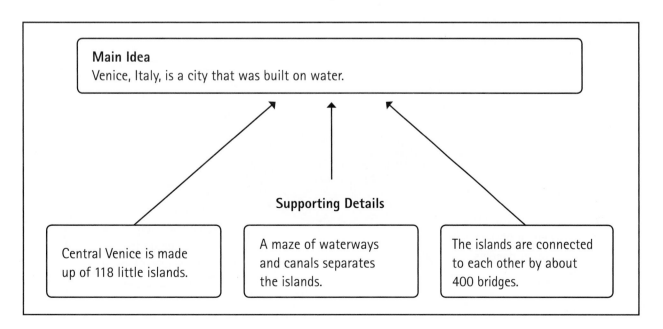

Main Idea
Venice, Italy, is a city that was built on water.

Supporting Details

Central Venice is made up of 118 little islands.

A maze of waterways and canals separates the islands.

The islands are connected to each other by about 400 bridges.

Reteach Comprehension
Draw Conclusions

When students move beyond the literal meaning of a text to draw conclusions, they get more ideas from what they read and understand better the points an author is trying to make. Use the following routine to guide students in drawing conclusions.

1 Discuss Drawing Conclusions

Tell students that a conclusion is a sensible decision they reach based on details or facts in a story or an article. Explain that when they draw conclusions, they think about information in the text and what they already know.

2 Model Drawing a Conclusion

Model using your own experiences to draw a conclusion.

Think Aloud **MODEL** I saw a motorcycle parked in the driveway and a duffel bag on the hall floor. I heard music booming from upstairs. I knew that my brother Lorre was home from college.

Discuss how you combined what you already knew with details (sight of motorcycle and duffel bag and sound of music) to draw a conclusion.

3 Ask Questions

Read aloud a passage and ask questions that foster drawing conclusions. For example:

- *What kind of person is the main character?*
- *How can you tell?*
- *Why do you think the character acts this way?*

4 Use a Graphic Organizer

Have partners read both fiction and nonfiction passages. Students can ask each other questions that lead to drawing conclusions. Suggest that they use webs or charts to show the facts or details that support their conclusions.

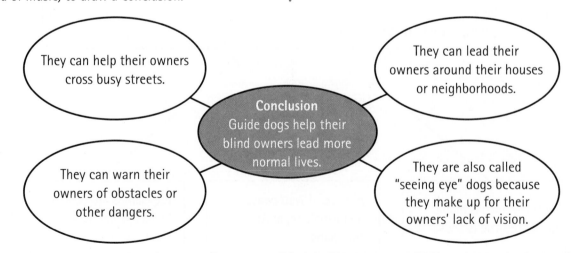

They can help their owners cross busy streets.

They can lead their owners around their houses or neighborhoods.

Conclusion
Guide dogs help their blind owners lead more normal lives.

They can warn their owners of obstacles or other dangers.

They are also called "seeing eye" dogs because they make up for their owners' lack of vision.

Reteach Comprehension
Plot

When students understand that stories have a structure and that that structure is somewhat predictable from story to story, they are better able to tell which events are most important and why they happen. Use this routine to support students' understanding of plot.

1 Review Plot

Review plot as the important events in a story. Explain that a plot has a beginning, middle, and end. Help students chart the beginning, middle, and end of familiar stories.

2 Discuss the Elements

What does it mean that a plot has a beginning, middle, and end? Discuss these elements in more detail:

- The beginning of a plot usually tells who the characters are and what they are doing right now. The beginning of a plot may also tell something about what those characters did in the past—what the reader needs to know about how and why they got here and perhaps what it is they want. The beginning of a plot also tells about the setting, if that is important.

- The middle of a plot usually contains more than one action. It may contain as many actions as are needed for the characters to try to get what they want.

- The end of a plot means that a story doesn't just stop, it comes to a satisfying conclusion. The conclusion usually tells whether or not the main character gets what he or she wants. A "satisfying conclusion" doesn't necessarily mean that it is the ending the reader wants; it means that the ending is "right" for the story.

3 Record Plot Structure

Have students identify and record the beginning, middle, and end of one or more stories they have read. Remind students that the middle may contain more than one action.

Title Holly's Helping Hand

Beginning
Holly decides she wants to do housework. She asks Mother what she can do to help. Mother tells her to clean up her room.

Middle
Holly looks at her room and decides that she doesn't want to bother.

She complains to Mother, and Mother gives her a different job: Follow her for a day and write down in a notebook everything Mother does.

Holly carefully records Mother's activities all day until late afternoon, when she is tired and takes a nap.

End
Holly and Mother talk about jobs, and Holly realizes that cleaning up her room is one of the many jobs Mother has to do. Holly decides that it will be her own personal "housework."

Reteach Comprehension
Graphic Sources

Graphic sources can be a valuable aid to readers in previewing and comprehending text. When students interpret and create graphics as they read, they often strengthen their understanding of the text. Use this routine to teach graphic sources.

1 Discuss Graphic Sources

Explain that a graphic is a way of showing information visually, or in a way that you can see. Graphics can include pictures, charts, graphs, maps, diagrams, schedules, and so on. Graphics often show information from the text in a visual way. They can organize many facts or ideas.

2 Use Graphics to Preview

Remind students to look for graphics when they preview. Graphics are often a good way to discover what the story or article is about.

3 Compare Graphics to Text

Have students compare the text with graphics in a selection and discuss the author's purpose for including graphics. Captions, charts, diagrams, and maps may present information that is nowhere else in the article, or they may help the reader better understand text information.

4 Create Graphics

Give students opportunities to create their own pictures, charts, and other graphics to help them organize and understand text information.

5 Use a Graphic Organizer

Have students create a graph from information in a selection or from a poll they take. Depending on the content, they may use the four-column graph shown below, or they may create their own graphs with as many columns as needed.

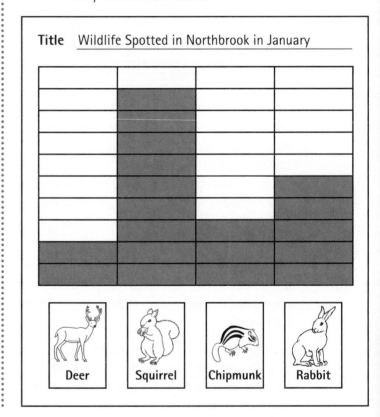

Reteach Comprehension
Generalize

Recognizing generalizations helps students judge the validity of an argument. Making their own generalizations helps students understand and summarize texts. Use this routine to teach generalizing.

1 Define Generalization

Explain that a generalization is a broad statement or rule that applies to many examples. A valid generalization is well supported by facts and logic. A faulty one is not well supported.

2 Teach Character Development

Students should look for clue words that signal generalizations as they read. List words on the board:

all	none
most	few
always	never
generally	in general

3 Model Generalizing

Explain that when readers generalize, they think about a number of examples and decide what they have in common. After reading a passage containing several facts, model how to generalize.

4 Scaffold Generalizing

Before students write their own generalizations, have them choose from several the one most valid for a paragraph. You may also ask them to complete stems, such as: *The first day of school each year is generally* _____.

5 Practice Generalizing

Have students record a generalization and examples in a web.

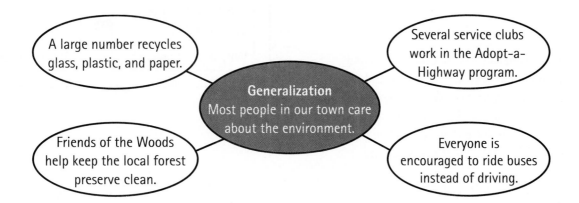

Reteach Comprehension
Cause and Effect

Students who are able to connect what happens in a selection to the reason why it happens can better understand what they read. In fiction, this skill will help them figure out why characters do what they do. In nonfiction, it will give them a better grasp of factual information. Use the following routine to teach cause and effect.

1 Demonstrate Cause and Effect

Remind students that a cause is why something happens and an effect is what happens. Demonstrate by setting a lightweight object, such as a paper cup, on a desk and batting it off with a pencil. Ask:

What is the effect? (The cup fell on the floor.)
What is the cause? (You hit it with a pencil.)

2 Identify Cause and Effect

Write this sentence on the board: *Because it was cold in the cabin, Dad put some more wood in the fireplace.* Explain that sometimes a sentence has a clue word such as *because, so,* or *since* that signals a cause-and-effect relationship. Have volunteers circle the cause *(it was cold in the cabin)* and the effect *(Dad put some more wood in the fireplace)* and underline the clue word *(because).*

3 Apply to a Selection

Read with students a story that has causes and effects. Explain that several causes can lead to one effect: *Torn jeans <u>and</u> a missing shoe made Jerry late to catch his school bus.* One cause can lead to several effects: *The lights going out made Jess bump into the door <u>and</u> Mary spill the milk she was pouring.*

4 Record Causes and Effects

Have students use a cause-effect chart to record the causes and effects in the selection.

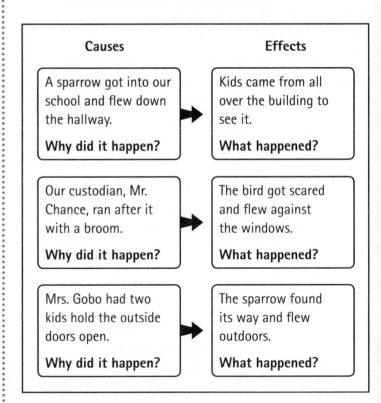

Causes	Effects
A sparrow got into our school and flew down the hallway. **Why did it happen?**	Kids came from all over the building to see it. **What happened?**
Our custodian, Mr. Chance, ran after it with a broom. **Why did it happen?**	The bird got scared and flew against the windows. **What happened?**
Mrs. Gobo had two kids hold the outside doors open. **Why did it happen?**	The sparrow found its way and flew outdoors. **What happened?**

Reteach Comprehension
Fact and Opinion

When students can identify statements of fact and opinion, they are able to make critical judgments concerning what they hear, read, and write. Use this routine to help students recognize statements of fact and statements of opinion and distinguish between them.

1 Define Fact and Opinion

Explain that a statement of fact can be proved true or false. A statement of opinion is someone's ideas or feelings. It cannot be proved true or false, but it can be supported or explained.

2 Give Examples

Write three statements on the board:

- *The Story of Ferdinand was written by Munro Leaf.*
- *Everybody should read The Story of Ferdinand.*
- *The Story of Ferdinand was first published in 1936.*

Ask: *Which sentences are statements of fact? (the first and the third) How can you tell?* Ask students to tell ways the facts could be proved true or false, such as looking at the book or asking the school librarian. Talk about other ways to check statements of fact *(observing, weighing, measuring, asking an expert).*

Ask: *Which sentence is a statement of opinion? (the second one)* Point out the judgment word *should.* Explain that opinions often contain judgment words such as *should, I think, cute,* and *best.*

3 Provide Practice

- Partners can read nonfiction selections and use a T-chart to list statements of fact and opinion.

- Have small groups read letters to the editor in a newspaper. Students can list opinions and their supporting arguments.

Statements of Fact	Statements of Opinion
1. The faces of Presidents Washington, Jefferson, Lincoln, and Roosevelt are carved into the stone of Mount Rushmore.	1. The sight of the monument is breathtaking, especially at sunset.
2. The sculpture took 14 years and was finished in 1941.	2. The Grand View Terrace is the best place to see this great work of art.
3. The presidents' faces are 60 feet high from their chins to the tops of their heads.	3. The monument is truly a "shrine to democracy."

Reteach Comprehension
Steps in a Process

For many activities, it is important that they be done in a certain order. When students understand the steps in a process, they can remember the process better and may better understand why certain steps are necessary.

1 Discuss Steps in a Process

Explain that a process is a series of actions that are done to get a certain result. Remind students that when they read about the order in which something happens, they are following the steps in a process. Instructions for making or doing something are also steps in a process.

2 Teach Clue Words

Clue words such as *first, second, next,* and *finally* can help a reader keep these steps in order. Sometimes the steps are numbered. When there are no clue words or numbers, a reader must use his or her common sense to put the steps in order. Usually, the order in which they are mentioned in writing is the order in which they should be done.

3 Order Sentence Strips with Steps

Write a clear sequence of steps in a process on sentence strips. Partners can work together to place the strips in the correct order. They can retell the process, inserting clue words to show the order.

4 Record Steps on a Chart

After reading about a process, students can work in pairs to create charts showing the steps in the process.

Process   Repotting a plant

Step 1
Choose a large enough pot with a hole in the bottom for drainage. Place a few pieces of broken flower pot over the hole, but be careful not to block the hole.

↓

Step 2
Put a layer of small stones to cover the bottom. Add a layer of crushed charcoal to keep the soil sweet.

↓

Step 3
Take the plant from its old pot, holding the stem just above the roots. Shake the plant gently to remove clods of old dirt.

↓

Step 4
Hold the plant in its new pot so that its roots are below the pot rim. Add potting soil a little at a time until the roots are covered. With your fingers, press the soil down firmly around the plant.

↓

Step 5
Water the plant thoroughly and set it somewhere to drain.

Reteach Comprehension
Classify and Categorize

Recognizing similarities in objects is a skill that begins in a child's earliest years. Classifying items is an important skill for comprehension in reading. Use this routine to teach classifying and categorizing.

1 Define the Terms

Explain that a group is a number of objects, people, or animals that are related, or have something in common. Two other names for *group* are *class* and *category*. We can group things, or we can classify or categorize them.

2 How We Classify

Classifying is something students probably do every day. For example, they might classify their toys as games or dolls and action figures. Explain that, to classify, students have to look at the characteristics, or qualities, of objects. Then they put each object into the group with other objects that share those characteristics.

3 Model Classifying and Categorizing

Point to classroom objects and model how they might be classified by color, by use, by where they came from, and so on. Point out that an object might be classified by more than one characteristic. (For example, the jacket is red; it also belongs to Caroline.) Have volunteers continue the exercise.

4 Practice Classifying and Categorizing

Have students use a graphic organizer like the one below to practice classifying different kinds of foods. Encourage them to add other foods to the list.

Food	Meat	Vegetable
potato	chicken	potato
chicken	ham	carrots
carrots	beef	peas
peas		beets
ham		
beets		
beef		

Student Edition
Glossary

How to Use This Glossary

This glossary can help you understand and pronounce some of the words in this book. The entries in this glossary are in alphabetical order. There are guide words at the top of each page to show you the first and last words on the page. A pronunciation key is at the bottom of the following page. Remember, if you can't find the word you are looking for, ask for help or check a dictionary.

The entry word is in dark type. It shows how the word is spelled and how the word is divided into syllables.

The pronunciation is in parentheses. It also shows which syllables are stressed.

Part-of-speech labels show the function or functions of an entry word and any listed form of that word.

a·dore (ə dôr′), *VERB.* to love and admire someone very greatly: *She adores her mother.* □ *VERB* **a·dores, a·dored, a·dor·ing.**

Sometimes, irregular and other special forms will be shown to help you use the word correctly.

The definition and example sentence show you what the word means and how it is used.

Aa

a·dor·a·ble (ə dôr′ə bəl), *ADJECTIVE.* attractive; delightful: *What an adorable kitten!*

ant·ler (ant′lər), *NOUN.* a bony, branching growth on the head of a male deer, elk, or moose. Antlers grow in pairs and are shed once a year. □ *PLURAL* **ant·lers.**

antlers

anx·ious·ly (angk′shəs lē) *ADVERB.* uneasily; with fear of what might happen: *We looked anxiously at the storm clouds.*

ar·e·a (âr′ē ə), *NOUN.* **1.** the amount of surface; extent: *The rug covers a large area.* **2.** a level, open space: *a playground area.* □ *PLURAL* **ar·e·as.**

ar·range (ə rānj′), *VERB.* to put things in a certain order: *She arranged the books on the library shelf.* □ *VERB* **ar·rang·es, ar·ranged, ar·rang·ing.**

ar·ti·fi·cial (är′tə fish′əl), *ADJECTIVE.* made by a person or machine; not natural: *Plastics are artificial substances that do not occur in nature.*

Bb

bat¹ (bat), *NOUN.* a small, flying mammal that comes out at night to feed, often on mosquitoes: *Bats have sensitive ears.*

bat² (bat), *NOUN.* a piece of wood or metal used for hitting the ball in baseball or softball.

bat 1.

bat·ter·y (bat′ə rē), *NOUN.* a container filled with chemicals that produces electrical power: *We needed a battery for the flashlight.*

bay (bā), *NOUN.* a part of a sea or lake partly surrounded by land.

bill (bil), *NOUN.* the beak of a bird.

bill

blew (blü), *VERB.* past tense of *blow.*

bliz·zard (bliz′ərd), *NOUN.* a blinding snowstorm with very strong, cold winds. □ *PLURAL* **bliz·zards.**

blow (blō), *VERB.* **1.** to make air come out of your mouth. **2.** to move in the wind: *The leaves blew around the yard.* □ *VERB* **blows, blew, blow·ing.**

a in hat	er in term	ô in order	ch in child	ə = a in about
ā in age	i in it	oi in oil	ng in long	ə = e in taken
â in care	ī in ice	ou in out	sh in she	ə = i in pencil
ä in far	o in hot	u in cup	th in thin	ə = o in lemon
e in let	ō in open	ù in put	ҭн in then	ə = u in circus
ē in equal	ò in all	ü in rule	zh in measure	

542

543

---

bot·tom (bot′əm), *NOUN.* the lowest part: *These berries at the bottom of the basket are crushed.*

bulb (bulb), *NOUN.* a round, underground part from which certain plants grow. *Onions and tulips grow from bulbs.* □ *PLURAL* **bulbs.**

bun·dle (bun′dl), *NOUN.* a number of things tied or wrapped together. □ *PLURAL* **bun·dles.**

but·ter·fly (but′ər flī), *NOUN.* an insect with large, often brightly colored wings: *Her flower garden attracted many butterflies.* □ *PLURAL* **but·ter·flies.**

butterfly

Cc

car·pen·ter (kär′pən tər), *NOUN.* someone whose work is building and repairing things made of wood.

carpenter

car·pet·ma·ker (kär′pit māk ər), *NOUN.* A person who makes carpets and rugs for floors: *The carpetmaker sold us a blue carpet.*

chan·nel (chan′l), *NOUN.* a body of water joining two larger bodies of water: *The small channel was too narrow for the boat's passage.*

cheat (chēt), *VERB.* to deceive or trick someone; to do business or play in a way that is not honest: *I hate to play games with someone who cheats.* □ *VERB* **cheats, cheat·ed, cheat·ing.**

chip (chip), *VERB.* to cut or break off a small thin piece of something: *I chipped the cup when I knocked it against the cupboard.* □ *VERB* **chips, chipped, chip·ping.**

clev·er (klev′ər), *ADJECTIVE.* bright; intelligent; having a quick mind: *She is a clever girl to have solved that math problem.*

col·lec·tion (kə lek′shən), *NOUN.* a group of things gathered from many places and belonging together: *Our library has a large collection of books.*

collection

com·pas·sion·ate (kəm pash′ə nit), *ADJECTIVE.* Wishing to help those who suffer; full of compassion: *The compassionate doctor treated people who could not afford to pay her.*

con·serve (kən sėrv′), *VERB.* to save something from loss or waste: *Fixing a leaky faucet helps to conserve water.* □ *VERB* **con·serves, con·served, con·serv·ing.**

crop (krop), *NOUN.* plants grown for food: *Wheat, corn, and soybeans are major crops in the United States.* □ *PLURAL* **crops.**

cud·dle (kud′l), *VERB.* to lie close and comfortably; to curl up: *The two puppies cuddled together in front of the fire.* □ *VERB* **cud·dles, cud·dled, cud·dling.**

Dd

dan·ger·ous·ly (dān′jər əs lē), *ADVERB.* not safely: *The car drove dangerously close to the wall.*

dim (dim), *ADJECTIVE.* somewhat dark; not bright: *The light from the candle was too dim for reading.*

Ee

e·nor·mous (i nôr′məs), *ADJECTIVE.* very, very large; huge: *Long ago, enormous animals lived on the Earth.*

enormous

er·rand (er′ənd), *NOUN.* a short trip that you take to do something: *She has errands to do downtown.* □ *PLURAL* **er·rands.**

ex·act·ly (eg zakt′lē), *ADVERB.* without any error; precisely: *I know exactly where I put the keys.*

ex·cit·ed·ly (ek sī′tid lē), *ADVERB.* with strong, lively feelings: *My heart beat excitedly as I opened the old trunk.*

544

545

Glossary

flipper • hatch

Ff

flip·per (flip′ər), *NOUN.* one of the broad, flat body parts used for swimming by animals such as seals and penguins. □ *PLURAL* **flip·pers.**

flippers

fro·zen (frō′zn), *ADJECTIVE.* hardened with cold; turned into ice: *frozen sherbet.*

fu·el (fyü′əl), *NOUN.* something that is used as a source of heat or energy, such as gasoline, coal, or wood: *The car wouldn't run because it was out of fuel.*

Gg

gas (gas), *NOUN.* a substance, such as air, that is neither a solid nor a liquid: *Sometimes balloons are filled with a gas called helium.*

gear (gir), *NOUN.* the equipment or clothing needed for a particular activity: *Their camping gear included tents, sleeping bags, and flashlights.*

gi·gan·tic (ji gan′tik), *ADJECTIVE.* huge or enormous: *The gigantic footprints must have been made by an elephant.*

goo (gü), *NOUN.* a sticky or messy substance: *Wash that goo off your hands.*

grape·vine (grāp′vīn), *NOUN.* **1.** a vine that grapes grow on. **2.** way that news and rumors are mysteriously spread: *We heard it on the grapevine.*

Hh

hatch (hach), *VERB.* to come out of an egg: *One of the chickens hatched today.* □ *VERB* **hatch·es, hatched, hatch·ing.**

hatch

546

hunter • language

hun·ter (hun′tər), *NOUN.* an animal or person who goes after animals for food or sport: *Owls and eagles are hunters.* □ *PLURAL* **hun·ters.**

hunter

Ii

i·guan·a (i gwä′nə), *NOUN.* a large lizard found in tropical America that has a row of spines along its back. □ *PLURAL* **i·guan·as.**

i·mag·ine (i maj′ən), *VERB.* to make a picture or idea of something in your mind: *We can hardly imagine life without cars.* □ *VERB* **i·mag·ines, i·mag·ined, i·mag·in·ing.**

in·cred·i·ble (in kred′ə bəl), *ADJECTIVE.* **1.** impossible to believe; unbelievable: *the hurricane's power was incredible.* **2.** very good: *what an incredible day it is!*

Kk

knowl·edge (nol′ij), *NOUN.* what you know: *Gardeners have great knowledge of flowers.*

Ll

la·dle (lā′dl), *NOUN.* a large spoon with a long handle and a deep bowl: *Dad used a ladle to serve the soup.*

ladle

lan·guage (lan′gwij), *NOUN.* human speech, spoken or written: *Civilization would be impossible without language.* □ *PLURAL* **lan·guag·es.**

547

Glossary

laundry • noble

laun·dry (lȯn′drē), **1.** *NOUN.* clothes, towels, and other such items that need to be washed or have just been washed: *One of my chores is folding the laundry.* **2.** *ADJECTIVE.* used for doing laundry: *The laundry basket was full of dirty clothes.*

laundry

la·zy (lā′zē), *ADJECTIVE.* not willing to work or move fast. *He lost his job because he was lazy.*

lof·ty (lȯf′tē), *ADJECTIVE.* **1.** very high: *lofty mountains.* **2.** proud; haughty: *He had a lofty contempt for others.*

Mm

mar·ket·place (mär′kət plās′), *NOUN.* a place where people meet to buy and sell things: *The marketplace was very crowded.*

ma·te·ri·al (mə tir′ē əl), *NOUN.* the substance from which something is made: *The Three Little Pigs used different materials to build their houses.* □ *PLURAL* **ma·te·ri·als.**

ma·ture (mə chúr′ or mə tür′), *ADJECTIVE.* **1.** ripe or full grown: *Grain is harvested when it is mature.* **2.** mentally or physically like an adult: *He is very mature for someone so young.*

mel·o·dy (mel′ə dē), *NOUN.* a pleasing or easily remembered series of musical notes; tune.

men·tion (men′shən), *VERB.* tell or speak about something: *I mentioned your idea to the group, and they liked it.* □ *VERB* **men·tions, men·tioned, men·tion·ing.**

mer·chant (mėr′chənt), *NOUN.* someone who buys and sells goods for a living: *Some merchants do most of their business with foreign countries.*

Nn

nar·ra·tor (nar′āt ər), *NOUN.* the person who tells the story or tale: *I was the narrator in the school play.*

no·ble (nō′bəl), *ADJECTIVE.* **1.** showing greatness of mind and character; good: *a noble person.* **2.** excellent; fine; splendid; magnificent: *Niagara Falls is a noble sight.*

548

overhead • preservative

Oo

o·ver·head (ō′vər hed′), *ADVERB.* over the head; on high; above: *The stars twinkled overhead.*

Pp

par·ka (pär′kə), *NOUN.* a warm, heavy jacket with a hood: *If you go out in this cold weather, you should wear your parka.*

parka

part·ner (pärt′nər), *NOUN.* a member of a company or firm who shares the risks and profits of the business. □ *PLURAL* **part·ners.**

pat·tern (pat′ėrn), *NOUN.* an arrangement or design: *The birthday cake was decorated with a pattern of balloons.* □ *PLURAL* **pat·terns.**

peck (pek), *VERB.* to strike with the beak: *The baby sparrow pecked its egg.* □ *VERB* **pecks, pecked, peck·ing.**

plat·form (plat′fôrm), *NOUN.* a flat, raised structure or surface: *He stepped up on the platform to give his speech.*

plen·ty (plen′tē), *NOUN.* a full supply; all that you need; a large enough number or amount: *You have plenty of time to catch the train.*

plug (plug), *NOUN.* a device at the end of a wire that is put into an outlet to make a connection with a source of electricity: *A plug has metal prongs.*

poke (pōk), *VERB.* to push with force against someone or something; jab: *He poked me in the ribs with his elbow.* □ *VERB* **pokes, poked, pok·ing.**

preen (prēn), *VERB.* to smooth or arrange the feathers with the beak. □ *VERB* **preens, preened, preen·ing.**

preen

pre·serv·a·tive (pri zėr′və tiv), *NOUN.* any substance that will prevent decay or injury: *Paint is a preservative for wood surfaces.*

549

Student Edition
Glossary

proof • snuggle

proof (prüf), *NOUN.* a way or means of showing that something is true: *Do you have proof of what you are saying?*

Rr

raise (rāz), **1.** *VERB.* to lift something up; put up: *We raised the flag. Raise your hand if you know the answer.* **2.** *NOUN.* an increase in amount, especially in wages, salary, or allowance: *He was happy with his raise.* □ *VERB* **rais·es, raised, rais·ing.** *PLURAL.* **raises.**

rai·sin (rā′zn), *NOUN.* a small, sweet, dried grape.

Ss

scat·ter (skat′ər), *VERB.* to separate and go in different directions: *The chickens scattered in fright when the truck honked at them.* □ *VERB* **scat·ters, scat·tered, scat·ter·ing.**

search (sérch), **1.** *VERB.* to look through; examine; try to find something by looking for it. **2.** *NOUN.* the act of searching: *She found her book after a long search.* □ *VERB* **search·es, searched, search·ing.**

sec·tion (sek′shən), *NOUN.* a part or division of something: *We visited the children's section of the library.*

shelf (shelf), *NOUN.* a horizontal board on a wall or in a cupboard, used for holding or storing things: *Meg placed the books on the shelves.* □ *PLURAL.* **shelves.**

shine (shīn), *VERB.* to give off light or reflect light; glow: *The candles on the cake shone for a moment before Rebecca blew them out.* □ *VERB* **shines, shone, shin·ing.**

shoe·lace (shü′lās), *NOUN.* a string or cord used for fastening a shoe: *The kindergartners practiced tying their shoelaces.* □ *PLURAL.* **shoe·la·ces.**

snug·gle (snug′əl), *VERB.* to lie closely and comfortably together; nestle; cuddle: *The kittens snuggled together in the basket.* □ *VERB* **snug·gles, snug·gled, snug·gling.**

snuggle

550

---

splendid • survivor

splen·did (splen′did), *ADJECTIVE.* very good; excellent: *James and his family had a splendid vacation in Colorado.*

spoil (spoil), *VERB.* **1.** to become bad or not good to eat: *The fruit spoiled because I kept it too long.* **2.** to injure the character or disposition of: *They spoiled her by always giving her what she wanted.* □ *VERB* **spoils, spoiled, spoil·ing.**

sprout (sprout), *VERB.* to produce new leaves, shoots, or buds; begin to grow: *Tulips sprout in the spring.* □ *VERB* **sprouts, sprout·ed, sprout·ing.**

sprout

stead·y (sted′ē), *ADJECTIVE.* firmly fixed; firm; not swaying or shaking: *This post is as steady as a rock.*

sting (sting), **1.** *VERB.* to pierce or wound with a sharp point: *The wasp will sting you if you're not careful.* **2.** *NOUN.* a sharp pain: *Our team felt the sting of defeat.* □ *VERB* **stings, stung, sting·ing.**

store (stôr), **1.** *NOUN.* a place where things are sold: *grocery store, toy store.* **2.** *VERB.* to put things away until they are needed: *We always store comforters in the closet during the summer.*

strain (strān), *VERB.* to draw tight; stretch too much: *The weight strained the rope.* □ *VERB* **strains, strained, strain·ing.**

stray (strā), *VERB.* to lose your way; wander; roam: *Their dog has strayed off somewhere.* □ *VERB* **strays, strayed, stray·ing.**

sup·plies (sə plīz′), *NOUN PLURAL.* the food and equipment necessary for an army exercise, camping trip, and so on.

sur·round (sə round′), *VERB.* to shut something in on all sides; encircle; enclose: *A high fence surrounded the field.* □ *VERB* **sur·rounds, sur·round·ed, sur·round·ing.**

sur·vi·vor (sər vī′vər), *NOUN.* someone or something that survives: *There were two survivors from the plane crash.* □ *PLURAL.* **sur·vi·vors.**

551

---

symphony • unwrap

sym·pho·ny (sim′fə nē), *NOUN.* a long, complicated musical composition for an orchestra.

Tt

tem·per·a·ture (tem′pər ə chər), *NOUN.* The degree of heat or cold in something, usually measured by a thermometer: *The water temperature was too cold for swimming.*

term (tèrm), *NOUN.* a definite or limited time: *The U.S. President's term in office is four years.*

thou·sand (thou′znd), *NOUN or ADJECTIVE.* ten hundred; 1,000. □ *PLURAL.* **thou·sands.**

thread (thred), *NOUN.* a very thin string made of strands of cotton, silk, wool, or nylon, spun and twisted together. *She fixed the sweater with cotton thread.*

thread

ton (tun), *NOUN.* a unit of weight equal to 2,000 pounds: *A small car weighs about one ton, and a minivan weighs about two tons.* □ *PLURAL.* **tons.**

top·ic (top′ik), *NOUN.* a subject that people think, write, or talk about: *Newspapers discuss the topics of the day.* □ *PLURAL.* **top·ics.**

trade (trād), *VERB.* to exchange one thing for another: *Rita traded her blue crayon for a red one.* □ *VERB* **trades, tra·ded, tra·ding.**

tro·phy (trō′fē), *NOUN.* **1.** an award, often in the form of a statue or cup, given as a symbol of victory. **2.** a prize in a race or contest. □ *PLURAL.* **tro·phies.**

twig (twig), *NOUN.* a small, thin branch of a tree or other woody plant: *The children collected small shells and twigs to decorate their sandcastles.* □ *PLURAL.* **twigs.**

twitch (twich), *VERB.* to make small, jerky movements: *The cat's tail twitched as he watched the bird outside the window.* □ *VERB* **twitch·es, twitched, twitch·ing.**

Uu

un·seen (un sēn′), *ADJECTIVE.* not seen; unnoticed: *An unseen error caused the plane crash.*

un·wrap (un rap′), *VERB.* to open: *She unwrapped the gift.* □ *VERB* **un·wraps, un·wrapped, un·wrap·ping.**

552

---

variety•yank

Vv

va·ri·e·ty (və rī′ə tē), *NOUN.* a selection of different things: *This market sells a wide variety of fruits and vegetables.*

vis·ion (vizh′ən), *NOUN.* the ability to think ahead and plan: *Our group needs a leader with vision.*

Ww

wa·ter·less (wô′tər lis), *ADJECTIVE.* **1.** containing little or no water. **2.** needing no water: *waterless cooking.*

wealth (welth), *NOUN.* riches; many valuable possessions; property: *people of wealth, the wealth of a city.*

wil·low (wil′ō), *NOUN.* a tree with narrow leaves and thin branches that bend easily: *She liked to sit under the curved branches of the willow.*

willow

wob·ble (wob′əl), *VERB.* to move unsteadily from side to side; shake; tremble: *The baby wobbled when she began to walk alone.* □ *VERB* **wob·bles, wob·bled, wob·bling.**

Yy

yank (yangk), *VERB.* to pull with a sudden, sharp movement: *Keith yanked open the heavy door.* □ *VERB* **yanks, yanked, yank·ing.**

553

Glossary

How to Use This Glossary

This glossary can help you understand and pronounce some of the words in this book. The entries in this glossary are in alphabetical order. There are guide words at the top of each page to show you the first and last words on the page. A pronunciation key is at the bottom of the following page. Remember, if you can't find the word you are looking for, ask for help or check a dictionary.

The entry word is in dark type. It shows how the word is spelled and how the word is divided into syllables.

The pronunciation is in parentheses. It also shows which syllables are stressed.

Part-of-speech labels show the function or functions of an entry word and any listed form of that word.

a·dore (ə dôr′), VERB. to love and admire someone very greatly: *She adores her mother.* ❏ VERB. **a·dores, a·dored, a·dor·ing.**

Sometimes, irregular and other special forms will be shown to help you use the word correctly.

The definition and example sentence show you what the word means and how it is used.

536

Aa

air·port (âr′pôrt′), NOUN. an area used regularly by aircraft to land and take off: *An airport has buildings for passengers and for keeping and repairing aircraft.*

airport

aq·ue·duct (ak′wə dukt), NOUN. a large pipe or channel for bringing water from a distance.

at·tic (at′ik), NOUN. the space in a house just below the roof and above the other rooms.

av·er·age (av′ər ij), NOUN. the quantity found by dividing the sum of all the quantities by the number of quantities. The average of 3 and 5 and 10 is 6 (because 3 + 5 + 10 = 18, and 18 divided by 3 = 6).

Bb

bak·er·y (bā′kər ē), NOUN. a place where bread, pies, cakes, and pastries are made or sold.

bakery

bas·ket·ball (bas′kit bôl), NOUN. **1.** a game played with a large, round ball between two teams of five players each. The players score points by tossing the ball through baskets hanging at either end of the court. **2.** the ball used in this game.

batch (bach), NOUN. a quantity of something made at the same time: *a batch of cookies.*

Cc

card·board (kärd′bôrd′), NOUN. a stiff material made of layers of paper pulp pressed together, used to make cards, posters, boxes, and so on.

board (bôrd), NOUN. **1.** a broad, thin piece of wood for use in building: *We used 10-inch boards for shelves.* **2.** a group of people managing something; council: *a board of directors.*

boil (boil), VERB. to cause a liquid to bubble and give off steam by heating it: *He boiled some water for tea.* ❏ VERB **boils, boiled, boil·ing.**

bou·quet (bū kā′), NOUN. a bunch of picked or cut flowers: *He picked a bouquet of wildflowers for his mother.*

bow (bou), VERB. to bend the head or body in greeting, respect, worship, or obedience: *The people bowed before the queen.* ❏ VERB **bows, bowed, bow·ing.**

braid·ed (brād′ed), ADJECTIVE. woven or twined together: *The warm, braided bread was delicious.*

a in *hat*	ér in *term*	ō in *order*	ch in *child*	ə = a in *about*
ā in *age*	i in *it*	oi in *oil*	ng in *long*	ə = e in *taken*
ä in *care*	ī in *ice*	ou in *out*	sh in *she*	ə = i in *pencil*
ä in *far*	o in *hot*	u in *cup*	th in *thin*	ə = o in *lemon*
e in *let*	ō in *open*	ù in *put*	ᴛʜ in *then*	ə = u in *circus*
ē in *equal*	ò in *all*	ü in *rule*	zh in *measure*	

537

Glossary

cel·e·brate (sel′ə brāt), VERB. to do something special in honor of a special person or day: *We celebrated my birthday with a party.* ❏ VERB **cel·e·brates, cel·e·brat·ed, cel·e·brat·ing.**

celebrate

cel·lar (sel′ər), NOUN. a room or rooms under a building where things are stored: *She went down to the cellar to get a can of peaches.*

chill·y (chil′ē), ADJECTIVE. cold; unpleasantly cool: *It is a rainy, chilly day.*

chore (chôr), NOUN. a small task or easy job that you have to do regularly: *Feeding our pets is one of my daily chores.* ❏ PLURAL **chores.**

538

cir·cus (sér′kəs), NOUN. a traveling show in which clowns, acrobats, and trained animals perform: *His favorite part of the circus was the elephant parade.* ❏ PLURAL. **circuses.**

clutch (kluch), VERB. to grasp something tightly: *I clutched the railing to keep from falling.* ❏ VERB **clutch·es, clutched, clutch·ing.**

con·tent¹ (kon′tent), NOUN. **1.** contents, all the things inside a box, a house, and so on: *An old chair and a bed were the only contents of the room.* **2.** chapters or sections in a book: *A table of contents gives a list of the sections in this book.*

con·tent² (kən tent′), **1.** VERB. to satisfy; please: *Nothing contents me when I am sick.* **2.** ADJECTIVE. satisfied; pleased: *Will you be content to wait till tomorrow?* ❏ VERB **con·tents, con·tent·ed, con·tent·ing.**

con·tin·ue (kən tin′yü), **1.** VERB. to keep up; keep on; go on: *The rain continued all day.* **2.** VERB. to go on with something after stopping for a while: *The story will be continued next week.* ❏ VERB **con·tin·ues, con·tin·ued, con·tin·u·ing.**

cot·ton (kot′n), ADJECTIVE. cloth made from soft, white fibers that grow in fluffy bunches on the cotton plant: *Light-colored cotton clothes keep me cool in hot weather.*

---

crouch (krouch), **1.** NOUN. a crouching position. **2.** VERB. to stoop over with the legs bent: *She was crouched beside the table.* ❏ VERB **crouch·es, crouched, crouch·ing.**

crown (kroun), NOUN. a head covering of precious metal worn by a royal person, such as a queen or a king.

crys·tal (kris′tl), NOUN. a hard, solid piece of some substance that is naturally formed of flat surfaces and angles: *Crystals can be small, like grains of salt, or large, like some kinds of stone.*

crystal

cur·i·ous (kyúr′ē əs), ADJECTIVE. strange; odd; unusual: *I found a curious, old box in the attic.*

cur·rent (kėr′ənt), **1.** NOUN. a flow or stream of water, electricity, air, or any fluid: *The current swept the stick down the river.* **2.** ADJECTIVE. of or about the present time: *current events.*

cus·tom·er (kus′tə mər), NOUN. someone who buys goods or services: *Just before the holidays, the store was full of customers.*

Dd

deep (dēp), ADJECTIVE. going a long way down from the top or surface: *a deep cut; a deeper pond; the deepest trench in the ocean.* **deep·er, deep·est.**

de·li·cious (di lish′əs), ADJECTIVE. very pleasing or satisfying; delightful, especially to the taste or smell: *a delicious cake.*

depth (depth), NOUN. the distance from the top to the bottom: *The depth of the well is about 25 feet.*

de·scribe (di skrīb′), VERB. to tell in words how someone looks, feels, or acts, or to record the most important things about a place, a thing, or an event: *The reporter described the awards ceremony in detail.* ❏ VERB **de·scribes, de·scribed, de·scrib·ing.**

des·ert (dez′ərt), NOUN. a dry, sandy region without water or trees: *In North Africa there is a great desert called the Sahara.*

539

Student Edition
Glossary

difficult • erupt

dif·fi·cult (dif′i kult), *ADJECTIVE*. hard to make, do, or understand: *The math test included some easy problems and some difficult ones.*

dis·ap·pear (dis′ə pir′), *VERB*. to vanish completely; stop existing: *When spring came, the snow disappeared.* □ *VERB* **dis·ap·pears, dis·ap·peared, dis·ap·pear·ing.**

dis·ease (də zēz′), *NOUN*. a sickness; illness; condition in which a bodily system, organ, or part does not work properly: *Diabetes is a disease.*

dis·cov·er·y (dis kuv′ər ē), *NOUN*. something found out: *One of Benjamin Franklin's discoveries was that lightning is electricity.*

dough (dō), *NOUN*. a soft, thick mixture of flour, liquid, and other things from which bread, biscuits, cake, and pie crusts are made.

dough

drown (droun), *VERB*. to die or cause to die under water or other liquid because of lack of air to breathe: *We almost drowned when our raft overturned.* □ *VERB* **drowns, drowned, drown·ing.**

Ee

ech·o (ek′ō), *VERB*. to be heard again: *Her shout echoed through the valley.* □ *VERB* **ech·oes, ech·oed, ech·o·ing.**

en·cour·age (en kér′ij), *VERB*. to give someone courage or confidence; urge on: *We encouraged our team with loud cheers.* □ *VERB* **en·cour·ag·es, en·cour·aged, en·cour·ag·ing.**

e·rupt (i rupt′), *VERB*. to burst out violently: *Lava and ash erupted from the volcano.* □ *VERB* **e·rupts, e·rupt·ed, e·rupt·ing.**

erupt

540

expression • goal

ex·pres·sion (ek spresh′ən), *NOUN*. the act of putting into words or visual medium: *freedom of expression.*

Ff

fare·well (fâr′wel′), *ADJECTIVE*. parting; last: *a farewell kiss.*

feast (fēst), *NOUN*. a big meal for a special occasion shared by a number of people: *The breakfast that she cooked was a real feast.*

fes·ti·val (fes′tə vəl), *NOUN*. a program of entertainment, often held annually: *a summer music festival.*

festival

fierce (firs), *ADJECTIVE*. wild and frightening: *The fierce lion paced in its cage.*

fierce

flight (flīt), *NOUN*. a set of stairs from one landing or one story of a building to the next.

fool·ish (fü′lish), *ADJECTIVE*. without any sense; unwise: *It is foolish to cross the street without looking both ways.*

fo·reign (fôr′ən), *ADJECTIVE*. outside your own country: *She travels often in foreign countries.*

freeze (frēz), *VERB*. **1.** to become hard from cold; turn into a solid. **2.** to become unable to move: *I froze in my tracks when I saw the bear.* □ *VERB* **freez·es, froze, freez·ing.**

Gg

goal (gōl), *NOUN*. something desired: *Her goal was to be a scientist.*

541

graceful • label

grace·ful (grās′fəl), *ADJECTIVE*. beautiful in form or movement: *He is a graceful dancer.*

guard (gärd), **1.** *NOUN*. (in basketball) a member of the backcourt. **2.** *NOUN*. a person or group that protects or watches. **3.** *VERB*. to watch over someone or something; keep safe; defend: *The dog guarded the child.* □ *VERB* **guards, guard·ed, guard·ing.**

guid·ance (gīd′ns), *NOUN*. helpful advice or instruction: *a teacher's guidance.*

gul·ly (gul′ē), *NOUN*. a ditch made by heavy rains or running water.

Hh

hand·ker·chief (hang′kər chif), *NOUN*. a soft, usually square piece of cloth used for wiping your nose, face, or hands.

handkerchief

home·sick (hōm′sik′), *ADJECTIVE*. very sad because you are far away from home.

hon·or (on′ər), **1.** *NOUN*. knowing what is right or proper and always doing it: *A person of honor always keeps his or her promises.* **2.** *VERB*. to show respect to someone: *We honor our country's dead soldiers on Memorial Day.* □ *VERB* **hon·ors, hon·ored, hon·or·ing.**

Ii

in·gre·di·ent (in grē′dē ənt), *NOUN*. one of the parts of a mixture: *The ingredients of a cake usually include eggs, sugar, flour, and flavoring.* □ *PLURAL* **in·gre·di·ents.**

Jj

jour·ney (jér′nē), *NOUN*. a long trip from one place to another: *I'd like to take a journey around the world.*

joy·ful (joi′fəl), *ADJECTIVE*. causing or showing joy; glad; happy: *joyful news.*

Ll

la·bel (lā′bəl), *VERB*. to put or write a name on something: *She labeled her backpack with her name and address.* □ *VERB* **labels, labeled, label·ing.**

542

liberty • pale

lib·er·ty (lib′ər tē), *NOUN*. freedom: *In 1865, the United States granted liberty to all people who were enslaved.*

lo·cal (lō′kəl), *ADJECTIVE*. about a certain place, especially nearby, not far away: *I go to a local doctor.*

Mm

med·al (med′l), *NOUN*. a piece of metal like a coin, given as a prize or award, usually with a picture or words stamped on it: *She received two medals in gymnastics.* □ *PLURAL* **med·als.**

medal

mem·or·y (mem′ər ē), *NOUN*. a person, thing, or event that you can remember: *One of my favorite memories is my seventh birthday party.* □ *PLURAL* **mem·or·ies.**

mix·ture (miks′chər), *NOUN*. a mixed condition: *At the end of the move, I felt a mixture of relief and disappointment.*

mod·el (mod′l), *NOUN*. a small copy of something: *A globe is a model of the Earth.* □ *PLURAL* **mod·els.**

Nn

nar·row (nar′ō), *ADJECTIVE*. not wide; having little width; less wide than usual for its kind: *a narrow path.*

na·tive (nā′tiv), *ADJECTIVE*. belonging to someone because of that person's birth: *The United States is my native land.*

nib·ble (nib′əl), *VERB*. to bite something gently or to eat with small, quick bites: *The rabbits were nibbling the lettuce in the garden.* □ *VERB* **nib·bles, nib·bled, nib·bling.**

Oo

out·run (out run′), *VERB*. to run faster than someone or something else: *She can outrun her older sister.* □ *VERB* **out·runs, out·ran, out·run·ning.**

Pp

pace (pās), *NOUN*. a step: *He took three paces into the room.* □ *PLURAL* **pac·es.**

pale (pāl), *ADJECTIVE*. not bright; dim: *a pale blue.*

543

Glossary

peak • rhythm

peak (pēk), *NOUN.* the pointed top of a mountain or hill: *We saw the snowy peak in the distance.*

perch (pėrch), *VERB.* to come to rest on something; settle; sit: *A robin perched on the branch.* ❑ *VERB* **perch·es, perched, perch·ing.**

pier (pir), *NOUN.* a platform that extends over water, used as a landing place for ships and boats: *The boys sat at the end of the pier and watched the boats on the lake.*

pier

pil·lar (pil′ər), *NOUN.* a slender, strong upright support used either to support or to decorate a building: *There were pillars on either side of the front door.* ❑ *PLURAL* **pil·lars.**

pitch·er (pich′ər), *NOUN.* a player on a baseball team who pitches to the catcher. *A batter tries to hit the ball before it gets to the catcher.*

pop·u·lar (pop′yə lər), *ADJECTIVE.* liked by most people: *a popular sport; a popular song.*

Rr

rain·drop (rān′drop′), *NOUN.* the water that falls in drops from the clouds. ❑ *PLURAL* **rain·drops.**

rec·i·pe (res′ə pē), *NOUN.* a set of written directions that show you how to fix something to eat: *Please give me your recipe for bread.*

reed (rēd), *NOUN.* a kind of tall grass that grows in wet places: *Reeds have hollow, jointed stalks.* ❑ *PLURAL* **reeds.**

reeds

rhythm (riŦH′əm), *NOUN.* the natural, strong beat that some music or poetry has: *Rhythm makes you want to clap your hands to keep time.*

544

ruin • sport

ru·in (rü′ən), *VERB.* to destroy or spoil something completely: *The rain ruined our picnic.* ❑ *VERB* **ru·ins, ru·ined, ru·in·ing.**

Ss

scoop (sküp), *NOUN.* a tool like a small shovel used to dip up things: *A cuplike scoop is used to serve ice cream.*

scoop

scram·ble (skram′bəl), *VERB.* to make your way, especially by climbing or crawling quickly: *We scrambled up the steep, rocky hill, trying to follow the guide.* ❑ *VERB* **scram·bles, scram·bled, scram·bling.**

set·tle (set′l), *VERB.* to set up the first towns and farms in an area: *The English settled New England.* ❑ *VERB* **set·tles, set·tled, set·tling.**

snug (snug), *ADJECTIVE.* fitting your body closely: *That coat is a little too snug with a sweater under it.*

soar (sôr), *VERB.* to rise, fly, or glide high in the air: *The hawk soars above the treetops.* ❑ *VERB* **soars, soared, soar·ing.**

soar

so·cial (sō′shəl), *ADJECTIVE.* concerned with human beings as a group: *Schools and hospitals are social institutions.*

spare (spâr), **1.** *ADJECTIVE.* extra: *a spare tire.* **2.** *VERB.* to show mercy to someone; decide not to harm or destroy: *He spared his enemy's life.* ❑ *VERB* **spares, spared, spar·ing.**

sport (spôrt), **1.** *NOUN.* A game or contest that requires some skill and usually a certain amount of physical exercise. **2.** *PLURAL* **sports,** *ADJECTIVE.* of, about, or suitable for sports: *sports clothes, sports medicine.*

545

Glossary

stamp • symbol

stamp (stamp), **1.** *NOUN.* a small piece of paper with glue on the back; postage stamp: *You put stamps on letters or packages before mailing them.* ❑ *PLURAL* **stamps. 2.** *VERB.* to bring down your foot with force: *He stamped his foot in anger.* ❑ *VERB* **stamps, stamped, stamp·ing.**

stir (stėr), *VERB.* **1.** to mix something by moving it around with a spoon, stick, and so on: *Stir the sugar into the lemonade.* **2.** to move something: *The wind stirred the leaves.* ❑ *VERB* **stirs, stirred, stir·ring.**

stoop (stüp), *NOUN.* a porch or platform at the entrance of a house.

stroke (strōk), *NOUN.* **1.** the act of hitting something; blow: *I drove in the nail with several strokes of the hammer.* **2.** a single complete movement made over and over again: *He rowed with strong strokes of the oars.*

stroke 1.

stud·y (stud′ē), **1.** *NOUN.* the effort to learn by reading or thinking: *After an hour's study, I knew my lesson.* **2.** *VERB.* to make an effort to learn: *She studied her spelling words for half an hour.* ❑ *PLURAL* **stud·ies.** ❑ *VERB* **stud·ies, stud·ied, stud·y·ing.**

sup·port (sə pôrt′), *VERB.* to help; aid: *Parents support and love their children.* ❑ *VERB* **sup·ports, sup·port·ed, sup·port·ing.**

swal·low (swäl′ō), *VERB.* to make food or drink travel from your mouth down your throat: *Swallow your food before you talk.* ❑ *VERB* **swal·lows, swal·lowed, swal·low·ing.**

sweep (swēp), *VERB.* to move or pass over a wide area: *A crow swept over the field.* ❑ *VERB* **sweeps, swept, sweep·ing.**

swoop (swüp), *VERB.* to come down fast on something, as a hawk does when it attacks: *Bats are swooping down from the roof of the cave.* ❑ *VERB* **swoops, swooped, swoop·ing.**

sym·bol (sim′bəl), *NOUN.* an object, diagram, icon, and so on, that stands for or represents something else: *The dove is a symbol of peace.*

546

tablet • waterfall

Tt

tab·let (tab′lit), *NOUN.* a small, flat surface with something written on it.

ter·ri·ble (ter′ə bəl), *ADJECTIVE.* causing great fear; dreadful; awful: *The terrible storm destroyed many homes.*

thatch (thach), *NOUN.* plant material, such as straw or reeds, that is used to make or cover a roof.

ther·mal (thėr′məl), *ADJECTIVE.* of or about heat: *They wear thermal socks when they go hiking in cold weather.*

tide (tīd), *NOUN.* the rise and fall of the ocean about every twelve hours that is caused by the gravitational pull of the moon and the sun.

torch (tôrch), *NOUN.* a long stick with material that burns at one end of it.

torch

treas·ure (trezh′ər), *NOUN.* any person or thing that is loved or valued a great deal: *The silver teapot is my parents' special treasure.*

Uu

un·a·ware (un′ə wâr′), *ADJECTIVE.* not aware; unconscious: *We were unaware of the approaching storm.*

un·for·get·ta·ble (un′fər get′ə bəl), *ADJECTIVE.* so good or so wonderful that you cannot forget it: *Winning the race was an unforgettable experience.*

un·veil (un vāl′), *VERB.* to remove a veil from; uncover; disclose; reveal: *The bride unveiled her face.* ❑ *VERB* **un·veils, un·veiled, un·veil·ing.**

Vv

val·ley (val′ē), *NOUN.* a region of low land that lies between hills or mountains: *Many valleys have rivers running through them.* ❑ *PLURAL* **val·leys.**

Ww

wa·ter·fall (wó′tər fól′), *NOUN.* a stream of water that falls from a high place: *The canoe turned back before it reached the waterfall.*

waterfall

547

Scope and Sequence

Reading

Concepts About Print	Pre-K	K	1	2	3	4	5	6
Hold book right side up, turn pages correctly, move from front to back of book	•	•	•					
Identify parts of a book and their functions (front cover, title page/title, back cover, page numbers)	•	•	•					
Identify information that different parts of a book provides (title, author, illustrator)	•	•	•	•				
Know uppercase and lowercase letter names and match them	•	•	•					
Know the order of the alphabet	•	•	•					
Demonstrate one-to-one correspondence between oral words and printed words		•	•					
Identify and distinguish between letters, words, and sentences	•	•	•					
Recognize distinguishing features of a paragraph		•	•					
Recognize environmental print		•	•	•				
Track print (front to back of book, top to bottom of page, left to right on line, sweep back left for next line)	•	•	•					
Recognize first name in print	•	•	•					

Phonological and Phonemic Awareness	Pre-K	K	1	2	3	4	5	6
Phonological Awareness								
Identify and produce rhyming words in response to an oral prompt	•	•	•					
Distinguish rhyming pairs of words from nonrhyming pairs	•	•						
Track and represent changes in simple syllables and words with two and three sounds as one sound is added, substituted, omitted, or changed		•	•					
Count each syllable in a spoken word		•	•					
Segment and blend syllables in spoken words		•						
Segment and blend onset and rime in one-syllable words		•	•					
Recognize and produce words beginning with the same sound	•	•	•					
Phonemic Awareness								
Identify and isolate initial, final, and medial sounds in spoken words	•	•	•	•				
Blend sounds orally to make words or syllables		•	•	•				
Segment a word or syllable into sounds		•	•	•				
Count sounds in spoken words or syllables and syllables in words		•	•	•				
Manipulate sounds in words (add, delete, and/or substitute phonemes)	•	•	•	•				
Distinguish long- and short-vowel sounds in orally stated single-syllable words				•				

Decoding and Word Recognition	Pre-K	K	1	2	3	4	5	6
Read simple one-syllable and high-frequency (sight) words		•T	•T	•T	•			
Phonics								
Understand and apply the *alphabetic principle* that spoken words are composed of sounds that are represented by letters; as letters change, so do sounds	•	•	•					
Know sound-letter relationships and match sounds to letters		•T	•T	•				
Generate sounds from letters and blend those sounds to decode		•	•T	•T	•T			
Consonants, consonant blends, and consonant digraphs		•	•T	•T	•T			
Short and long vowels		•	•T	•T	•T			
r-controlled vowels; vowel digraphs; diphthongs; common vowel patterns			•T	•T	•T			
Phonograms/word families		•	•	•				

• instructional opportunity   **T** tested in standardized test format

Decoding and Word Recognition *continued*	Pre-K	K	1	2	3	4	5	6
Word Structure								
Decode multisyllabic words with common word parts and spelling patterns		•	•T	•T	•T	•T	•T	•T
Base words and inflected endings; plurals			•T	•T	•T	•T	•T	•T
Contractions and compound words			•T	•T	•T	•T	•T	•T
Prefixes and suffixes			•T	•T	•T	•T	•T	•T
Greek and Latin roots						•	•	•
Apply knowledge of syllabication rules to decode words			•T	•T	•T	•T	•T	•T
Recognize common abbreviations			•	•	•			
Decoding Strategies								
Blending strategy: Apply knowledge of sound-letter relationships to decode unfamiliar words		•	•	•	•			
Apply knowledge of word structure to decode unfamiliar words		•	•	•	•	•	•	•
Use context along with sound-letter relationships and word structure to decode		•	•	•	•	•	•	•
Self-monitor accuracy of decoding and self-correct			•	•	•	•	•	•
Fluency								
Read aloud grade level text fluently with accuracy, comprehension, appropriate pace/rate; with expression/intonation (prosody); with attention to punctuation and appropriate phrasing			•T	•T	•T	•T	•T	•T
Practice fluency in a variety of ways, including choral reading, partner/paired reading, Readers' Theater, repeated oral reading, and tape-assisted reading		•	•	•	•	•	•	•
Work toward appropriate fluency goals by the end of each grade			•	•	•	•	•	•
Read regularly and with comprehension in independent-level material		•	•	•	•	•	•	•
Read silently for increasing periods of time		•	•	•	•	•	•	•
Vocabulary and Concept Development	Pre-K	K	1	2	3	4	5	6
Recognize and understand selection vocabulary		•	•	•T	•T	•T	•T	•T
Understand content-area vocabulary and specialized, technical, or topical words		•	•	•	•	•	•	•
Word Learning Strategies								
Develop vocabulary through direct instruction, concrete experiences, reading, listening to text read aloud	•	•	•	•	•	•	•	•
Use knowledge of word structure to figure out meanings of words		•		•T	•T	•T	•T	•T
Use context clues for meanings of unfamiliar words, multiple-meaning words, homonyms, homographs		•		•T	•T	•T	•T	•T
Use grade-appropriate reference sources to learn word meanings	•	•	•	•	•T	•T	•T	•T
Use picture clues to help determine word meanings	•	•	•	•	•			
Use new words in a variety of contexts	•	•	•	•	•	•	•	•
Create and use graphic organizers to group, study, and retain vocabulary			•	•	•	•	•	•
Monitor expository text for unknown words or words with novel meanings by using word, sentence, and paragraph clues to determine meaning						•	•	•
Extend Concepts and Word Knowledge								
Academic language	•	•	•	•	•	•	•	•
Classify and categorize	•	•	•	•	•	•	•	•
Abbreviations			•	•	•			•
Antonyms and synonyms		•	•	•T	•T	•T	•T	•T
Prefixes and suffixes			•	•	•	•	•	•T

• instructional opportunity   **T** tested in standardized test format

Vocabulary and Concept Development *continued*	Pre-K	K	1	2	3	4	5	6
Homographs and homophones				•	•T	•T	•T	•T
Multiple-meaning words			•	•T	•T	•T	•T	•T
Related words and derivations					•	•	•	•
Compound words			•	•	•	•	•	•
Figurative language and idioms			•	•	•	•	•	•
Descriptive words (location, size, color, shape, number, ideas, feelings)	•	•	•	•				
High-utility words (shapes, colors, question words, position/directional words, and so on)	•	•	•	•				
Time and order words	•	•	•	•	•	•	•	•
Word origins: etymologies/word histories; words from other languages, regions, or cultures						•	•	•
Adages and sayings							•	
Analogies							•	•

Reading Comprehension	Pre-K	K	1	2	3	4	5	6
Comprehension Strategies								
Predict and set purpose to guide reading	•	•	•	•	•	•	•	•
Use background knowledge before, during, and after reading	•	•	•	•	•	•	•	•
Monitor and clarify by using fix-up strategies to resolve difficulties in meaning: adjust reading rate, reread and read on, seek help from references sources and/or other people, skim and scan		•	•	•	•	•	•	•
Inferring		•	•	•	•	•	•	•
Questioning before, during, and after reading	•	•	•	•	•	•	•	•
Visualize—use mental imagery		•	•	•	•	•	•	•
Summarize text		•	•	•	•	•	•	•
Recall and retell stories	•	•	•					
Important ideas (nonfiction) that provide clues to an author's meaning		•	•	•	•	•	•	•
Text structure (nonfiction—such as cause/effect, chronological, compare/contrast, description)	•		•	•	•	•	•	•
Story structure (fiction—such as plot, problem/solution)	•		•	•	•	•	•	•
Create and use graphic and semantic organizers, including outlines, notes, summaries			•	•	•	•	•	•
Use strategies flexibly and in combination			•	•	•	•		•
Comprehension Skills								
Author's purpose			•T	•T	•T	•T	•T	•T
Author's viewpoint/bias							•T	•T
Categorize and classify	•	•	•	•				
Cause and effect			•	•T	•T	•T	•T	•T
Compare and contrast			•	•T	•T	•T	•T	•T
Draw conclusions and make inferences			•	•T	•T	•T	•T	•T
Facts and details			•	•T	•T	•	•	•T
Fact and opinion (statements of fact and opinion)			•T	•T	•T	•T	•T	•T
Follow directions/steps in a process	•	•	•	•	•	•	•	•
Generalize					•T	•T	•T	•

• instructional opportunity   **T** tested in standardized test format

Reading Comprehension *continued*	Pre-K	K	1	2	3	4	5	6
Graphic sources (illustrations, photos, maps, charts, graphs, font styles, etc.)		•	•	•	•	•T	•T	•T
Main idea and supporting details		•T	•T	•T	•T	•T	•T	•T
Paraphrase				•	•	•	•	•
Persuasive devices and propaganda					•	•	•	•
Realism/fantasy	•	•T	•T					
Sequence of events	•	•T	•T	•T	•T	•T	•T	•T
Higher Order Thinking Skills								
Analyze					•	•	•	•
Analyze text with various organizational patterns					•	•	•	•
Describe and connect the essential ideas, arguments, and perspectives of a text				•	•	•	•	•
Evaluate and critique ideas and text				•	•	•	•	•
Draw inferences, conclusions, or generalizations; support them with textual evidence and prior knowledge	•	•T	•T	•T	•T	•T	•T	•T
Make judgments about ideas and texts				•	•	•	•	•
Hypothesize					•	•	•	•
Make connections (text to self, text to text, text to world)	•	•	•	•	•	•	•	•
Organize and synthesize ideas and information				•	•	•	•	•T

Literary Response and Analysis	Pre-K	K	1	2	3	4	5	6
Genre and Its Characteristics								
Identify types of everyday print materials (storybooks, poems, newspapers, signs, labels)	•	•	•	•	•	•	•	•
Recognize characteristics of a variety of genre	•	•	•	•	•	•	•	•
Distinguish common forms of literature		•	•	•	•	•	•	•
Identify characteristics of literary texts, including drama, fantasy, traditional tales		•	•	•	•	•	•	•
Identify characteristics of nonfiction texts, including biography, interviews, newspaper articles		•	•	•	•	•	•	•
Identify characteristics of poetry and song, including nursery rhymes, limericks, blank verse	•	•	•	•	•	•	•	•
Literary Elements and Story Structure								
Character	•	•T	•T	•T	•T	•T	•T	•T
Recognize and describe traits, actions, feelings, and motives of characters		•	•	•	•	•	•	•
Analyze characters' relationships, changes, and points of view		•	•	•	•	•	•	•
Analyze characters' conflicts					•	•	•	•
Analyze the effect of character on plot and conflict						•	•	•
Plot and Plot Structure	•	•T	•T	•T	•T	•T	•T	•T
Beginning, middle, end	•	•	•	•	•	•		
Goal and outcome or problem and solution/resolution		•	•	•	•	•	•	•
Rising action, climax, and falling action/denouement; setbacks						•	•	•
Setting	•	•T	•T	•T	•T	•T	•T	•T
Relate setting to problem/solution		•	•	•	•	•	•	•
Explain ways setting contributes to mood						•	•	•
Theme				•T	•T	•T	•T	•T

• instructional opportunity   **T** tested in standardized test format

Literary Response and Analysis *continued*	Pre-K	K	1	2	3	4	5	6
Use Literary Elements and Story Structure	•	•	•	•	•	•	•	•
Analyze and evaluate author's use of setting, plot, character, and compare among authors				•	•	•	•	•
Identify similarities and differences of characters, events, and settings within or across selections/cultures		•	•	•	•	•	•	•
Literary Devices								
Dialect						•	•	
Dialogue and narration	•		•	•	•	•	•	•
Identify the speaker or narrator in a selection		•	•	•	•	•		•
Exaggeration/hyperbole				•	•	•	•	•
Figurative language: idiom, jargon, metaphor, simile, slang				•	•	•	•	•
Flashback						•	•	•
Foreshadowing				•	•	•	•	•
Formal and informal language				•	•	•	•	•
Humor				•	•	•	•	•
Imagery and sensory words			•	•	•	•	•	•
Mood				•	•	•	•	•
Personification						•	•	•
Point of view (first-person, third-person, omniscient)					•	•	•	•
Puns and word play						•	•	•
Sound devices and poetic elements	•	•	•	•	•	•	•	•
Alliteration, assonance, onomatopoeia	•	•	•	•	•	•	•	•
Rhyme, rhythm, repetition, and cadence	•	•	•	•	•	•	•	•
Word choice	•	•	•	•	•	•	•	•
Symbolism							•	•
Tone						•	•	•
Author's and Illustrator's Craft								
Distinguish the roles of author and illustrator	•	•	•	•				
Recognize/analyze author's and illustrator's craft or style				•	•	•	•	•
Evaluate author's use of various techniques to influence readers' perspectives						•	•	•
Literary Response								
Recollect, talk, and write about books	•	•	•	•	•	•	•	•
Reflect on reading and respond (through talk, movement, art, and so on)	•	•	•	•	•	•	•	•
Ask and answer questions about text	•	•	•	•	•	•	•	•
Write about what is read		•	•	•	•	•	•	•
Use evidence from the text to support opinions, interpretations, or conclusions		•	•	•	•	•	•	•
Support ideas through reference to other texts and personal knowledge				•	•	•	•	•
Locate materials on related topic, theme, or idea				•	•	•	•	•
Make connections: text to self, text to text, text to world			•	•	•	•	•	•
Offer observations, react, speculate in response to text				•	•	•	•	•

• instructional opportunity   **T** tested in standardized test format

Literary Response and Analysis *continued*	Pre-K	K	1	2	3	4	5	6
Literary Appreciation/Motivation								
Show an interest in books and reading; engage voluntarily in social interaction about books	•	•	•	•	•	•	•	•
Choose text by drawing on personal interests, relying on knowledge of authors and genres, estimating text difficulty, and using recommendations of others	•	•	•	•	•	•	•	•
Read a variety of grade-level-appropriate narrative and expository texts		•	•	•	•	•	•	•
Read from a wide variety of genres for a variety of purposes		•	•	•	•	•	•	•
Read independently		•	•	•	•	•	•	•
Establish familiarity with a topic		•	•	•	•	•	•	•
Cultural Awareness								
Comprehend basic plots of classic tales from around the world			•	•	•	•	•	•
Compare and contrast tales from different cultures			•	•	•	•	•	•
Develop attitudes and abilities to interact with diverse groups and cultures	•	•	•	•	•	•	•	•
Connect experiences and ideas with those from a variety of languages, cultures, customs, perspectives	•	•	•	•	•	•	•	•
Compare language and oral traditions (family stories) that reflect customs, regions, and cultures		•	•	•	•	•	•	•
Recognize themes that cross cultures and bind them together in their common humanness		•	•	•	•	•	•	•

Language Arts

Writing	Pre-K	K	1	2	3	4	5	6
Concepts About Print for Writing								
Write uppercase and lowercase letters		•	•					
Print own name and other important words	•	•	•					
Write using pictures, some letters, some phonetically spelled words, and transitional spelling to convey meaning	•	•	•					
Write consonant-vowel-consonant words		•	•					
Dictate messages or stories for others to write	•	•	•					
Create own written texts for others to read; write left to right on a line and top to bottom on a page	•	•	•					
Participate in shared and interactive writing	•	•	•					
Traits of Writing								
Focus/Ideas		•	•	•	•	•	•	•
State a clear purpose and maintain focus; sharpen ideas		•	•	•	•	•	•	•
Use sensory details and concrete examples; elaborate			•	•	•	•	•	•
Delete extraneous information			•	•	•	•	•	•
Use strategies, such as tone, style, consistent point of view, to achieve a sense of completeness						•	•	•
Organization		•	•	•	•	•T	•T	•T
Use graphic organizers to group ideas	•	•	•	•	•	•	•	•
Write coherent paragraphs that develop a central idea and have topic sentences and facts and details			•	•	•	•	•	•
Use transitions to connect sentences and paragraphs and establish coherence			•	•	•	•	•	•

• instructional opportunity   T tested in standardized test format

Writing *continued*	Pre-K	K	1	2	3	4	5	6
Select an organizational structure, such as comparison and contrast, categories, spatial order, climactic order, based on purpose, audience, length							•	•
Organize ideas in a logical progression, such as chronological order or order of importance	•	•	•	•	•	•	•	•
Write introductory, supporting, and concluding paragraphs					•	•	•	•
Use strategies of note-taking, outlining, and summarizing to impose structure on composition drafts					•	•	•	•
Write a multi-paragraph paper				•	•	•	•	•
Voice			•	•	•	•	•	•
Develop personal, identifiable voice and an individual tone/style			•	•	•	•	•	•
Maintain consistent voice and point of view						•	•	•
Use voice appropriate to audience, message, and purpose						•	•	•
Word Choice		•	•	•	•T	•T	•T	•T
Use clear, precise, appropriate language		•	•	•	•	•	•	•
Use figurative language and vivid words				•	•	•	•	•
Use sensory details, imagery, characterization				•	•	•	•	•
Select effective vocabulary using word walls, dictionary, or thesaurus		•	•	•	•	•	•	•
Sentences		•	•	•	•T	•T	•T	•T
Combine, elaborate, and vary sentences	•	•	•	•	•T	•T	•T	•T
Write topic sentence, supporting sentences with facts and details, and concluding sentence		•	•	•	•	•	•	•
Use correct word order		•	•	•	•	•	•	•
Conventions		•	•	•	•T	•T	•T	•T
Use correct spelling and grammar; capitalize and punctuate correctly		•	•	•	•	•	•	•
Correct sentence fragments and run-ons					•	•	•	•
Use correct paragraph indentation				•	•	•	•	•
The Writing Process								
Prewrite using various strategies	•	•	•	•	•	•	•	•
Develop first drafts of single- and multiple-paragraph compositions		•	•	•	•	•	•	•
Revise drafts for varied purposes, including to clarify and to achieve purpose, sense of audience, improve focus and coherence, precise word choice, vivid images, and elaboration	•	•	•	•	•	•	•	•
Edit and proofread for correct conventions (spelling, grammar, usage, and mechanics)		•	•	•	•	•	•	•
Publish own work	•	•	•	•	•	•	•	•
Writing Genres								
Narrative writing (such as personal narratives, stories, biographies, autobiographies)	•	•	•T	•T	•T	•T	•T	•T
Expository writing (such as comparison and contrast, problem and solution, essays, directions, explanations, news stories, research reports, summaries)		•	•	•T	•T	•T	•T	•T
Descriptive writing (such as labels, captions, lists, plays, poems, response logs, songs)	•	•	•T	•T	•T	•T	•T	•T
Persuasive writing (such as ads, editorials, essays, letters to the editor, opinions, posters)		•	•	•T	•T	•T	•T	•T
Notes and letters (such as personal, formal, and friendly letters, thank-you notes, and invitations)		•	•	•	•	•	•	•

• instructional opportunity   **T** tested in standardized test format

Writing *continued*	Pre-K	K	1	2	3	4	5	6
Responses to literature			•	•	•	•	•	•
Writing Habits and Practices								
Write on a daily basis	•	•	•	•	•	•	•	•
Use writing as a tool for learning		•	•	•	•	•	•	•
Write independently for extended periods of time			•	•	•	•	•	•
Penmanship								
Gain increasing control of penmanship, including pencil grip, paper position, posture, stroke	•	•	•	•				
Write legibly, with control over letter size and form; letter slant; and letter, word, and sentence spacing		•	•	•	•	•	•	•
Write lowercase and uppercase letters	•	•	•	•	•	•	•	•
Manuscript	•	•	•	•	•	•	•	•
Cursive				•	•	•	•	•
Write numerals	•	•	•					
Written and Oral English Language Conventions	Pre-K	K	1	2	3	4	5	6
Grammar and Usage in Speaking and Writing								
Sentences								
Correct word order in written sentences		•	•	•				
Types (declarative, interrogative, exclamatory, imperative)	•	•	•T	•T	•T	•T	•T	•T
Structure (complete, incomplete, simple, compound, complex, compound-complex)	•	•	•	•T	•T	•T	•T	•T
Parts (subjects/predicates: complete, simple, compound; phrases; clauses)			•	•T	•T	•T	•T	•T
Fragments and run-on sentences			•	•	•	•	•	•
Combine and rearrange sentences; use appositives, participial phrases, adjectives, adverbs, and prepositional phrases				•	•	•	•	•
Transitions and conjunctions to connect ideas; independent and dependent clauses				•	•	•	•	•
Varied sentence types and sentence openings to present effective style						•		•
Parts of speech: nouns (singular and plural), verbs and verb tenses, adjectives, adverbs, pronouns and antecedents, conjunctions, prepositions, interjections, articles		•	•	•T	•T	•T	•T	•T
Contractions			•	•T	•T	•T	•T	•T
Usage								
Subject-verb agreement		•	•	•T	•T	•T	•T	•T
Pronoun agreement/referents			•	•	•T	•T	•T	•T
Misplaced modifiers							•	•
Misused words						•		•
Negatives; avoid double negatives						•	•	•
Mechanics in Writing								
Capitalization (first word in sentence, proper nouns and adjectives, pronoun *I*, titles, months, days of the week, holidays, and so on)	•	•	•T	•T	•T	•T	•T	•T
Punctuation (period, question mark, exclamation mark, apostrophe, comma, quotation marks, parentheses, colon, and so on)		•	•T	•T	•T	•T	•T	•T

• instructional opportunity   **T** tested in standardized test format

Written and Oral English Language Conventions *continued*	Pre-K	K	1	2	3	4	5	6
Spelling								
Spell independently by using pre-phonetic knowledge, knowledge of letter names, sounds of the alphabet	•	•	•T	•	•	•	•	•
Consonants: single, double, blends, digraphs, silent letters, and unusual consonant spellings		•	•T	•T	•T	•T	•T	•T
Vowels: short, long, *r*-controlled, digraphs, diphthongs, less-common vowel patterns, schwa		•	•T	•T	•T	•T	•T	•T
Use knowledge of word structure to spell				•	•	•	•	•
Base words and affixes (inflections, prefixes, suffixes), possessives, contractions, and compound words				•	•T	•T	•T	•T
Greek and Latin roots, syllable patterns, multisyllabic words				•	•	•	•	•
Spell high-frequency, irregular words			•T	•T	•	•	•	•
Spell frequently misspelled words correctly, including homophones or homonyms				•	•	•	•	•
Use meaning relationships to spell						•	•	•
Listening and Speaking	Pre-K	K	1	2	3	4	5	6
Listening Skills and Strategies								
Listen to a variety of presentations attentively and politely	•	•	•	•	•	•	•	•
Self-monitor comprehension while listening, using a variety of skills and strategies, e.g., ask questions	•	•	•	•	•	•	•	•
Listen for a purpose								
For enjoyment and appreciation	•	•	•	•	•	•	•	•
To expand vocabulary and concepts	•	•	•	•	•	•	•	•
To obtain information and ideas	•	•	•	•	•	•	•	•
To follow oral directions	•	•	•	•	•	•	•	•
To answer questions and solve problems	•	•	•	•	•	•	•	•
To participate in group discussions	•	•	•	•	•	•	•	•
To identify and analyze the musical elements of literary language	•	•	•	•	•	•	•	•
To gain knowledge of one's own culture, the culture of others, and the common elements of cultures	•	•	•	•	•	•	•	•
To respond to persuasive messages with questions or affirmations						•	•	•
Determine purpose of listening				•	•	•	•	•
Recognize formal and informal language				•	•	•	•	•
Connect prior experiences to those of a speaker	•	•	•	•	•	•	•	•
Listen critically to distinguish fact from opinion and to analyze and evaluate ideas, information, experiences				•	•	•	•	•
Paraphrase, retell, or summarize information that has been shared orally				•	•	•	•	•
Evaluate a speaker's delivery; identify tone, mood, and emotion					•	•	•	•
Interpret and critique a speaker's purpose, perspective, persuasive techniques, verbal and nonverbal messages, and use of rhetorical devices; draw conclusions						•	•	•
Speaking Skills and Strategies								
Speak clearly, accurately, and fluently, using appropriate delivery for a variety of audiences, and purposes; sustain audience interest, attention	•	•	•	•	•	•	•	•
Use proper intonation, volume, pitch, modulation, and phrasing		•	•	•	•	•	•	•
Speak with a command of standard English conventions	•	•	•	•	•	•	•	•
Use appropriate language for formal and informal settings	•	•	•	•	•	•	•	•

• instructional opportunity   **T** tested in standardized test format

Listening and Speaking *continued*	Pre-K	K	1	2	3	4	5	6
Use visual aids to clarify oral presentations	•	•	•	•	•	•	•	•
Organize ideas and convey information in a logical sequence or structure with a beginning, middle, and end and an effective introduction and conclusion			•	•	•	•	•	•
Support opinions with detailed evidence and with visual or media displays					•	•	•	•
Emphasize key points to assist listener						•	•	•
Speak for a purpose								
To ask and answer questions	•	•	•	•	•	•	•	•
To give directions and instructions	•	•	•	•	•	•	•	•
To retell, paraphrase, or explain information	•	•	•	•	•	•	•	•
To communicate needs and share ideas and experiences	•	•	•	•	•	•	•	•
To describe people, places, things, locations, events, and actions		•	•	•	•	•	•	•
To participate in conversations and discussions	•	•	•	•	•	•	•	•
To express an opinion	•	•	•	•	•	•	•	•
To recite poems or songs or deliver dramatic recitations, interpretations, or performances	•	•	•	•	•	•	•	•
To deliver oral responses to literature	•	•	•	•	•	•	•	•
To deliver presentations or oral reports (narrative, descriptive, persuasive, problems and solutions, and informational based on research)	•	•	•	•	•	•	•	•
Stay on topic; maintain a clear focus	•	•	•	•	•	•	•	•
Support spoken ideas with details and examples		•	•	•	•	•	•	•
Use appropriate verbal and nonverbal elements (such as facial expression, gestures, eye contact, posture)	•	•	•	•	•	•	•	•

Viewing/Media	Pre-K	K	1	2	3	4	5	6
Interact with and respond to a variety of media for a range of purposes	•	•	•	•	•	•	•	•
Compare and contrast print, visual, and electronic media				•	•	•	•	•
Analyze media						•	•	•
Evaluate media				•	•	•	•	•
Recognize bias and propaganda in media message						•	•	•
Recognize purpose and persuasion in media messages			•	•	•	•	•	•

Research Skills

Understand and Use Graphic Sources	Pre-K	K	1	2	3	4	5	6
Advertisement				•	•	•	•	•
Chart/table	•	•	•	•	•	•	•	•
Diagram/scale drawing				•	•	•	•	•
Graph (bar, circle, line, picture)			•	•	•	•	•	•
Illustration, photograph, caption, label	•	•	•	•	•	•	•	•
Map/globe	•	•	•	•	•	•	•	•
Poster/announcement	•	•	•	•	•	•	•	•
Schedule						•	•	•
Sign	•	•	•	•		•	•	•
Time line				•	•	•	•	•

• instructional opportunity   **T** tested in standardized test format

Understand and Use Reference Sources	Pre-K	K	1	2	3	4	5	6
Know and use organizational features and parts of a book to locate information	•	•	•	•	•	•	•	•
Use alphabetical order			•	•	•	•	•	•
Understand purpose, structure, and organization of reference sources (print, electronic, media, Internet)	•	•	•	•	•	•	•	•
Almanac						•	•	•
Atlas					•	•	•	•
Card catalog/library database					•	•	•	•
Picture Dictionary		•	•	•				•
Dictionary/glossary					•	•T	•T	•T
Encyclopedia					•	•	•	•
Magazine/periodical					•	•	•	•
Newspaper and newsletter					•	•	•	•
Readers' Guide to Periodical Literature						•	•	•
Technology (on- and offline electronic media)		•	•	•	•	•	•	•
Thesaurus					•	•	•	•
Study Skills and Strategies	**Pre-K**	**K**	**1**	**2**	**3**	**4**	**5**	**6**
Adjust reading rate			•	•	•	•	•	•
Clarify directions	•	•	•	•	•	•	•	•
Outline				•	•	•	•	•
Skim and scan			•	•	•	•	•	•
SQP3R						•	•	•
Summarize			•	•	•	•	•	•
Take notes, paraphrase, and synthesize			•	•	•	•	•	•
Use graphic and semantic organizers to organize information		•	•	•	•	•	•	•
Test-Taking Skills and Strategies	**Pre-K**	**K**	**1**	**2**	**3**	**4**	**5**	**6**
Understand the question, the vocabulary of tests, and key words			•	•	•	•	•	•
Answer the question; use information from the text (stated or inferred)	•	•	•	•	•	•	•	•
Write across texts				•	•	•	•	•
Complete the sentence				•	•	•	•	•
Technology/New Literacies	**Pre-K**	**K**	**1**	**2**	**3**	**4**	**5**	**6**
Non-Computer Electronic Media								
Audiotapes/CDs, videotapes/DVDs	•	•	•	•	•	•	•	•
Computer Programs/Services: Basic Operations and Concepts								
Use accurate computer terminology	•	•	•	•	•	•	•	•
Create, name, locate, open, save, delete, and organize files		•	•	•	•	•	•	•
Use input and output devices (such as mouse, keyboard, monitor, printer, touch screen)	•	•	•	•	•	•	•	•
Use basic keyboarding skills		•	•	•	•	•	•	•
Responsible Use of Technology Systems and Software								
Work cooperatively and collaboratively with others; follow acceptable-use policies	•	•	•	•	•	•	•	•
Recognize hazards of Internet searches						•	•	•
Respect intellectual property						•	•	•

• instructional opportunity   T tested in standardized test format

Technology/New Literacies *continued*	Pre-K	K	1	2	3	4	5	6
Information and Communication Technologies:								
Information Acquisition								
Use electronic Web (nonlinear) navigation, online resources, databases, keyword searches				•	•	•	•	•
Use visual and nontextual features of online resources	•	•	•	•	•	•	•	•
Internet inquiry				•	•	•	•	•
Identify questions				•	•	•	•	•
Locate, select, and collect information				•	•	•	•	•
Analyze information				•	•	•	•	•
Evaluate electronic information sources for accuracy, relevance, bias					•	•	•	•
Understand bias/subjectivity of electronic content (about this site, author search, date created)					•	•	•	•
Synthesize information					•	•	•	•
Communicate findings				•	•	•	•	•
Use fix-up strategies (such as clicking *Back, Forward,* or *Undo;* redoing a search; trimming the URL)					•	•	•	•
Communication								
Collaborate, publish, present, and interact with others		•	•	•	•	•	•	•
Use online resources (e-mail, bulletin boards, newsgroups)			•	•	•	•	•	•
Use a variety of multimedia formats			•	•	•	•	•	•
Problem Solving								
Use technology resources for solving problems and making informed decisions					•	•	•	•
Determine when technology is useful			•	•	•	•	•	•

The Research Process	Pre-K	K	1	2	3	4	5	6
Identify topics; ask and evaluate questions; develop ideas leading to inquiry, investigation, and research		•	•	•	•	•	•	•
Choose and evaluate appropriate reference sources		•	•	•	•	•	•	•
Locate and collect information including using organizational features of electronic text	•	•	•	•	•	•	•	•
Take notes/record findings		•	•	•	•	•	•	•
Combine and compare information			•	•	•	•	•	•
Evaluate, interpret, and draw conclusions about key information		•	•	•	•	•	•	•
Paraphrase and summarize information		•	•	•	•	•	•	•
Make an outline				•	•	•	•	•
Organize content systematically		•	•	•	•	•	•	•
Communicate information		•	•	•	•	•	•	•
Write and present a report		•	•	•	•	•	•	•
Include citations					•	•	•	•
Respect intellectual property/avoid plagiarism						•	•	•
Select and organize visual aids		•	•	•	•	•	•	•

• instructional opportunity   **T** tested in standardized test format

Pacing

BACK TO SCHOOL!

	UNIT 1					WEEK 6 Cumulative Review	UNIT 2	
	WEEK 1	WEEK 2	WEEK 3	WEEK 4	WEEK 5		WEEK 7	WEEK 8
Comprehension Skill	Character, Setting, and Theme	Sequence of Events	Sequence of Events	Compare and Contrast	Author's Purpose		Main Idea and Details	Compare and Contrast
Comprehension Strategy	Background Knowledge	Summarize	Visualize	Background Knowledge	Story Structure		Monitor and Clarify	Visualize
Vocabulary Strategy/Skill	Context Clues/ Homonyms	Word Structure/ Compound Words	Reference Sources/ Unfamiliar Words	Context Clues/ Multiple-Meaning Words	Word Structure/ Prefixes and Suffixes		Context Clues/ Synonyms	Context Clues/ Unfamiliar Words
Fluency	Accuracy	Rate	Express Character-ization	Accuracy	Appropriate Phrasing		Accuracy	Expression
Phonics and Spelling	Short Vowels VCCV	Plurals -s, -es, -ies	Adding -ed, -ing, -er, -est	Long Vowel Digraphs	Vowel Sounds in out and toy		Syllable Patterns V/CV, VC/V	Words Ending in le

	UNIT 4					WEEK 24 Cumulative Review	UNIT 5	
	WEEK 19	WEEK 20	WEEK 21	WEEK 22	WEEK 23		WEEK 25	WEEK 26
Comprehension Skill	Generalize	Graphic Sources	Fact and Opinion	Fact and Opinion	Cause and Effect		Compare and Contrast	Main Idea and Details
Comprehension Strategy	Summarize	Important Ideas	Inferring	Questioning	Monitor and Clarify		Visualize	Inferring
Vocabulary Strategy/Skill	Context Clues/ Unfamiliar Words	Dictionary/ Glossary/ Unfamiliar Words	Context Clues/ Multiple-Meaning Words	Context Clues/ Multiple-Meaning Words	Dictionary/ Glossary/ Unfamiliar Words		Context Clues/ Synonyms	Context Clues/ Homophones
Fluency	Accuracy	Appropriate Phrasing and Punctuation	Expression	Appropriate Phrasing	Rate		Rate	Accuracy
Phonics and Spelling	Plurals	Vowels with r	Prefixes pre-, mid-, over-, out-, by-	Suffixes -er, -or, -ess, -ist	Syllable Pattern VCCCV		Syllable Pattern CVVC	Homophones

IT'S TEST TIME!

How do I cover all the skills before the test?

This chart shows the instructional sequence from Scott Foresman Reading Street. *You can use this pacing guide as is to ensure you're following a comprehensive scope and sequence, or you can adjust the sequence to match your school/district focus calendar, curriculum map, or testing schedule.*

UNIT 3

WEEK 9	WEEK 10	WEEK 11	WEEK 12	WEEK 13	WEEK 14	WEEK 15	WEEK 16	WEEK 17	WEEK 18
Draw Conclusions	Author's Purpose	Main Idea and Details	Cumulative Review	Draw Conclusions	Character, Setting, Plot	Graphic Sources	Generalize	Cause and Effect	Cumulative Review
Questioning	Predict and Set Purpose	Text Structure		Important Ideas	Inferring	Text Structure	Story Structure	Predict and Set Purpose	
Word Structure/ Compound Words	Context Clues/ Antonyms	Context Clues/ Unfamiliar Words		Context Clues/ Homophones	Dictionary/ Glossary/ Unfamiliar Words	Dictionary/ Unfamiliar Words	Context Clues/ Unfamiliar Words	Word Structure/ Prefixes and Suffixes	
Rate	Appropriate Phrasing	Rate		Expression	Accuracy	Appropriate Phrasing	Rate	Expression	
Compound Words	Words with *spl, thr, squ, str*	Digraphs *sh, th, ph, ch, tch*		Contractions	Prefixes *un-, re-, mis-, dis-, non-*	Consonant Sounds /j/, /s/ and /k/	Suffixes *-ly, -ful, -ness, -less, -able, -ible*	Consonants with *wr, kn, mb, gn, st*	

UNIT 6

WEEK 27	WEEK 28	WEEK 29	WEEK 30	WEEK 31	WEEK 32	WEEK 33	WEEK 34	WEEK 35	WEEK 36
Sequence	Draw Conclusions	Author's Purpose	Cumulative Review	Fact and Opinion	Cause and Effect	Graphic Sources	Plot and Theme	Generalize	Cumulative Review
Monitor and Clarify	Summarize	Background Knowledge		Questioning	Inferring	Important Ideas	Story Structure	Inferring	
Word Structure/ Compound Words	Context Clues/ Unfamiliar Words	Context Clues/ Homonyms		Word Structure/ Prefixes	Context Clues/ Antonyms	Glossary/ Unfamiliar Words	Word Structure/ Prefixes and Suffixes	Context Clues/ Homographs	
Expression and Punctuation	Accuracy	Appropriate Phrasing		Rate	Appropriate Phrasing	Accuracy	Rate	Expression	
Vowel Sound in *ball*	Vowel patterns *ei, eigh*	Suffixes *-y, -ish, -hood, -ment*		Vowels in *tooth, cook*	Schwa	Words with *-tion, -sion, -ture*	Prefixes *im-, in-*	Related Words	

WHEN IS YOUR STATE TEST?

Pacing

BACK TO SCHOOL!

	UNIT 1					WEEK 6 Cumulative Review	UNIT 2	
	WEEK 1	WEEK 2	WEEK 3	WEEK 4	WEEK 5		WEEK 7	WEEK 8
Speaking and Listening	News Report	Description	Narrate a Story	Panel Discussion	Book Report		Speech	Persuasive Speech
Grammar	Sentences	Subjects and Predicates	Statements and Questions	Commands and Exclamations	Compound Sentences		Common and Proper Nouns	Singular and Plural Nouns
Weekly Writing	Narrative Poem	Fable	Friendly Letter	Description	Realistic Fiction		Poem	Fairy Tale
Trait of the Week	Word Choice	Conventions	Organization	Voice	Sentences		Word Choice	Word Choice
Writing	E-Pen Pals/Personal Narrative							

	UNIT 4					WEEK 24 Cumulative Review	UNIT 5	
	WEEK 19	WEEK 20	WEEK 21	WEEK 22	WEEK 23		WEEK 25	WEEK 26
Speaking and Listening	Presentation	Weather Forecast	Interview	Sportscast	Book Review		Introductions	Readers' Theater
Grammar	Singular and Plural Pronouns	Subject and Object Pronouns	Possessive Pronouns	Contractions	Prepositions		Adjectives and Articles	Adjectives That Compare
Weekly Writing	Persuasive Text	Story	Biography	Autobiography	Summary		Editorial	Personal Narrative
Trait of the Week	Conventions	Conventions	Sentences	Organization/ Paragraphs	Word Choice		Organization	Conventions
Writing	Classroom Profile/Problem-Solution Essay							

IT'S TEST TIME!

WEEK 9	WEEK 10	WEEK 11	WEEK 12
Presentation	Interview	Description	Cumulative Review
Irregular Plural Nouns	Singular Possessive Nouns	Plural Possessive Nouns	
Persuasive Ad	Friendly Letter	Directions	
Focus/Ideas	Conventions	Organization/Paragraphs	
Story Exchange/How-to Report			

WEEK 13	WEEK 14	WEEK 15	WEEK 16	WEEK 17	WEEK 18
Commercial	Dramatize	How-to Demonstration	Description	Oral Report	Cumulative Review
Action and Linking Verbs	Main and Helping Verbs	Subject-Verb Agreement	Present, Past, and Future Tense	Irregular Verbs	
Fiction	Drama: Play	Formal letter	News Story	Compare/Contrast Paragraph	
Voice	Sentences	Conventions	Sentences	Word Choice	
Photo Writing/Cause-and-Effect Essay					

WEEK 27	WEEK 28	WEEK 29	WEEK 30
Song or Poem	Radio Ad	Retelling	Cumulative Review
Adverbs	Adverbs That Compare	Conjunctions	
Poem	Invitation	Story Review	
Word Choice	Focus/Ideas	Conventions	
E-Newsletter/Persuasive Essay			

WEEK 31	WEEK 32	WEEK 33	WEEK 34	WEEK 35	WEEK 36
Announcement	Express an Opinion	Talk Show	Description	Song	Cumulative Review
Capital Letters	Abbreviations	Combining Sentences	Commas	Quotations and Parentheses	
Taking Notes	Poem	Description	Comic Book	Historical Fiction	
Focus/Ideas	Organization	Conventions	Organization	Word Choice	
Discussion Forum/Research Report					

WHEN IS YOUR STATE TEST?

Student Progress Report: Grade 3

Name _____

This chart lists the skills taught in this program. On this reproducible chart, record your student's progress toward mastery of the skills covered in this school year here. Use the chart below to track the coverage of these skills.

Skill	Date	Date	Date
Read aloud written words in which the final "e" has been dropped in order to add a word ending.			
Read aloud words in which the final consonant is doubled when adding a word ending.			
Read aloud words in which the final "y" has been changed to "i" in order to add a word ending.			
Read aloud written words in which common suffixes or pre-fixes are added to the beginning or end of the words.			
Read aloud words with common spelling patterns.			
Read aloud words with closed syllable patterns.			
Read aloud words with open syllable patterns.			
Read aloud words with final stable-syllable patterns.			
Read aloud words with r-controlled vowels.			
Read aloud words with vowel combinations.			
Read aloud words with common spelling patterns.			
Read aloud contractions.			
Monitor reading accuracy.			
Use ideas from text features to make and confirm predictions.			

Skill	Date	Date	Date
Ask relevant questions, clarify what's read, and find facts and details about stories and other texts. Support answers with evidence.			
Understand a variety of texts by establishing a purpose for reading and checking comprehension. Make corrections and adjustments when that understanding breaks down.			
Smoothly read aloud and understand grade-level texts.			
Understand the meaning of common prefixes and common suffixes, and understand how they affect the root word.			
Figure out unfamiliar words or words with multiple meanings based on context.			
Identify and use antonyms, synonyms, words with multiple meanings, and words that are pronounced the same but differ in meaning.			
Identify and apply playful uses of language.			
Alphabetize a series of words to the third letter. Use a dictionary or a glossary to determine the meanings, syllable patterns, and pronunciation of unknown words.			
Paraphrase the themes and supporting details of fables, legends, myths, or stories.			
Compare and contrast the settings in myths and folktales.			
Describe different forms of poetry and how they create images in the reader's mind.			

Skill	Date	Date	Date
Explain how the elements of plot and character are presented through dialogue.			
Sequence and summarize the main events in the plot and explain their influence on future events.			
Describe how characters relate to each other and the changes they undergo.			
Identify whether the narrator or speaker of a story is first or third person.			
Explain the difference in point of view between a biography and autobiography.			
Identify language that creates visual images in a readers mind and appeals to the senses.			
Read quietly to oneself for long periods of time and produce evidence of reading. Explain in one's own words the meaning of what is read, and the order in which events occurred.			
Identify the topic and locate the author's purposes for writing the text.			
Identify the details or facts that support the main idea.			
Analyze, make inferences, and draw conclusions from the facts presented in the text and support those conclusions with evidence.			
Identify cause-and-effect relationships among ideas in texts.			

Skill	Date	Date	Date
Use text features to find information, and to make and verify predictions about the contents of the text.			
Identify what the author is trying to persuade the reader to think or do.			
Follow and explain a set of written multi-step directions.			
Understand how to look for and use information found in graphics.			
Understand how communication changes when moving from one type of media to another.			
Explain how various techniques in media are used to affect the message being delivered.			
Compare how different writing styles are used to communicate different kinds of information on the Internet.			
Plan a first draft and choose the appropriate genre for communicating ideas to an audience. Generate ideas through a range of strategies.			
Develop drafts and organize ideas into paragraphs.			
Revise drafts to make them clear and well organized for their audience. Include simple and compound sentences.			
Edit drafts for grammar, mechanics, and spelling using a teacher-developed rubric.			
Publish work for an audience.			
Write literary texts that are imaginative, build to an ending, and contain details about the characters and setting.			

239

Skill	Date	Date	Date
Use sensory details and the conventions of poetry.			
Write about important personal experiences.			
Establish a central idea in a topic sentence.			
Include supporting sentences with simple facts, details, and explanations.			
Write compositions that contain a concluding statement.			
Write essays tailored for a specific audience and purpose.			
Write responses to stories, poems, and nonfiction essays using evidence from the text to show understanding.			
Write persuasive essays for specific audiences on specific issues. Include personal opinions and use supporting details.			
Use and understand verbs.			
Use and understand nouns.			
Use and understand adjectives.			
Use and understand adverbs.			
Use and understand prepositions and prepositional phrases.			
Use and understand possessive pronouns.			
Use and understand conjunctions.			
Use and understand time and sequence transition-words.			
Form the complete subject and verb in a sentence.			

Skill	Date	Date	Date
Show agreement between subjects and verbs in simple and compound sentences.			
Print or write in script with spacing between words.			
Correctly capitalize geographical names and places.			
Correctly capitalize historical periods.			
Correctly capitalize official titles of people.			
Recognize and correctly use apostrophes in contractions and possessives.			
Recognize and correctly use commas in series and dates.			
Use correct mechanics and indent paragraphs.			
Use knowledge of letter sounds, word parts, how words break into syllables, and syllable patterns to spell.			
Develop a plan for gathering relevant information about the major research question.			
Spell words that double their final consonant when adding an ending.			
Spell words that drop their final "e" when adding an ending.			
Spell words that change their final "y" to "i" when adding an ending.			
Spell words that double their final consonant when adding an ending.			
Spell words that use complex combinations of consonants.			
Spell words that form vowel sounds from more than one letter.			

Skill	Date	Date	Date
Spell frequently used words and compound words from a common list.			
Spell words with common syllable constructions.			
Spell one-syllable words that sound the same but are spelled differently.			
Spell complex contractions.			
Use knowledge of spelling, and print and online dictionaries, to find the correct spellings of words.			
Develop research topics based on interests or the results of brainstorming sessions. Narrow topic and generate questions about it.			
Follow a research plan that includes the use of surveys, visiting places, and interviewing people.			
Collect information from experts, encyclopedias, and online searches.			
Use visual sources for information.			
Skim and scan text features.			
Take notes and organize information.			
Identify the author, title, publisher, and publication year of sources.			
Understand the difference between paraphrasing information and committing plagiarism. Identify why it is important to use reliable sources.			
Make research questions more specific based on the information collected from expert sources.			

Skill	Date	Date	Date
Draw conclusions about a topic in a brief written report, including a works-cited page showing author, title, publisher, and publication year for each source used.			
Listen closely to speakers, ask relevant questions, and make relevant comments.			
Give instructions that involve following directions, and retell instructions in one's own words.			
Speak clearly about a topic, make eye contact, have appropriate speaking rate, volume, and clarity to communicate ideas effectively.			
Work together with other students. Participate in discussions led by teachers and other students, ask and answer questions, and offer suggestions that build upon the ideas of others.			
Establish purposes for reading selected texts based upon own or others' desired outcome to enhance comprehension.			
Ask literal, interpretive, and evaluative questions of a text.			
Monitor and adjust comprehension using a variety of strategies.			
Make inferences about a text and use evidence from the text to support understanding.			
Summarize information in a text, maintaining meaning and logical order.			
Make connections between literary and informational texts with similar ideas and provide evidence from the text.			

21st Century Skills

English/Language Arts and Cross-Disciplinary Connections

Grade 3

English/Language Arts Standards

Writing

Compose a variety of texts that demonstrate clear focus, the logical development of ideas in well-organized paragraphs, and the use of appropriate language that advances the author's purpose. • Determine effective approaches, forms, and rhetorical techniques that demonstrate understanding of the writer's purpose and audience. • Generate ideas and gather information relevant to the topic and purpose, keeping careful records of outside sources. • Evaluate relevance, quality, sufficiency, and depth of preliminary ideas and information, organize material generated, and formulate thesis. • Recognize the importance of revision as the key to effective writing.	U1W1, U1W2, U1W3, U1W4, U1W5, U2W1, U2W2, U2W3, U2W4, U2W5, U3W1, U3W2, U3W3, U3W4, U3W5, U4W1, U4W2, U4W3, U4W4, U4W5, U5W1, U5W2, U5W3, U5W4, U5W5, U6W1, U6W2, U6W3, U6W4, U6W5

Reading

Locate explicit textual information and draw complex inferences, analyze, and evaluate the information within and across texts of varying lengths. • Use effective reading strategies to determine a written work's purpose and intended audience. • Use text features and graphics to form an overview of informational texts and to determine where to locate information. • Identify explicit and implicit textual information including main ideas and author's purpose. • Draw and support complex inferences from text to summarize, draw conclusions, and distinguish facts from simple assertions and opinions. • Analyze the presentation of information and the strength and quality of evidence used by the author, and judge the coherence and logic of the presentation and the credibility of an argument. • Analyze imagery in literary texts. • Evaluate the use of both literal and figurative language to inform and shape the perceptions of readers. • Compare and analyze how generic features are used across texts. • Identify and analyze the audience, purpose, and message of an informational or persuasive text. • Identify and analyze how an author's use of language appeals to the senses, creates imagery, and suggests mood. • Identify, analyze, and evaluate similarities and differences in how multiple texts present information, argue a position, or relate a theme.	U1W2, U1W3, U1W4, U1W5, U2W1, U2W2, U2W3, U2W4, U2W5, U3W1, U3W2, U3W3, U3W4, U4W1, U4W2, U4W3, U4W4, U4W5, U5W1, U5W2, U5W3, U5W4, U5W5, U6W1, U6W3, U6W5
Understand new vocabulary and concepts and use them accurately in reading, speaking, and writing. • Identify new words and concepts acquired through study of their relationships to other words and concepts. • Apply knowledge of roots and affixes to infer the meanings of new words. • Use reference guides to confirm the meanings of new words or concepts.	U1W1, U1W2, U1W3, U1W4, U1W5, U2W1, U2W2, U2W3, U2W4, U2W5, U3W1, U3W2, U3W3, U3W4, U3W5, U4W1, U4W2, U4W3, U4W4, U4W5, U5W1, U5W2, U5W3, U5W4, U5W5, U6W1, U6W2, U6W3, U6W4, U6W5

Describe, analyze, and evaluate information within and across literary and other texts from a variety of cultures and historical periods. • Read a wide variety of texts from American, European, and world literatures. • Analyze themes, structures, and elements of myths, traditional narratives, and classical and contemporary literature. • Analyze works of literature for what they suggest about the historical period and cultural contexts in which they were written. • Analyze and compare the use of language in literary works from a variety of world cultures.	U1W1, U1W2, U1W3, U1W4, U1W5, U2W1, U2W2, U2W3, U2W4, U2W5, U3W1, U3W2, U3W3, U3W4, U3W5, U4W1, U4W2, U4W3, U4W4, U4W5, U5W1, U5W2, U5W3, U5W4, U5W5, U6W1, U6W2, U6W3, U6W4, U6W5
Explain how literary and other texts evoke personal experience and reveal character in particular historical circumstances. • Describe insights gained about oneself, others, or the world from reading specific texts. • Analyze the influence of myths, folktales, fables, and classical literature from a variety of world cultures on later literature and film.	U1W1, U1W2, U1W3, U1W4, U1W5, U2W1, U2W2, U2W3, U2W4, U2W5, U3W1, U3W2, U3W3, U3W4, U3W5, U4W1, U4W2, U4W3, U4W4, U4W5, U5W1, U5W2, U5W3, U5W4, U5W5, U6W1, U6W2, U6W3, U6W4, U6W5

Speaking

Understand the elements of communication both in informal group discussions and formal presentations (e.g., accuracy, relevance, rhetorical features, and organization of information). • Understand how style and content of spoken language varies in different contexts and influences the listener's understanding. • Adjust presentation (delivery, vocabulary, length) to particular audiences and purposes.	U1W1, U1W2, U1W3, U1W4, U1W5, U2W1, U2W2, U2W3, U2W4, U2W5, U3W1, U3W2, U3W3, U3W4, U3W5, U4W1, U4W2, U4W3, U4W4, U4W5, U5W1, U5W2, U5W3, U5W4, U5W5, U6W1, U6W2, U6W3, U6W4, U6W5
Develop effective speaking styles for both group and one-on-one situations. • Participate actively and effectively in one-on-one oral communication situations. • Participate actively and effectively in group discussions. • Plan and deliver focused and coherent presentations that convey clear and distinct perspectives and demonstrate solid reasoning.	U1W1, U1W2, U1W3, U1W4, U1W5, U2W1, U2W2, U2W3, U2W4, U2W5, U3W1, U3W2, U3W3, U3W4, U3W5, U4W1, U4W2, U4W3, U4W4, U4W5, U5W1, U5W2, U5W3, U5W4, U5W5, U6W1, U6W2, U6W3, U6W4, U6W5

Listening

Apply listening skills as an individual and as a member of a group in a variety of settings (e.g., lectures, discussions, conversations, team projects, presentations, interviews). • Analyze and evaluate the effectiveness of a public presentation. • Interpret a speaker's message; identify the position taken and the evidence in support of that position. • Use a variety of strategies to enhance listening comprehension (e.g., focus attention on message, monitor message for clarity and understanding, provide verbal and nonverbal feedback, note cues such as change of pace or particular words that indicate a new point is about to be made, select and organize key information).	U1W1, U1W2, U1W3, U1W4, U1W5, U2W1, U2W2, U2W3, U2W4, U2W5, U3W1, U3W2, U3W3, U3W4, U3W5, U4W1, U4W2, U4W3, U4W4, U4W5, U5W1, U5W2, U5W3, U5W4, U5W5, U6W1, U6W2, U6W3, U6W4, U6W5
Listen effectively in informal and formal situations. • Listen critically and respond appropriately to presentations. • Listen actively and effectively in one-on-one communication situations. • Listen actively and effectively in group discussions.	U1W1, U1W2, U1W3, U1W4, U1W5, U2W1, U2W2, U2W3, U2W4, U2W5, U3W1, U3W2, U3W3, U3W4, U3W5, U4W1, U4W2, U4W3, U4W4, U4W5, U5W1, U5W2, U5W3, U5W4, U5W5, U6W1, U6W2, U6W3, U6W4, U6W5

Research

Formulate topic and questions. • Formulate research questions. • Explore a research topic. • Refine research topic and devise a timeline for completing work.	U1W1, U1W2, U1W3, U1W4, U1W5, U2W1, U2W2, U2W3, U2W4, U2W5, U3W1, U3W2, U3W3, U3W4, U3W5, U4W1, U4W2, U4W3, U4W4, U4W5, U5W1, U5W2, U5W3, U5W4, U5W5, U6W1, U6W2, U6W3, U6W4, U6W5
Select information from a variety of sources. • Gather relevant sources. • Evaluate the validity and reliability of sources. • Synthesize and organize information effectively. • Use source material ethically.	U1W1, U1W2, U1W3, U1W4, U1W5, U2W1, U2W2, U2W3, U2W4, U2W5, U3W1, U3W2, U3W3, U3W4, U3W5, U4W1, U4W2, U4W3, U4W4, U4W5, U5W1, U5W2, U5W3, U5W4, U5W5, U6W1, U6W2, U6W3, U6W4, U6W5
Produce and design a document. • Design and present an effective product. • Use source material ethically.	U1W1, U1W2, U1W3, U1W4, U1W5, U2W1, U2W2, U2W3, U2W4, U2W5, U3W1, U3W2, U3W3, U3W4, U3W5, U4W1, U4W2, U4W3, U4W4, U4W5, U5W1, U5W2, U5W3, U5W4, U5W5, U6W1, U6W2, U6W3, U6W4, U6W5

Cross-Disciplinary Standards

Key Cognitive Skills

Intellectual curiosity • Engage in scholarly inquiry and dialogue. • Accept constructive criticism and revise personal views when valid evidence warrants.	U1W1, U1W2, U1W3, U1W4, U1W5, U2W1, U2W2, U2W3, U2W4, U2W5, U3W1, U3W2, U3W3, U3W4, U3W5, U4W1, U4W2, U4W3, U4W4, U4W5, U5W1, U5W2, U5W3, U5W4, U5W5, U6W1, U6W2, U6W3, U6W4, U6W5
Reasoning • Consider arguments and conclusions of self and others. • Construct well-reasoned arguments to explain phenomena, validate conjectures, or support positions. • Gather evidence to support arguments, findings, or lines of reasoning. • Support or modify claims based on the results of an inquiry.	U2W2, U6W2
Problem solving • Analyze a situation to identify a problem to be solved. • Develop and apply multiple strategies to solving a problem. • Collect evidence and data systematically and directly relate to solving a problem.	U2W3
Academic behaviors • Self-monitor learning needs and seek assistance when needed. • Use study habits necessary to manage academic pursuits and requirements. • Strive for accuracy and precision. • Persevere to complete and master tasks.	U1W1, U1W2, U1W3, U1W4, U1W5, U2W1, U2W2, U2W3, U2W4, U2W5, U3W1, U3W2, U3W3, U3W4, U3W5, U4W1, U4W2, U4W3, U4W4, U4W5, U5W1, U5W2, U5W3, U5W4, U5W5, U6W1, U6W2, U6W3, U6W4, U6W5
Work habits • Work independently. • Work collaboratively.	U1W1, U1W2, U1W3, U1W4, U1W5, U2W1, U2W2, U2W3, U2W4, U2W5, U3W1, U3W2, U3W3, U3W4, U3W5, U4W1, U4W2, U4W3, U4W4, U4W5, U5W1, U5W2, U5W3, U5W4, U5W5, U6W1, U6W2, U6W3, U6W4, U6W5

Academic integrity

- Attribute ideas and information to source materials and people.
- Evaluate sources for quality of content, validity, credibility, and relevance.
- Include the ideas of others and the complexities of the debate, issue, or problem.
- Understand and adhere to ethical codes of conduct.

U1W2, U2W5, U3W4, U4W3, U6W4, U6W5

Foundational Skills

Reading across the curriculum

- Use effective prereading strategies.
- Use a variety of strategies to understand the meanings of new words.
- Identify the intended purpose and audience of the text.
- Identify the key information and supporting details.
- Analyze textual information critically.
- Annotate, summarize, paraphrase, and outline texts when appropriate.
- Adapt reading strategies according to structure of texts.
- Connect reading to historical and current events and personal interest.

U1W1, U1W2, U1W3, U1W4, U1W5, U2W1, U2W2, U2W3, U2W4, U2W5, U3W1, U3W2, U3W3, U3W4, U3W5, U4W1, U4W2, U4W3, U4W4, U4W5, U5W1, U5W2, U5W3, U5W4, U5W5, U6W1, U6W2, U6W3, U6W4, U6W5

Writing across the curriculum

- Write clearly and coherently using standard writing conventions.
- Write in a variety of forms for various audiences and purposes.
- Compose and revise drafts.

U1W1, U1W2, U1W3, U1W4, U1W5, U2W1, U2W2, U2W3, U2W4, U2W5, U3W1, U3W2, U3W3, U3W4, U3W5, U4W1, U4W2, U4W3, U4W4, U4W5, U5W1, U5W2, U5W3, U5W4, U5W5, U6W1, U6W2, U6W3, U6W4, U6W5

Research across the curriculum

- Understand which topics or questions are to be investigated.
- Explore a research topic.
- Refine research topic based on preliminary research and devise a timeline for completing work.
- Evaluate the validity and reliability of sources.
- Synthesize and organize information effectively.
- Design and present an effective product.
- Integrate source material.
- Present final product.

U1W1, U1W2, U1W3, U1W4, U1W5, U2W1, U2W2, U2W3, U2W4, U2W5, U3W1, U3W2, U3W3, U3W4, U3W5, U4W1, U4W2, U4W3, U4W4, U4W5, U5W1, U5W2, U5W3, U5W4, U5W5, U6W1, U6W2, U6W3, U6W4, U6W5

Use of data

- Identify patterns or departures from patterns among data.
- Use statistical and probabilistic skills necessary for planning an investigation, and collecting, analyzing, and interpreting data.
- Present analyzed data and communicate findings in a variety of formats.

U2W3, U5W2

Technology

- Use technology to gather information.
- Use technology to organize, manage, and analyze information.
- Use technology to communicate and display findings in a clear and coherent manner.
- Use technology appropriately.

U1W5, U2W2, U3W1, U3W5, U4W2, U4W3, U5W5, U6W4

Science Connections on Reading Street

Grade 3

Nature of Science: Scientific Ways of Learning and Thinking

Cognitive skills in science • Utilize skepticism, logic, and professional ethics in science. • Use creativity and insight to recognize and describe patterns in natural phenomena. • Formulate appropriate questions to test understanding of natural phenomena. • Rely on reproducible observations of empirical evidence when constructing, analyzing, and evaluating explanations of natural events and processes.	U1W1, U3W3

Science, Technology, and Society

History of science • Understand the historical development of major theories in science. • Recognize the role of people in important contributions to scientific knowledge.	U4W3

Biology

Evolution and populations • Know multiple categories of evidence for evolutionary change and how this evidence is used to infer evolutionary relationships among organisms. • Recognize variations in population sizes, including extinction, and describe mechanisms and conditions that produce these variations.	U2W5, U3W4
Systems and homeostasis • Know that organisms possess various structures and processes (feedback loops) that maintain steady internal conditions. • Describe, compare, and contrast structures and processes that allow gas exchange, nutrient uptake and processing, waste excretion, nervous and hormonal regulation, and reproduction in plants, animals, and fungi; give examples of each.	U2W1, U3W4, U4W5
Ecology • Identify Earth's major biomes, giving their locations, typical climate conditions, and characteristic organisms present in each. • Know patterns of energy flow and material cycling in Earth's ecosystems. • Understand typical forms of organismal behavior. • Know the process of succession.	U3W5, U4W2

Environmental Science

Human practices and their impacts • Describe the different uses for land (land management). • Understand the use and consequences of pest management. • Know the different methods used to increase food production. • Understand land and water usage and management practices. • Understand how human practices affect air, water, and soil quality.	U3W1, U3W4

Social Studies Connections on Reading Street

Grade 3

Spatial analysis of physical and cultural processes that shape the human experience • Use the tools and concepts of geography appropriately and accurately. • Analyze the interaction between human communities and the environment. • Analyze how physical and cultural processes have shaped human communities over time. • Evaluate the causes and effects of human migration patterns over time. • Analyze how various cultural regions have changed over time. • Analyze the relationship between geography and the development of human communities.	U3W1, U3W2, U5W5
Change and continuity of political ideologies, constitutions, and political behavior • Evaluate different governmental systems and functions. • Evaluate changes in the functions and structures of government across time. • Explain and analyze the importance of civic engagement.	U6W2, U6W3, U6W4, U6W5
Change and continuity of economic systems and processes • Identify and evaluate the strengths and weaknesses of different economic systems. • Analyze the basic functions and structures of international economics.	U1W5
Change and continuity of social groups, civic organizations, institutions, and their interaction • Identify different social groups (e.g., clubs, religious organizations) and examine how they form and how and why they sustain themselves. • Define the concept of socialization and analyze the role socialization plays in human development and behavior. • Analyze how social institutions (e.g., marriage, family, churches, schools) function and meet the needs of society. • Identify and evaluate the sources and consequences of social conflict.	U1W2, U1W4
Problem-solving and decision-making skills • Use a variety of research and analytical tools to explore questions or issues thoroughly and fairly. • Analyze ethical issues in historical, cultural, and social contexts.	U2W2, U2W3, U2W4, U6W2, U6W4

Multicultural societies • Define a "multicultural society" and consider both the positive and negative qualities of multiculturalism. • Evaluate the experiences and contributions of diverse groups to multicultural societies.	U5W1, U5W2, U5W3, U5W4

Factors that influence personal and group identities, (e.g., race, ethnicity, gender, nationality, institutional affiliations, socioeconomic status)	U1W3, U4W1, U4W5, U5W1, U6W1

- Explain and evaluate the concepts of race, ethnicity, and nationalism.
- Explain and evaluate the concept of gender.
- Analyze diverse religious concepts, structures, and institutions around the world.
- Evaluate how major philosophical and intellectual concepts influence human behavior or identity.
- Explain the concepts of socioeconomic status and stratification.
- Analyze how individual and group identities are established and change over time.

Analysis, Synthesis and Evaluation of Information

Critical examination of texts, images, and other sources of information	U1W1, U1W2, U1W3, U1W4, U1W5, U2W1, U2W2, U2W3, U2W4, U2W5, U3W1, U3W2, U3W3, U3W4, U3W5, U4W1, U4W2, U4W3, U4W4, U4W5, U5W1, U5W2, U5W3, U5W4, U5W5, U6W1, U6W2, U6W3, U6W4, U6W5

- Identify and analyze the main idea(s) and point(s) of view in sources.
- Situate an informational source in its appropriate contexts (contemporary, historical, cultural).
- Evaluate sources from multiple perspectives.
- Understand the differences between a primary and secondary source and use each appropriately to conduct research and construct arguments.
- Read narrative texts critically.
- Read research data critically.

Research and methods	U1W1, U1W2, U1W3, U1W4, U1W5, U2W1, U2W2, U2W3, U2W4, U2W5, U3W1, U3W2, U3W3, U3W4, U3W5, U4W1, U4W2, U4W3, U4W4, U4W5, U5W1, U5W2, U5W3, U5W4, U5W5, U6W1, U6W2, U6W3, U6W4, U6W5

- Use established research methodologies.
- Explain how historians and other social scientists develop new and competing views of past phenomena.
- Gather, organize and display the results of data and research.
- Identify and collect sources.

Critical listening	U1W1, U1W2, U1W3, U1W4, U1W5, U2W1, U2W2, U2W3, U2W4, U2W5, U3W1, U3W2, U3W3, U3W4, U3W5, U4W1, U4W2, U4W3, U4W4, U4W5, U5W1, U5W2, U5W3, U5W4, U5W5, U6W1, U6W2, U6W3, U6W4, U6W5

- Understand/interpret presentations (e.g., speeches, lectures, less formal presentations) critically.

Effective Communication

Clear and coherent oral and written communication	U1W1, U1W2, U1W3, U1W4, U1W5, U2W1, U2W2, U2W3, U2W4, U2W5, U3W1, U3W2, U3W3, U3W4, U3W5, U4W1, U4W2, U4W3, U4W4, U4W5, U5W1, U5W2, U5W3, U5W4, U5W5, U6W1, U6W2, U6W3, U6W4, U6W5

- Use appropriate oral communication techniques depending on the context or nature of the interaction.
- Use conventions of standard written English.

Academic integrity	U1W2, U2W5, U3W4, U4W3, U6W5

- Attribute ideas and information to source materials and authors.

Index

A

B

C

254

E-mail. *See* Genres; Technology, new literacies.

Encyclopedia. *See* Reference sources.

Encyclopedia article. *See* Genres.

Endings. *See* Spelling, word analysis; Word analysis.

End punctuation. *See* Exclamation mark, Period, Question mark.

English, conventions of. *See* Abbreviations; Adjectives; Adverbs; Apostrophe; Articles; Capitalization; Clauses; Commas; Conjunctions; Contractions; Exclamation mark; Gerunds; Nouns; Parentheses; Period; Prepositions; Pronoun/antecedent agreement; Pronouns; Question mark; Quotation mark; Semicolon; Sentences; Subject/verb agreement; Verbs; Writing process, proofread/edit.

ESL (English as a Second Language). *See* ELL (English Language Learners) suggestions.

Essential message. *See* Main idea and details, Theme.

Etymologies. *See* Vocabulary development.

Evaluate online sources. *See* Technology, skills for using technology.

Evaluation. *See* Assessment, Higher-order thinking skills.

Exaggeration. *See* Literary terms.

Exclamation mark, 3.1v2: 127d, 139c, 151e, 152–153, 159c, 159o, **3.1v2:** IR47

Expository nonfiction. *See* Genres.

Expository text/article. *See* Genres, Text features.

Expression/intonation. *See* Fluency, reading.

F

Fable. *See* Genres.

Fact and fiction. *See* Fact and opinion.

Fact and opinion, 3.1v2: 133a, 134–135, 135a, 137a, 141a, 144–145, 145a, 147a, **3.2v1:** 247a, 251a, **3.2v2:** 347a, **3.3v1:** 381a, **3.4v1:** 51a, 90a, 90–91, 96–97, 97a, 100e, 101a, 102–103, 103a, 107a, 111a, 115h, 115l–115m, CL12–CL13, **3.4v2:** 120a, 120–121, 126–127, 127a, 132e, 133a, 134–135, 135a, 141a, 147a, 149h, 149l–149m, IR32–IR33, IR35, **3.5v1:** 233a, CL8–CL9, **3.5v2:** 305a, **3.6v1:** 370a, 370–371, 376–377, 377a, 382e, 382–383, 383a, 387a, 391a, 393h, 393l–393m, 441a, 444–445, 445a, 447a, **3.6v2:** CL8–CL9, IR10–IR11, IR13–IR15

H

Logs, strategy response

background knowledge, **3.5v1:** 238e

genre, **3.1v1:** 29a, 38e, 50a, 65a, 72e, 82a, 99a, 106e, 118a, **3.2v1:** 275a, 282e, 294a, **3.2v2:** 343a, 350e, 358a, **3.3v1:** 413a, 418e, 428a, **3.3v2:** 477a, 486e, 496a, 511a, 518e, 532a, **3.4v1:** 95a, 100e, 110a, **3.4v2:** 158a, 168e, **3.5v1:** 199a, 206e, 216a, **3.5v2:** 329a, 340e, 354e, **3.6v1:** 439a, 446e, 456a, **3.6v2:** 469a, 503a, 512e, 524a

graphic organizers, **3.1v2:** 131a, 140e, 154a, 188a, **3.6v2:** 478e

important ideas, **3.3v1:** 379a, 388e, 398a, **3.4v1:** 63a, 70e, 80a

inferring, **3.5v1:** 231a, 238e, 250a, **3.6v1:** 403a, 412e, 424a

monitor and clarify, **3.1v2:** 176e, **3.2v1:** 209a, 216e, 226h, **3.5v1:** 263a, 272e, 284a

predict and set purpose, **3.2v2:** 309a, 318e

questioning, **3.4v2:** 125a, 132e, 144a, **3.6v1:** 375a, 382e, 390a

story structure, **3.1v2:** 169a

summarize, **3.2v1:** 226h, 260a, **3.2v2:** 330a, **3.3v1:** 398a, **3.4v1:** 29a, 36e, 46a, 80a, **3.5v1:** 284a, **3.5v2:** 297a, 304e, 309a, 314a

text structure, **3.3v1:** 447a, 452e

visualize, **3.2v1:** 241a, 248e

M

Magazine article. *See* Genres.

Magazine/periodical (as reference source). *See* Reference sources.

Main idea and details, 3.2v1: 204a, 204–205, 210–211, 211a, 213a, 216e, 218–219, 219a, 223a, 227a, 229a, 231h, 231l–231m, 276–277, 277a, 279a, 284–285, 285a, 288–289, 289a, CL8–CL9, **3.2v2:** 321a, 323a, 325a, 338a, 338–339, 344–345, 345a, 349a, 350e, 352–353, 353a, 355a, 363h, 363l–363m, CL10–CL11, **3.3v2:** 515a, 523a, 525a, **3.4v1:** 66–67, 67a, 69a, 75a, 83a, **3.5v1:** 226a, 226–227, 232–233, 233a, 238e, 244–245, 245a, 247a, 251a, 253h, 253l–253m, **3.5v2:** IR20–IR21, IR23–IR25, **3.6v1:** 381a, 426–427, 427a, 441a

Making connections. *See* Connections, making.

Map/globe. *See* Graphic sources.

Mapping selections. *See* Graphic and semantic organizers, types.

Mass media. *See* Media literacy.

Mechanics (of English grammar and writing). *See* Capitalization, Comma, Exclamation mark, Period, Question mark.

Media. *See* Media literacy.

Media literacy

creation of media

commercial, **3.3v1:** 403a

documentary, **3.1v1:** 55a

news report, **3.1v1:** 55a

radio advertisement, **3.5v2:** 319a

kinds of media

advertisement/commercial, **3.3v1:** 403a, **3.5v2:** 319a

CD-ROM, **3.6v2:** 487c

drama, **3.3v1:** 437a

illustration/photographs **3.2v1:** 226g

Internet, **3.1v2:** 188g, 188–191, 191a, **3.4v1:** 85a, **3.4v2:** 144g, 144–147, **3.5v2:** 319a, 354g, 354–357, **3.6v2:** 487c, 490g, 490–491

interview, **3.2v2:** 333a

magazine, **3.2v1:** 291c, **3.3v2:** 496g, 496–499, **3.5v2:** 319a

newsletter, **3.5v1:** 213c

newspaper, **3.1v1:** 118g, 118–119, 119a, **3.3v2:** 529c, **3.4v1:** 85a, **3.5v2:** 319a

news report, **3.1v1:** 55a

radio, **3.2v2:** 333a, **3.4v1:** 85a, **3.5v2:** 319a

talk show, **3.6v1:** 459a

television/videos/film, **3.3v1:** 403a, **3.4v1:** 85a

weather report, **3.4v1:** 85a

Metacognition. *See* Monitor and clarify.

Metaphor. *See* Figurative language, Literary terms.

Modeling. Teacher modeling and think-alouds are presented throughout Skills/Strategies in Content lessons and After Reading lessons.

P

U

V

W